T0319471

REASONS TO PASS

REASONS

to PASS

A Guide to Making Fewer and Better Investments

RALPH BIRCHMEIER

Columbia Business School
Publishing

Columbia University Press
Publishers Since 1893
New York   Chichester, West Sussex
cup.columbia.edu

Library of Congress Cataloging-in-Publication Data
Names: Birchmeier, Ralph, author.
Title: Reasons to pass : a guide to making fewer and better investments /
Ralph Birchmeier.
Description: New York : Columbia University Press, 2023. | Includes index.
Identifiers: LCCN 2022018678 | ISBN 9780231207089 (hardback) |
ISBN 9780231556804 (ebook)
Subjects: LCSH: Investments. | Investments—Psychological aspects. | Confidence.
Classification: LCC HG4521 .B57 2023 | DDC 332.6—dc23/eng/20220509
LC record available at https://lccn.loc.gov/2022018678

Cover design: Noah Arlow

CONTENTS

1

Principles and More

Introduction

Becoming a successful investor requires answering two important questions: What is your investment disposition, and what is your circle of competence? These primary considerations are behavioral, not analytical.

Consider the decision between two career paths: aeronautical engineering or equity investing. The engineering route requires an undergraduate degree filled with calculus, differential equations, analytical geometry, and computer science from a university accredited by the Accreditation Board for Engineering and Technology. A graduate degree comes next, followed by licensing requirements. These steps to success are well defined—challenging but attainable.

In contrast, the path to becoming an equity investor is anything but well defined. As Warren Buffett cautioned in his 1988 Berkshire Hathaway annual letter, "Our experience with newly-minted MBAs has not been that great. Their academic records always look terrific and the candidates always know just what to say; but too often they are short on personal commitment to the company and general business savvy. It's difficult to teach a new dog old tricks."

Many professional investors have earned finance undergraduate degrees and MBAs from top schools, or have earned their CFA designation, but paths to success vary widely. Philosophy majors often make excellent investors because they are taught to question convention. Management consultants also can do very well because of their expertise tearing apart corporate strategies. Lawyers deal with risks and operational complexity and sometimes can convert their analytical skills into investment success. Business managers have seen how companies work from the inside, giving them other distinct advantages. No one educational or career path guarantees investment success. In his 1992 Berkshire Hathaway annual letter, Buffett explained:

> Though the mathematical calculations required to evaluate equities are not difficult, an analyst—even one who is experienced and intelligent—can easily go wrong in estimating future "coupons." At Berkshire, we attempt to deal with this problem in two ways. First, we try to stick to businesses we believe we understand. That means they must be relatively simple and stable in character. Second, and equally important, we insist on a margin of safety in our purchase price. If we calculate the value of a common stock to be only slightly higher than its price, we're not interested. We believe this margin-of-safety principle, so strongly emphasized by Ben Graham, to be the cornerstone of investment success.

Couple this with the fact that valuation is simple in theory, not complex like calculating the lift of a newly engineered wing design. Let me repeat, valuation is simple. You calculate and forecast future cash flows available to equity investors and discount them back to today, sum these present values, and divide by shares outstanding. A basic accounting class and what is affectionately called "baby finance" in graduate school will get you most of the way toward gaining the skill set required to value most investments.

The trick with forecasting is that future free cash flows are hard to predict, with the primary problem being that the world is multivariate. Individual variables are almost impossible to predict on their own, and their interaction with each other adds complexity. Macroeconomic variables include interest rates, gross domestic product (GDP), inflation, change in consumer leverage, credit spreads, changes in taxation, and foreign exchange movements. Microeconomic forces must also be anticipated. What happens with new entry and exit, rivalry, technology shifts, regulatory changes, litigation, and corporate governance? Porter's Five Forces are a good analogy. Management actions and reactions—including mergers and acquisitions, operational changes, capital allocation, and balance sheet management—are unpredictable. Every one of these factors influences future free cash flows.

As Charlie Munger puts it in layman's terms in *Poor Charlie's Almanack*, "People have always had this craving to have someone tell them the future. Long ago, kings would hire people to read sheep guts. There's always been a market for people who pretend to know the future. Listening to today's forecasters is just as crazy as when the king hired the guy to look at the sheep guts. It happens over and over and over" (2005).

Even if free cash flows can be predicted perfectly, market sentiment can vacillate widely from fundamentals, which inherently makes stock prices unpredictable in the short to medium run. Bullish sentiment can drive stock prices far ahead of fundamentals, as we witnessed in technology stocks globally between 1998 and 2000. The China macro environment was strong between 2012 and 2015, yet the Chinese equity market experienced severe underperformance. Growth stocks through 2021 had an incredible ten-year run against value stocks. Some of the outperformance experienced during this time was an overdue convergence resulting from the fact that value stocks did quite well in the early and mid-2000s. The divide at year-end 2021 between sentiment and fundamentals, however, was the widest on record in favor of growth. These and many other examples demonstrate the magnitude of short-term price dislocations, each of which is driven by behavioral biases and cognitive errors. Valuation, indeed, is a precarious exercise.

Target Audience and Conceptual Overview

The target audience of this book is investors who want to adopt particular strategies. These lessons will find broad applicability, although they are best suited for investors with the following dispositions:

1. Time Horizon—Fundamentally oriented investors seek assets that are mispriced relative to their underlying fundamentals. Convergence between price and value can occur slowly, making the strategies endorsed by this book well suited for patient investors willing to hold assets over the long run. Patience is an underappreciated yet valuable temperament in investing.

2. Market Timing—Few investors can consistently predict economic tops and bottoms, the equity market, interest rates, or real estate cycles. Fundamentals and valuation do poor jobs as factors predicting market vicissitudes in the short run. This book is heavy on behavioral lessons and fundamental analysis. Practitioners of market timing should look elsewhere as picking tops and bottoms may be one of the most difficult assignments in all of investing.

3. Macro- Versus Micro-Investing—This is not a macroeconomic book and offers no clues about how to predict the Fed's next move or German GDP. Predicting macro movements is really hard and is tougher than evaluating microeconomic actions and reactions. Most professional macroeconomists, steeped in years of study and volumes of data, get the inflection points wrong. No economist would have dared predict ex ante that Australia would go on a twenty-five-year run of strong GDP growth without a recession, and nobody predicted that the ten-year government yield in Germany would drift negative for many quarters. The micro is in some cases analyzable, and the emphasis of this book is determining when the micro is analyzable and how that translates into a viable investment.

4. Index Investing—This book is focused on the purchase of individual equities, although its lessons are relevant for all asset classes and asset allocation across time. Those interested only in low-cost index funds will still find valuable insight relevant to asset allocation. Indexing is easy, in theory, and thus is appealing to those who have an investment strategy looking for simplicity. The challenge with indexing is selecting asset allocations, in which case the same behavioral pitfalls can interrupt sound decision-making. Those seeking guidance on how to flex asset allocation over time will find enough nuggets of wisdom to warrant further reading.

5. Momentum Investing—Robust research indicates that chasing price momentum works over the short run, defined as one year or less. Stocks in an uptrend tend to remain in an uptrend on average for the following few quarters. Confirmation bias drives trend investing because improving fundamentals are not often appropriately weighted right out of the gate. Rather, investors remain skeptical in line with their original thesis as they seek other confirming data. After several quarters, the improving fundamentals

increasingly disprove the investors' original thesis, which leads to a capitulation, a rerating of the stock price at which point the momentum effect wears off. Utilizing a momentum overlay on a fundamental strategy makes some sense, although relying solely on a momentum strategy is challenging because all investors have access to the same price charts.

6. Concentration—Applied properly, a portfolio with twenty to forty names in an investment portfolio has sufficient diversification. Some investors focus heavily on massive diversification, relying on many equity and bond funds spread around the globe to maximize risk management. Some of this diversification is illusory as material market downturns push correlations of most risk assets toward 1.0. Many investors build individual equity portfolios consisting of one hundred or more names. These portfolios can still outperform, although conviction invariably declines as one adds more names, and analytical challenges make portfolio management more complex when additional moving parts are introduced. It is really hard to properly evaluate long-term structural risks of a large overly diversified portfolio. This book advocates a small, high-conviction, but still diversified portfolio.

Humility

The best defense (against overconfidence) is that of the best physicists, who systematically criticize themselves to an extreme degree, using a mindset described by Nobel Laureate Richard Feynman as follows: "The first principle is that you must not fool yourself and you're the easiest person to fool."

—CHARLIE MUNGER, INVESTMENT PRACTICES OF
LEADING CHARITABLE FOUNDATIONS SPEECH, 1998

Human beings are not programmed to be humble. The average driver votes themselves a seven out of ten, the same as the average investor's self-ranking. We are all mostly better looking than average and keen to demonstrate our superior intellect. Overconfidence, humility's evil twin, is prone to raising havoc during the decision-making process, and it can have severe consequences in the investment industry.

Professional analysts presenting investment ideas to portfolio managers must speak with conviction to be taken seriously at most investment firms. Anything less is deemed lacking in confidence and will be discredited. Portfolio managers speaking with clients must herald an authoritative voice about why their investment thesis will prove correct. CEOs who speak with investors must express absolute confidence that their business plans will accrete value for shareholders. This confidence becomes embedded in investors' valuations, leading to bolder bets and reinforced conviction in their investment idea and their overall portfolio. The historically high industry compensation often triggers even greater self-esteem, catalyzing more overconfidence.

Benjamin Graham understood the inevitable consequences of this cycle, and his words still ring true today: "Rarely does one find a brokerage-house study that points out, with a convincing array of facts, that a popular industry is heading for a fall or that an unpopular one is due to prosper. Wall Street's view of the longer future is notoriously fallible" (*The Intelligent Investor*, 1973, chap. 11).

Indeed, the future is utterly unpredictable. Because many variables are completely unknowable, extrapolation becomes the mental shortcut, causing investors to miss the turns. Why do humans have such reluctance to accept their lack of "vision"? Behavioral factors, too many to count, push us to seek fortune-tellers, economists, and market experts to shed light. We try to avert ambiguity, and on this quest, we develop an illusion of control. Or more likely, this illusion of control drives us to seek forecasters. Complexity quickly overloads our Neanderthal brains, and heuristics built as defense mechanisms against complexity are ill equipped to deal with the multifactor ambiguity our modern-day world imposes.

Wall Street forecasts for the equity markets and the economy are structurally too optimistic. This optimism is well aligned with incentives because analysts get paid more when markets are strong. Aggregated bottom-up stock forecasts are even higher than macroeconomic predictions. C-suite executives overestimate future revenues and returns, which frequently leads to disappointment. Acquisitions are often unsuccessful for acquirors because companies overpay and because they overestimate benefits from synergies. Households save less during economic peaks because they are overly optimistic, tightening their belts only after recessions hit. Individuals upgrade to more expensive houses and cars than warranted in the good times, levering themselves up irrationally in the process. Likewise, corporate leverage increases during peaks even as risks are downplayed, and managers favor aggressive expansion strategies or generous shareholder distributions. Amateur and professional traders alike trade more actively when markets are strong, hurting after-tax returns. This systemic lack of humility leads to poor decisions and disappointing consequences for individuals, corporations, and investors.

Reality is different from overconfident perceptions. Philip Tetlock, a psychologist and professor at the University of Pennsylvania, has made a career of tracking the success rates of expert predictions, or rather, their collective failure to predict future events with precision. Humility is not a tendency broadly shared by professionals in any field. In *Expert Political Judgment: How Good Is It? How Can We Know?*, Tetlock offers a clue about how to get off the prediction hamster wheel: "We shall discover that the best forecasters and timeliest belief updaters shared a self-deprecating style of thinking that spared them some of the big mistakes to which their more ideologically exuberant colleagues were prone" (2005).

Do not despair. The solution is surprisingly simple: stay humble, always. The world is complicated and has too many moving parts. Have the humility to admit what you don't know, and then focus your investment efforts on the small amount that remains. Certain unknowables will not be material. Even high-conviction investments embed immaterial unknowables. Rather, remain vigilant for material unknowables, accepting your limitations, and then eliminate all investments so exposed. You will find thousands of investment options, but take comfort in knowing that you need only a handful to build a successful portfolio. Pass on the rest.

Principles Are the Bedrock

Principles are timeless, whereas plots capture a specific moment. Consider that nonfiction and fiction works alike weave enduring principles into the lens of the current environment. *Reasons to Pass* is no exception, and herein I present modern-era case studies to support the reasons to pass discussed in the conceptual overview. Although the reasons to pass may change over time, the principles guiding your investment process will persist.

Ayn Rand's *Atlas Shrugged* is one such example of a fiction work with enduring principles. Rand weaves these principles into an intriguing tale of businesses struggling against government overreach. Written in 1957, she frames these principles through the lens of a railroad baron and a steel tycoon. The morals are clear: property rights, proper incentives for labor, and the unintended consequences of government should be carefully considered. Her philosophy of objectivism still resonates today, evidenced by recent annual sales volumes up fourfold since the 1980s. She took more than one thousand pages to capture her principles in full, calling this work her magnum opus.

The Star Wars, Harry Potter, and Lord of the Rings franchises also weave captivating stories with enduring principles. Although they are fantasies, each is a dark versus light tale featuring an antagonist driven to expand power. Institutional greed is the central theme of each. The Ministry of Magic is no different than the Republic, which eventually morphs into the Empire. Principles guide the behavior of every protagonist and antagonist, villain and hero.

Effective politicians articulate their principles to the voting public. These principles define the foundation of their decision-making in the nuanced world in which they will be asked to govern. Statements such as "I am a progressive Democrat" or "I am a conservative Republican" do not suffice, because they do not define the belief system within which these politicians will frame specific decisions too numerous to list. When will the military be called into action? How are trade-offs between an increased social safety net and spiraling deficits weighed? We live in a world of scarce resources. How will they balance the need for greater school lunch programs against equally critical services for people experiencing homelessness or for military veterans? Principles come first, with specific legislation second. A progressive Democrat in California running for national office might begin with a mission statement that targets the principle of basic equality for all, whereas a conservative Republican could begin their mission statement with the principle of equal opportunity.

In his bestselling book *The Intelligent Investor*, Graham writes, "In the old legend the wise men finally boiled down the history of mortal affairs into the single phrase, 'This too will pass.' Confronted with a like challenge to distill the secret of sound investment into three words, we venture the motto, MARGIN OF SAFETY. This is the thread that runs through all the preceding discussion of investment policy—often explicitly, sometimes in a less direct fashion" (1973, chap. 20).

The Intelligent Investor is crafted from enduring principles. First written in 1949 and laboriously updated through the fourth edition in 1973, Graham cites examples such as National Presto to illustrate basic principles underlying investing success. His principles are timeless—follow them and be assured of a reasonable long-term outcome. He is rightfully credited with surviving, then thriving, through the Great Depression, the most challenging investment terrain for equity investors in U.S. history. He created the world's first true hedge fund, generating outstanding performance until its closure in 1958. He was a behavioralist at heart, understanding before academia the fallacies of the human brain. He was a prolific lecturer, and while a professor at Columbia Business School, he taught thousands of investors how to analyze companies. His most famous student, Buffett, wrote in his 1994 Berkshire Hathaway annual letter that "Ben Graham taught me 45 years ago that in investing it is not necessary to do extraordinary things to get extraordinary results."

Critics of Graham, those who consider his methods outdated and primitive, abound. Many define his investment philosophy simplistically as buying cheap broken-down stocks at a discount. Buy stocks at a highly discounted price to book, without considering growth or quality, or build portfolios of net-nets, companies whose market cap is below their working capital liquidation value.

Confusion is understandable. Examples of attractive investment candidates in Graham's literature are overweight asset-heavy companies, utilities, and old-world industrials. He coined the phrase "value investor" and was identified as the first value investor, but that definition became synonymous with low price to book. The Russell 1000 Value Index, the most followed U.S. value index, is differentiated from the Russell 1000 Growth Index by price to book. Low price to book equals value, whereas high price to book equals growth.

Even detractors of Graham agree that his work on equity analysis was ahead of his time. They acknowledge that he gathered data not widely available to create reasonable formulas that worked in the first half of the twentieth century, when companies were more capital intensive and industrially oriented. Pointing to these formulas and outdated examples, these readers assume little relevance to today's "more sophisticated" investment era. Many critics claim that Graham's message was focused on buying cigar-butt companies, those stocks cast on the ground trading at deep discounts with a quick puff or two left before discarding the filter.

Those readers completely misinterpret his principles. I encourage a thoughtful reread of his work, focused this time on his depth of thought and his underlying principles, rather than on his formulas or so-called antiquated examples. His principles, dispersed widely across his writings, created the cornerstone of pragmatic and modern valuation and are as relevant today as when first written in his 1934 work *Security Analysis*. These principles have proven the test of time and remain the foundation of the long-term-oriented fundamental investor. Focus on *The Intelligent Investor*, his personal magnus opus. It is thick on principles, with a host of chapters intended to educate. Chapters 8, 14, and 20 are particularly illuminating. *The Intelligent Investor* gets to the core of what it means to be a value investor. Interestingly, note that references to growth (or the lack of growth) are spare. His principles are mostly growth agnostic.

Consider Graham's fundamental principles:

1. Equities are not pieces of paper. They are pieces of ownership in an underlying business.
2. Most underlying businesses can be valued. Value the business, divide by shares outstanding, and you arrive at the intrinsic value per share.
3. The intrinsic value is an estimate. You could be wrong because the future is difficult to predict.
4. To protect from this uncertainty, only purchase equities at discounts to your intrinsic value. This is the margin of safety, and it protects the downside against these unforeseen events.
5. Stocks are not always efficiently priced in the marketplace. Oft repeated, Graham coined the Mr. Market parable. He will be manic, sometimes depressed, sometimes overjoyed. Be patient when investing, letting Mr. Market bring you opportunities to both buy and sell stocks.
6. When a material mismatch between price and value emerges, have the conviction to act. Don't worry if the crowd doesn't respond. Do your own analysis, draw conclusions, and then act independently.

Value Investors

But basically all investment is value investment in the sense that you're always trying to get better prospects than you're paying for.
—CHARLIE MUNGER, DAILY JOURNAL ANNUAL MEETING, 2019

Value investing is not bottom feeding on discarded low-growth stocks. It is a state of mind—that is, looking for mispriced assets in an uncertain world. The margin-of-safety principle is paramount, and this state of mind often extends to other aspects of value investors' lives. Living well below their means, regardless of income, is a frequently observed trait shared by value investors. This provides a financial cushion in the event the future unfolds differently from expectations. Many drive conservatively, preferring a wider margin of safety to protect against unexpected human error. The use of leverage is deployed prudently because value investors understand the risks that come with a possible overextension of debt. Borrow for education and other productive investments but not for consumption. Personal growth initiatives make skill sets more valuable and thus provide an additional intangible margin of safety against downside events. Delayed gratification offers similar benefits. Save today and let the powers of compound interest increase your life's margin of safety.

Many well-regarded investors have provided the inspiration for this book. These extraordinary capital allocators have benefited from Graham's teachings. Most are generous with their thought leadership and extensively share their mental models that frame or have framed their investment decisions. Many have written books, interweaving their principles with investment successes. Unfortunately, their principles are often hidden from plain sight because they are so widely dispersed across their literature—leading to the risk faced by Graham—the risk of misinterpretation. Peter Lynch, the famed portfolio manager for the Fidelity Magellan Fund, is often pigeonholed into (1) buy what you know or (2) buy at low price-to-earnings ratios. Marty Whitman, the founder and long-time portfolio manager of the Third Avenue Value Fund, was reduced simplistically to buying asset-heavy companies at fifty cents on the dollar. Bill Miller, the former star portfolio manager of the Legg Mason Value Trust, is seen as ebulliently optimistic about economic prospects and thus favors deep cyclicals at distressed prices. Seth Klarman, the hedge fund manager at Baupost, is reputed to be completely fixated on downside protection. Joel Greenblatt of Gotham Capital blends high return on capital with moderate earnings multiples. These investors have all shared their knowledge extensively yet are boxed in philosophically. Each investing philosophy has complexity not given fair justice by these stereotypes, and like Graham's writings, risk being misinterpreted.

Build the foundation and then the building. This book is titled *Reasons to Pass* to illustrate the principle of uncertainty, an explicit acknowledgment of the many unknowables that cannot be adequately quantified. Begin with this premise, and then overlay the fundamentals. Consider this text as one lens through which to view the world, equally applicable to doctoral students developing their thesis as it is to college graduates collecting their first paycheck as it is to those seeking greater clarity in their investment decision-making.

1

Reasons to Pass
Investment Principles

Equity Investments Are Pieces of Ownership
in Underlying Assets

Long-term thinking is both a requirement and an outcome of
true ownership. Owners are different from tenants. I know of a
couple who rented out their house, and the family who moved
in nailed their Christmas tree to the hardwood floors instead of
using a tree stand. Expedient, I suppose, and admittedly these
were particularly bad tenants, but no owner would be so short-
sighted. Similarly, many investors are effectively short-term tenants, turning their portfolios so quickly they are really just renting
the stocks that they temporarily "own."

—JEFF BEZOS, AMAZON ANNUAL LETTER, 2003

Some investments are outright ownership decisions. The purchase of a primary residence is a 100 percent ownership in an underlying asset, with
benefits of appreciation accruing fully to the homeowner. A lawyer who
makes partner may buy a 1 percent interest in exchange for 1 percent of the

firm's earnings. Purchases of equities are no different: they are an equity ownership proportional to the shares owned. Although shares may be treated as pieces of paper intended for speculation, that is not how investors think about them. Investors buy shares in a business as they would buy the neighborhood coffee shop—that is, by analyzing the underlying long-term fundamentals.

The distinction of time is important. In the 1950s, the average holding period of an equity investment was eight years, which has declined since then and crossed below one year around 2005. Declining transaction costs justify some decrease in the holding period, although capital gains taxes still account for the largest single transaction cost. The analysis of fundamentals lends itself only to investors with long-term time horizons. Short-term forecasts are speculative, mostly guesswork. Few investors can consistently predict whether actual quarterly results will come in below, at, or above forecasts, and even fewer have insight into subsequent stock price movements.

One Needs to Understand the Economics of the Underlying Assets to Determine Whether They Make Viable Long-Term Investments

Does Bitcoin have an intrinsic value? The cryptocurrency has no earnings, pays no interest, has no liquidation value, and does not fundamentally compound in any way. It might be worth $1 or $100,000, and were it trading there, you would have no fundamental basis for justifying ownership or future value. By comparison, consider whether Samsung Electronics has an intrinsic value. It generates a massive amount of revenue and substantial operating profits through the economic cycle, and it is heavily net cash. Its portfolio of patents and products is impressive, as is the strength of its diversified operations. Clearly, Samsung can be bought at some price as determined by its fundamentals, whereas a bitcoin purchase is speculative at any price because it always depends on a greater fool buying it off your hands at a premium.

Returning to the coffee shop analogy, what questions would you ask the current owner listing it for sale? Why are you selling the business? What is the history of revenues and operating profits? Do the profits include your salary? What capital investments have you made and will need to be made?

What is the structure of the lease? Details of employee arrangements would be helpful. Is labor tough to find without paying higher wages, or is the government requiring higher minimum wages for workers? Are regulations stable or changing? Perhaps the area is being zoned for more restaurants or to allow home kitchens, which will induce greater competition. Are there threats or opportunities with the customer base? A wealthier population with more retirees might be a nice long-term tailwind. How well capitalized is your business? Is it in need of new equity capital, or can capital be released? Finally, how are competitors doing? Struggling competitors may face closure and thus could reduce capacity in this neighborhood.

Fundamental equity investing is an identical process. Make it your goal to understand the underlying fundamentals facing each potential investment candidate and you will be on your way to successful investing. If you cannot understand the underlying economics, then pass!

Most Assets Globally Cannot Be Valued with Confidence

The world is awash in investment candidates. The abundance of choice is massive and overwhelming. Consider that each primary asset class, including fixed income, real estate, and equity markets, offers thousands of investment possibilities globally. Each of these possibilities generates income, or the expectation of income at some point in the future. Income tomorrow warrants some value today. When you discount these flows back to today, any investment can seem viable at some price.

The primary problem with this mindset is the uncertainty surrounding lifetime income generation. Rest assured that future income is unpredictable and quite often highly unpredictable. Large variances in actual versus expected income can become too hard to quantify beyond a certain threshold. Because these asset classes vary in their structural uncertainty, a brief discussion of major asset classes is warranted.

Fixed Income Securities

Most fixed income instruments have some price at which a purchase seems possible. Reliability of interest and principal repayment varies. The less reliable the future repayment is, the lower the warranted valuation, to the point at which the best decision is to pass. The higher the asset backing, seniority of repayment, or other protections, the higher the justified valuation will be. *Some fixed income investing is investment, and some is speculation.*

Developed Government Securities

U.S. government debt is considered to be "reliable." A thirty-year government bond bought in 2021 will pay 2 percent interest each year regardless of exogenous events, with principal repayment at maturity ensured. Other developed market government debt is perceived to be similarly safe. Deteriorating fiscal conditions seen globally over the past twenty years could cause stress at some point, but outright defaults of major government debts are unlikely. The deterioration of value from the suppression of interest rates is more likely and would be seen through negative real rates and higher inflation.

Short-duration government securities—two years or less—offer reasonable capital protection, whereas long duration fixed rate instruments are too tough to call given the record low interest rate environment of the early 2020s. Yes, these securities likely will do well if a recession approaches in the short term, as long bond yields decline. Taking a long-term perspective, yields in the United States near one-hundred-year lows are unlikely to offer a positive real return, especially with nominal yields at or below reasonable inflation expectations.

Speculators might engage in targeted buying of long-dated government bonds if they believe long rates are likely to compress. Conversely, investors who believe in reversion to the mean might short a long-duration bond hoping to profit from rising rates. Investors have different mindsets, looking to avoid material unknowables. Forecasting interest rates is virtually impossible. No strategist the world over would have predicted near zero long-term bond yields as recently as 2005. The investment implications of such a call would have been massive, yet impossible to justify. *When it's too hard to predict, and a call on future interest rates falls at the tail of our certainty distribution, just pass on long-term bonds.*

Emerging Market Government Securities

Emerging market (EM) government debt, especially in countries with outsized external investors and with less local "skin in the game," historically have been prone to defaults. Argentina, Russia, and Greece each have experienced outright defaults in recent history. Interest rates offered by EM's generally are higher to account for the greater risk of default, foreign exchange devaluation, and unexpected inflation. Higher structural risks, to some extent, can be incorporated into valuation, although many investors have fooled themselves into believing they could balance this equation. Foreign investors are drawn to EM government debt because of relatively higher current yields. A proper understanding of investment risks requires an evaluation of future economic developments, political decisions, and capital flows. These are highly unpredictable, multivariate, complex systems that are prone to behavioral errors, and almost all macroeconomists fall flat trying to predict these uncertainties.

Argentina sold $2.75 billion one-hundred-year government bonds at a yield of 8 percent as recently as 2017, only to ask for a $30 billion bailout from the International Monetary Fund one year later and then defaulting on its government debt in 2020. Why would any investor provide one-hundred-year fixed rate capital to a country that has defaulted on its debts nine times in the past two hundred years, including the largest sovereign default in history in 2001? High yields relative to other options available globally have enticed speculators to commit capital. Maybe this loan could have worked: systems do change, and the nature of people is to seek improvement over time. *Buying most any EM government debt is challenging, but extremely long-dated fixed rate bonds from a questionable credit, in an era of record-low global interest rates seen during 2021, is speculation, not investment. Pass.*

Investment-Grade Corporate Debt

Most corporations globally issue debt as a component of their capital structure. Corporate bonds, typically from five- to ten-year maturities, are issued to investors. A large portion are senior unsecured, meaning that payment of interest and repayment of principal depends on companies' free cash flow generation or the issuance of future capital to cover maturities.

Throughout history, more than 95 percent of investment grade bonds have been repaid as contracted, making investment-grade (IG) bond purchases a viable and attractive asset allocation. Spreads versus government securities vary over time. Tight spreads, as has been the case in much of the world over the past several years through 2021, make corporate debt less attractive. Recessions lead to spreads gapping out, and the wider the spreads, the more appealing the asset class. *Companies whose equity passes the harsh equity screens espoused herein will make excellent candidates for corporate bond investments in normal times and offer even better opportunities during times of distress.*

Noninvestment-Grade Corporate Debt

The 1980s vernacular for this was "junk bonds." Noninvestment-Grade (NIG) corporate debt is a related asset class grouped into its own category by consultants, with credit ratings below BBB. The United States has the deepest NIG market, with most other countries relying on banks to fund corporate NIG debt. Spreads vary over the cycle from 2 percent at the peak to 20 percent during the Great Financial Crisis (GFC) of 2008. Terms and conditions are also cyclical, with debt written that currently rivals the loosest terms with the least protections for investors seen in many years. Generally, credit peaks see few bondholder protections and tight spreads. Troughs see tough covenants and other terms and conditions that protect investors along with pricing at wide spreads over IG debt. NIG debt traded at par for most of the last three years with easy access for even the weakest credits, gapping out only temporarily through the COVID crisis until the U.S. central bank announced it would become a buyer of last resort in the corporate debt market. This decision disrupted the natural state of the economic cycle, as even low-quality credit found confident bids at high prices. The world is indeed an unpredictable place. Expectations continue to be that virtually all NIG bonds will repay as contracted. This asymmetry of expectations (i.e., little upside with large possible downside) made NIG bonds an unappealing asset class in 2021.

Distressed NIG bonds trade down to 10–50 percent of par during times of distress. Few go to zero because bankruptcy restructurings result in bondholders converting their debt into new equity, wiping out leverage, and making previously unmanageable capital structures viable. Bankruptcy law outside the United States varies, with most countries requiring liquidation rather than chapter 11–type restructurings. This changes the dynamics of NIG investing materially. Certain deep restructuring situations (the majority) fall in the too-tough-to-analyze pile because asset backing is uncertain or because sophisticated distressed debt investors that are not aligned with minority shareholders extract disproportionate value from restructurings. Restructurings require a high and intense attention span and specialized expertise. *Faced with a restructuring or bankruptcy situation, pass! It's too hard to add value unless you are a specialist in both credit markets and that industry.*

NIG debt is unlikely to be found in companies targeted within this book, although investment into the asset class is reasonable when spreads gap out. For our purposes, invest through an actively managed high-yield bond fund. High-yield exchange-traded fund (ETF) offerings are increasing, although uncertain liquidity risks in downturns make fixed income ETFs less desirable for our purposes. *Keep it simple: buy credit mutual funds low and sell high.*

Real Estate

Underlying commercial and residential real estate have been great sources of wealth creation over the past fifty years. Rents have grown in line with inflation, while cap rates have compressed. Loan to values (LTV) of 50 percent at public real estate investment trusts (REITs) and up to 80 percent in private markets have elevated returns on equity. In the United States, 1031 exchanges have shielded tax, allowing for tax-deferred real estate portfolios to compound over time. Where were equity lobbyists in 1921 when the 1031 regulations were being drafted?

Predicting real estate income introduces multiple complexities. Inflation is unpredictable, and lease terms vary in their ability to pass through inflation. Rental rates vary based on local demand and supply imbalances, and high vacancy rates can lead to large rent reductions. Governments can and will impose rent controls in high-inflation environments, weakening inflation protection. Most important, leverage availability varies through the cycle. Loose credit conditions seen in peak times allow for greater access to leverage, pushing real estate prices even higher. At some point, a mostly unpredictable inflection point causes credit to tighten, lowering prices and triggering defaults by those who are most indebted. Withdrawal by banks and credit investors can affect clearing prices dramatically. Buyers become scarce and those still present will lower their bids, sometimes precipitously so. In the most extreme scenario, real estate hits bottom when only cash buyers remain.

Greece class A office space saw a 50 percent reduction in rents per meter between 2007 and 2017 because of the large reduction in the demand for office space as unemployment rose from 8 percent to 30 percent. Ireland saw material rental increases between 2000 and 2007 as the economy boomed, and then witnessed roughly a halving of rents per meter in the subsequent bust. Since then, rents have inflated dramatically, returning back to and then moving well beyond previous peak levels. It took just over five years for rents in Ireland to regain their highs, whereas it has taken well over ten years in Greece. Rental demand moves more quickly than supply, which takes years to adjust to market conditions. This causes local and sometimes countrywide temporary dislocations. Finally, government intervention often occurs to protect renters particularly during periods of high inflation. Germany offers nationwide rent control on housing, as does the state of California as of 2019. Neither effort has been seen as a risk to asset prices so far because controls have not forced rents below natural market conditions. The next inflationary burst, when it occurs, likely will leave residential investors disappointed.

Real estate is an interesting asset class and should be a core portion of an investor's portfolio. The key to asset protection with reasonable upside is (1) normalizing rents at realistic levels, (2) embedding reasonable cap rates and (3) leveraging conservatively with long-duration fixed borrowings.

Equities

Equities sit at the bottom of the capital structure, the residual after all other stakeholders' claims are satisfied. Any movements in payments to the four major stakeholders (i.e., creditors, employees, customers, and government) will affect the earnings available to shareholders. *Equity income flows are the tip of the dog's tail, whipping around mercilessly and unpredictably.*

Macroeconomic conditions, the microeconomic environment, and company-specific factors all contribute to residual income left over for equity shareholders.

Macroeconomic conditions fluctuate narrowly for many years then widely for some period of time. Poor economic conditions produce high unemployment, financial distress, and bankruptcies, which the government will attempt to remedy through unpredictable means. High levels of government debt or large fiscal deficits may lead to political outcries, calls that more heavily regulate business, raise taxes, or drastically cut government spending. Current concerns surrounding the wide disparity of wealth may lead to uncertain, possibly negative consequences for corporate earnings power. Changes in capital gains tax rates alter the perceived benefit of equity investing, and interest rate shifts and credit spreads impact funding costs.

Microeconomic analysis encompasses industry conditions, competitive threats and responses, game theory, demand and supply issues, management quality, corporate governance, and technological advances. Most situations are too ambiguous, unclear, and lacking in long-term visibility with structural threats that precede robust conclusions. Understanding microeconomics is a cornerstone of equity analysis and provides long-term-oriented investors with their primary competitive advantage. The key is to identify those select cases in which unknowables are unlikely to overwhelm the investment thesis.

The goal of an equity analyst, the primary emphasis of this book, is simple: *Determine what is knowable, what is unknowable, and what is materially unknowable.*

Some companies' equity can be analyzed within a band of reasonableness, whereas others undulate widely, making predictions of income streams futile. On occasion, answers can be found but only with inordinate analytical efforts. Every analyst has one scarce resource that cannot be multiplied—time. Every investor, no matter how wealthy, faces some scarcity of capital. Time and capital each have value. Investing your time is no different than investing your capital; prize each as a scarce resource and deploy it only to situations that are likely to result in materially knowable investment decisions. As Charlie Munger explained,

> What makes investment hard, as I said at USC, is that it's easy to see that some companies have better businesses than others. But the price of the stock goes up so high that, all of a sudden, the question of which stock is the best to buy gets quite difficult. We've never eliminated the difficulty of that problem and 98 percent of the time, our attitude toward the market is, that we're agnostics. We don't know. Is GM valued properly vis-a-vis Ford? We don't know. We're always looking for something where we think we have an insight which gives us a big statistical advantage. And sometimes it comes from psychology, but often it comes from something else. And we only find a few—maybe one or two a year. ("A Lesson on Elementary, Worldly Wisdom Revisited," Stanford University speech, 1996)

There is no scarcity of available investment opportunities over time. Investment opportunities will manifest at unexpected times and places.

Marc Faber, the famed investor and publisher of the *Gloom, Boom & Doom* newsletter, utilizes the analogy of a cast-iron cauldron resting on bamboo support pillars. Water, a metaphor for global liquidity, washes into the bucket, while the bendable bamboo supports flex in unpredictable directions. Water spilling over the side signals investment excess, while the other side, elevated and dry, indicates investment opportunity. The span of time will provide a variety of investment options over one's investment lifetime as the cauldron tilts in unexpected directions of varying angles.

At a 2003 Berkshire Hathaway annual meeting, Munger said, "We have this investment discipline of waiting for a fat pitch. If I was offered the chance to go into business where people would measure me against benchmarks, force me to be fully invested, crawl around looking over my shoulder, I would hate it. I would regard it as putting me into shackles."

Lifetime opportunities will be plentiful, the cup truly runneth over! Why invest one moment of time or one dollar of capital on any idea that requires an opinion in something materially unknowable or that requires an overburdensome commitment of time to properly understand? Why invest any scarce resource into a name with ranges of outcomes too wide to be properly bracketed with odds that are no more than guesswork? Some ideas face highly uncertain odds of success. The world will be awash in investment opportunities over your lifetime. *Look carefully and patiently and you will find occasional equity opportunities. For everything else, just pass.*

Remaining Securities Have a Calculable Intrinsic Value per Share: This Intrinsic Value Is Not a Static Point, but a Best Estimate Around a Distribution

Fixed income investors concern themselves with future income plus certainty of principal repayment at maturity. Real estate investors consider competitive conditions, including imminent new supply, cap rates, lease contracts, upside options to brownfield development opportunities, and other factors to determine future income expectations. Equity investors, the primary focus of this book, calculate residual income into perpetuity after all other constituencies have been satisfied.

The intrinsic value is a range because no investor possesses a crystal ball. Few investors in 2007 saw a vicious downward economic cycle beginning in the middle of 2008. Discounted cash flow (DCF) valuations in

2007 forecast future years with strong profits and growing revenues, only to be redrawn in 2008 with several years of much depressed income, followed by several more years of lackluster recovery. The impact to cumulative earnings power was material to intrinsic value calculations.

The reference to a per share number is important. Bank earnings in 2005–2007 globally were above long-term average levels. Preprovision profits (PPP; think of this as operating profits before the cost of credit losses) were moderately elevated because of higher net interest income from stronger loan growth alongside greater use of leverage. PPP shrank modestly through the financial crisis, dropping 20 percent for the U.S. banking system. Intrinsic values per share, however, plummeted 50 percent for the average regional bank because all banks were forced to raise equity at highly depressed prices. Citigroup was the ultimate disappointment, engaging in a sizeable recapitalization at $3.25 per share for its convertible preferred in February 2009, down 95 percent from the previous year's stock price. PPP dropped slightly, whereas intrinsic value dropped by 80 percent because of this incredibly expensive dilution. Always think about value per share! At a Wesco annual meeting in 2010, Munger explained: "What happened is that all our elites failed us, especially academic elites. Faulty risk control mechanisms were taught in business schools and eventually law schools adopted the belief that everything is based on a Gaussian distribution. This turned out to be very wrong, despite all the high IQ people analyzing the financial markets."

The distribution of intrinsic value per share is not typically a normal distribution. High-quality consumer staples, Unilever, for example, will see intrinsic value range roughly within a normal distribution. It may earn margins plus or minus two or three points around its long-term average, while revenue growth may slow or go slightly negative in a worst case scenario, but it also will not surprise massively on the upside. Financial leverage is moderate while fixed costs are navigable over time. Altogether, intrinsic value will fluctuate within a fairly tight band, say 10 percent either way, in a symmetrical fashion. Vulnerable business models, highly leveraged companies, high–fixed cost businesses near economic peaks with poor management teams will see a capped upside coupled with large downsides, including the risk of complete loss for equity investors. Fixed costs burden all businesses to some degree and are a primary reason that distributions are abnormal. Financial debt, really just another fixed cost, further skews these distributions. Slightly declining business size leads to larger intrinsic value declines because fixed costs are spread over fewer units.

A 10 percent reduction in "normal" revenues rarely leads to a 10 percent decline in intrinsic value.

This asymmetry is most extreme near (1) an economic peak because market prices reflect continuing high expectations, and as a result, do not reflect potential downside risk (asymmetric risks to the downside); and (2) in trough conditions because the expectation of continuing malaise does not reflect potential operating improvements (asymmetric risks to the upside).

Say It with Me: "A Margin of Safety"

$20 billion would be the absolute minimum (cash at Berkshire). Since I've said $20 billion is a minimum, I'm not going to operate with $21 billion any more than I'm going to see a highway, a truck sign that says maximum load 30,000 pounds or something and then drive 29,800 across.

—WARREN BUFFETT, BERKSHIRE HATHAWAY ANNUAL MEETING, 2017

Purchase assets below their intrinsic value. That advice sounds obvious and is the language spoken by all fundamentally oriented investors, growth and value investors alike. The margin-of-safety concept is designed to protect against the original sin of investing, a permanent loss of capital. Invented by Benjamin Graham, this principle has become an investor staple among fundamentally oriented investors: *Predict for fun. Protect to win.*

The future is unknown. Good things can happen, such as strong productivity growth, research and development (R&D) success, market share gains, and opportunistic acquisitions, that enhance intrinsic value and lead to unexpected outperformance. Bad things can happen, too, unexpected events that negatively impact your intrinsic value.

Two necessary steps allow you to incorporate a margin of safety into your process. First, protect from permanent impairment of your investments through price. Buy at a low enough price to provide all the necessary cushion to protect from loss. Certain investments lend themselves well to this mechanism, in particular, those whose downside risks can be adequately captured in your valuation work. A second protection mechanism, the basis of *Reasons to Pass*, is to simply avoid investments prone to unquantifiable downside. Eliminate those without regard to price, and then be disciplined in your buy price for the remainder.

The Required Margin of Safety to Invest in a Stock Depends Heavily on the Intrinsic Value Range

> Intrinsic value is terribly important but very fuzzy. Two people looking at the same set of facts, moreover, and this would apply even to Charlie and me, will almost inevitably come up with at least slightly different intrinsic value figures.
> —WARREN BUFFETT, BERKSHIRE HATHAWAY ANNUAL MEETING, 2003

Each potential investment has a range of possible intrinsic values. Buy decisions are not formulaic, forcing a buy at an X percent margin of safety. Rather, they depend on the width and distribution of the likely range of outcomes. An ideal investment is made below a downside intrinsic value, but accommodations can be made depending on the nature of asymmetry. This concept is best illustrated with the following example:

> Example 1: Purchase one share of IBM at $150, assuming an intrinsic value of $200 based upon your fundamental work. The stock declines to $130 due to an unexpected revenue decline, but further analysis determines that IBM is merely pruning its least profitable businesses without impacting intrinsic value. Mr. Market has overreacted. The stock price decline is not concerning, as future upside has improved. Short term returns are negative but forward returns should be higher as the stock price converges with its fundamental value. Your investment in IBM at $150 appears sound.
>
> Subsequently, IBM announces a large acquisition of Red Hat for $34 billion, a price you determine to be materially above intrinsic value. The stock price responds negatively, dropping to $120. This value destruction also leads to a large new debt burden, making the company's fundamentals riskier. A new analysis calculates an adjusted intrinsic value of $100 per share, leading to a negative margin of safety.

The investment in IBM just experienced a permanent impairment of capital because your $150 investment is now worth only $100. This situation occurs regularly because the world is an unpredictable place and negative surprises are common. A margin of safety protects against some but not all negative surprises.

IBM's base case intrinsic *estimate* was $200, but as one legendary Brandes insider quipped repeatedly to clients, intrinsic value is a neighborhood, not an address. The size of the neighborhood will vary. Rather than focusing on the quantitative margin of safety, it helps to reframe the question. Ask what buy price offers the necessary protection against your downside intrinsic value. Initially, a range of intrinsic values for IBM might have been $150 to $250 given uncertainties around your base case. The discipline to refrain from purchase until IBM demonstrated a margin of safety in a downside scenario would have at least partially protected invested capital.

The Sell Discipline Is Heavily Influenced by a Range of Intrinsic Values

Selling when it approaches your calculation of its intrinsic value is hard. But if you buy a few great companies, then you can just sit on your ass. That's a good thing.
—CHARLIE MUNGER, BERKSHIRE HATHAWAY ANNUAL MEETING, 2000

The downside intrinsic value protects against permanent loss of capital, while the upside intrinsic value turbo charges the alpha. Large differences between stock prices and the upside intrinsic lead to greater compounding opportunities. An upside intrinsic for IBM may be $250, assuming a return to growth for its remaining core segments and a higher multiple ascribed to its cloud and artificial intelligence initiatives. A $120 stock price against an upside intrinsic provides enormously accretive return potential.

Sell discipline introduces two behavioral elements that make objective decision-making challenging. First, the nature of establishing an intrinsic value introduces a powerful anchor. The instinct will be to sell that stock when it hits that intrinsic value. The second and opposing force creates a loyalty to investments that have performed well, and this similarly powerful force compels investors to hold winners too long. You can't help but fall in love with Tesla in 2021 after its massive outperformance. Knowing which force proves dominant is a difficult question.

Several variables can offer guideposts that make the decision to sell more manageable. First, the base case intrinsic value does offer informational content. Second, evaluating the range and odds of various intrinsic values provides additional information. Decent odds of upside options materializing may compel continued holding. Higher conviction of the upside should increase the confidence to hold. The decision is fraught with behavioral difficulties, so consider any conclusion with reservation.

Two items of note offer worthy discussion. First, Munger has a point. Selling is hard—harder than buying because no protection from a large margin of safety cushions the decision. High-quality businesses most likely to grow intrinsic value over time offer an intangible margin of safety, providing investors comfort when stocks hover around intrinsic value. Second, study your sales decisions over time for clues about your behavioral biases. Some investors routinely sell early, some late.

Tax considerations are significant for taxable investors. A security trading at its intrinsic value will compound at its required rate of return, effectively compounding at its equity discount rate. A security bought at a discounted price will generate material capital gains taxes when sold at intrinsic value, reducing the amount of capital available for redeployment. This interrupts the power of compounding. After-tax reinvested capital is smaller, so less capital is available with which to generate future returns. Rotations into a new generation of high-margin-of-safety names might or might not offset the benefit of portfolio turnover. Many investors are overconfident in their ability to compound and thus are willing to make this trade-off too hastily.

Speaking at a 2003 Berkshire Hathaway annual meeting, Munger offered this: "Intelligent people make decisions based on opportunity costs. In other words, it's your alternatives that matter. That's how we make all of our decisions."

Notice the omission of relative margin of safety trade-offs. The opportunity cost of existing versus new names is an obvious point of focus. Selling expensive stocks to buy cheap stocks is intuitive. The problem with this state of mind is the potential degradation of this concept into a purely relative return investment process. A margin of safety is not a relative concept. It is absolute and unique to each name to protect against adverse outcomes. Each investment candidate worthy of consideration possesses an absolute margin of safety at which point an investment becomes viable. The framing of this decision into a comparison of what else is available runs the risk of polluting the investment process.

Buffett wrote in a 1996 Berkshire Hathaway annual letter that "to suggest that this investor should sell off portions of his most successful investments simply because they have come to dominate his portfolio is akin to suggesting that the Bulls trade Michael Jordan because he has become so important to the team."

Be very patient on sales. The more durable the franchise and the higher its barriers to entry, the more likely the company is to generate upside surprises. Equities trading around intrinsic value should continue to compound, but should do so at a rate that is more in line with the market rather than generating large excesses. Capital gains taxes are concrete and impair the compounding effect. The greater the capital gains tax rate, the greater the interruption. Rotation into new names offers no guarantee of excess returns relative to continued holding, so rotate judiciously only when the benefits of rotation are obvious and material. Cash is the default parking lot when viable investment alternatives cannot be found. It has a margin of safety of zero. It offers no real return but in return downside protection. Why sell a good quality equity around intrinsic to let it sit in cash?

Mr. Market Is Real

The tribute to Graham, the inventor of the margin of safety concept, is obvious. On average, stock prices float within striking distance of reasonable intrinsic values, incorporating everything knowable into an intrinsic value. Disconnects occur, however, because of behavioral biases and forced selling. Investors, like people generally, feel more secure in herds and thus are innately programmed to group together. Herding causes the masses to move in tandem. Leverage, the root cause of forced selling, creates indiscriminate selling regardless of price.

Margin calls in the Great Depression are the most obvious example of herding, driving stocks to repeated lows. Margin debt, equating to almost 20 percent of GDP in the late 1920s, spiraled into an out-of-control selling cycle. The Resolution Trust Corp (RTC) assumed several hundred billion dollars of foreclosed assets in the early 1990s with a mandate to liquidate its real estate portfolio regardless of price. Buyers benefited while taxpayers paid. The world's banks retreated from extending credit during the 2008 Great Financial Crisis, and overextended customers, and banks' asset workout groups, pushed through sales of foreclosed assets at any price. The Russian default of 1998 triggered unexpected losses by Long Term Capital Management, an investment firm that held more than $1 trillion of notional derivative exposure. The threat of forced selling rattled markets and forced the Federal Reserve to step in to stabilize markets.

Systematic fear and greed cause wild occasional swings of stock prices away from fundamentals. Investors have a low tolerance for investment gains they missed out on. Investment gains seen by early-inning participation of friends, family, and neighbors leads to heightened interest during the middle innings of an upward-sloping market cycle. Sharks are content to relax after a large meal, but humans instinctively demand more. The cycle of greed accelerates and then typically crescendos in one final burst. The U.S. equity market in January 2020, before the start of the COVID crisis, had what felt like the beginning of a final burst of euphoria. The end of 2021 headed directionally along a similar path as the vaccine-induced recovery took hold.

At the 2020 Berkshire Hathaway annual meeting, Buffett explained:

> Imagine for a moment that you decided to invest money now, and you bought a farm. And the farmland around here, let's say you bought 160 acres, and you bought it for x per share, or per acre. And the farmer next to you had 160 identical acres. And that farmer next door to you was a very peculiar character because every day that farmer with the identical farm said, "I'll sell you my farm, or I'll buy your farm at a certain price," which he would name. . . . you get the added advantage that you do have this neighbor who you're not obliged to listen to at all who is going to give you a price every day. And he's going to have his ups and downs. And maybe he'll name a selling price that they'll buy at, and in which case you sell if you want to. Or maybe he'll name you a very low price, and you'll buy his farm from him. But you don't have to.

The tech bubble of 1995 to 2000 was one of the greatest examples of Mr. Market at work. Just like all large moves away from fundamentals, the technology boom was real. It began around 1980 with the advent of the IBM PC and the Apple 2. Microsoft designed the operating system for the IBM PC in the late 1970s and all IBM clones to follow. Intel fueled growth with ever-faster processors. Meanwhile, the internet came of age, allowing these devices to become interconnected for the first time in the early 1990s. I recall the first email I sent in 1993 with an attachment to my CFO. He was baffled, not unlike the previous generation was with a fax machine. Browsers came online in the mid-1990s, and content followed. The progression was logical, with early content providers seen as having first-mover advantage and innovation expertise. Site design was a nascent skill, and designers commanded large salaries. Several successful technology initial public offerings (IPOs) encouraged many others toward the well of prosperity. The stories are numerous, but no company better highlights the transition from rationality to blind greed than Cisco Systems.

Cisco Systems manufactured routers that helped connect devices to the internet. It issued its IPO in 1990 with an initial-day pop of 24 percent, appreciating 61,000 percent through year-end 2000. In the winter of 1998, it carried a market cap of $400 billion against sales of $20 billion. Had their only expense been income tax, they would have traded at thirty times earnings.

Priceline, the online airfare first mover, is another classic tech bubble story. It judiciously timed its IPO for March of 1999, precisely one year before the absolute peak. It priced at $16, soaring to $70 in its first day of trading, and then appreciated 400 percent in the first twelve months. Given weak fundamentals and a hugely excessive valuation, it fell to $2 by year-end 2000 just nine months into the tech collapse. Did it follow the efficient market hypothesis?

The tech bubble was distinct in one way: it was not a highly leveraged bubble. The greatest price dislocations over time occur because of the benefits of purchases using leverage and the subsequent forced deleveraging. Leverage feels great in up markets, but in down markets, it acts as a burdensome fixed cost. Forced sellers are an integral conclusion to bubbles, most of which are, at their core, debt driven. Declining assets collateralize shorter duration debt, and lenders demand quick repayment. "Never throw good money after bad" is a typical banker's mantra. Both Tulipomania in the 1600s and the Swedish housing crisis of the early 1990s depended on leverage to fuel the climactic rises, and then crashes, as price-insensitive selling to stem further losses overwhelmed the market's ability to remain rational. The Asian crisis in 1997 saw Korean corporate debt-to-equity ratios rise to 500 percent. The Great Depression, to a large extent, was a forced deleveraging of overextended investors who purchased equity securities on margin. Installment lending pushed consumers deeper in debt. The U.S. housing crisis of 2008 saw banks issuing short-duration 100 percent LTVs in the previous few years that foreclosed quickly once mortgage payments rose. Banks are notoriously price insensitive about price when trying to get these assets off their books. Oil service providers were overleveraged in 2020 with debt maturities becoming visible in future years. Low oil and gas prices at the time and impending debt maturities would have forced distressed asset sales had commodity prices not spiked upward in 2021. *Forced selling at any price, untethered to underlying fundamentals, is a natural part of capitalism that pushes prices far from intrinsic value. Any time huge increases in leverage are seen, pain and market dislocations will follow.*

Properly Size Your Investment Allocations

Sizing positions is a universal dilemma applying equally to consumption or investment. You purchase an item, running shoes for example, only to see that same pair the following month at half off. Increase the materiality, and now it's a car, or a tract home in the perfect neighborhood. Immaterial purchases, such as toilet paper or running shoes, can be bought in advance by price-sensitive consumers as there is little consequence to being overallocated. When making more material purchases, including real estate and other investments, two primary issues are at play. The first is a scarcity of capital: all investors have a limited amount of capital available for allocations. Few individuals can purchase a primary residence only to afford a second residence even at half price. Even large funds and the wealthiest individuals face some scarcity of capital with large purchases. Capital has value precisely because it is scarce. The second issue relates to maximum desired exposure to an asset class. Few people want one thousand rolls of toilet paper, or ten pairs of running shoes, no matter what the discounted price of those assets in a fire sale. Purchasing at a discount works only to a certain maximum allocation.

Economic theory dictates that price acts as the mechanism to create an equilibrium between buyers and sellers. Investor appetite for an asset increases after price declines. This generally holds true for the system at large, although it frequently breaks down with specific assets. Maximum allocations will vary based on the asset—the more certainty around your estimate of intrinsic value, the higher the maximum allocation. Once maximum allocations are reached, price ceases to matter.

Improperly Sized Investments

There have been two times that my Berkshire stockholdings have fallen by more than 50 percent. So what? Warren has always said that if you're not prepared to experience a 50 percent quotational loss, you shouldn't be in stocks.
—CHARLIE MUNGER, WESCO FINANCIAL ANNUAL MEETING, 2003

The goal of investors is to buy assets at discounted prices—the larger the discount, the more shares should be bought. Inevitably, investors will purchase an investment that subsequently declines. It happens to even the best investors and is a normal scenario. Don't get discouraged when stocks trade below, even far below, your average purchase price. Average cost is sunk and is not consequential to your investment decision-making.

Fundamental investors look for wide margins of safety. Stocks decline, leading to a review and, if necessary, a downward adjustment to an intrinsic value. The margin of safety may decline, remain steady, or increase. If the margin of safety expands, an investor should contemplate an increased allocation.

Whether an investor increases an asset allocation is heavily dependent on the size of the legacy position. Highly overallocated assets that subsequently decline provide less room for averaging down. Investors or their clients force maximum constraints to allocations for risk management purposes. It is prudent to set some diversification constraints. The problem arises if large allocations were taken too early at higher prices, leaving little room for additional purchases regardless of price. An investment process needs to be set up to minimize this risk. Buy low, and buy more when lower.

A behavioral element at play also distorts rational thinking. Overallocate too early when the asset price is high and the pain of loss will be amplified after a large price decline. Large paper losses make further purchases unpalatable. Size a position appropriately and your appetite for further purchases at lower prices will remain rationally anchored. When initiating an investment position, imagine the mix of frustration and enthusiasm if that asset declines by half.

Price × 50% = Enthusiasm > Frustration = Increased asset allocation

vs.

Price × 50% = Enthusiasm < Frustration = Stable or decreased asset allocation

As Graham wrote, "It is our argument that a sufficiently low price can turn a security of mediocre quality into a sound investment opportunity— provided that the buyer is informed and experienced and that he practices adequate diversification. For, if the price is low enough to create a substantial margin of safety, the security thereby meets our criterion of investment" (*The Intelligent Investor*, 1973, chap. 20).

Low-Quality Names

Special caution should be taken with companies whose intrinsic value range includes zero at the lower bound. Typically, you will size your initial position responsibly, and then average down after a large price decline.

The stock declines again, leading to another allocation of capital. This scenario will occur multiple times with names headed into bankruptcy, for which a complete wipe out of your investment is likely. Beware of multiple average downs with low quality names. These stocks can always go lower: let your perceived margin of safety expand materially before averaging down, and then limit your additional purchases to one or maybe two additional buys, each at materially higher margins of safety.

Equity Allocations in Total

Individual and institutional investors globally demonstrated high conviction in equities going into the 2008 financial crisis. Equity allocations were high, cash balances were low, and margin debt was at record levels. Declining markets in the second half of 2008 and resultant compelling valuations should have been a super-magnet for cash, but instead, what cash existed was left on the sidelines. Equity allocations were too high going into the crisis. Investors saw their paper losses mount and rationally determined that those losses exceeded their maximum tolerance to pain. How can one argue for more exposure when their overall allocations were too large to begin with? Anyone contemplating an equity allocation should prepare themselves mentally for declines by asking (1) do I need this money in the next five to ten years, and (2) if I do, can I still make do with a theoretical 30 percent immediate decline in my equity portfolio?

Conclusion

Properly sized investments allow for increased allocations when margins of safety become hugely compelling. Your ownership of any asset is zero to maximum. Ask yourself three questions: What price warrants an initial allocation? What is the maximum allocation for this asset? What price warrants a maximum allocation?

Think Independently

A contrarian approach is just as foolish as a follow-the-crowd strategy. What's required is thinking rather than polling.
—WARREN BUFFETT, BERKSHIRE HATHAWAY ANNUAL LETTER, 1990

Thinking independently is an obvious trait for contrarians, but it is not enough to be blindly contrarian to gain large excess returns. The heuristic of seeking out the most contrarian investments is no better than not thinking at all. Contrarian investments feel good to value investors because hatred of a name makes it more likely that it becomes undervalued. Herds will often force prices lower. The complexity arises because uncertainty leads to revulsion, which leads to lower stock prices. Some uncertainty is quantifiable, and some is not. The famed Tiger hedge fund manager Julian Robertson once postulated that he made more money off consensus bets than contrarian bets. Rest assured that your definition of consensus overlaps little with his. Fortunately, you don't need access to his sphere of influence to do well. Do your own independent work, and when confident, buy with conviction.

Risk Management

> In assessing risk, a beta purist will disdain examining what a company produces, what its competitors are doing, or how much borrowed money the business employs. He may even prefer not to know the company's name. What he treasures is the price history of its stock. In contrast, we'll happily forgo knowing the price history and instead will seek whatever information will further our understanding of the company's business.
> —WARREN BUFFETT, BERKSHIRE HATHAWAY ANNUAL LETTER, 1993

Anyone familiar with the capital asset pricing model (CAPM) will easily recall that equities contain a general equity risk premium and beta. The equity risk premium is a nebulous concept with an honorable intent requiring equities to generate a higher return to compensate for higher risk. Beta then applies to individual equities to adjust that company's riskiness as compared with the stock market. Riskier names warrant a beta greater than one. Per the academics, beta is calculated as a volatility measure of a company's stock price. Stocks with greater historical price volatility receive higher betas.

Now imagine how you would define risk as an owner of a business. Factors to consider are many, but prominent ones would include the following:

1. Porter's Five Forces (i.e., barriers to entry, rivalry, substitution, and threats from suppliers or threats from customers)
2. Technology or obsolescence risk

3. How profits will evolve in and beyond the next downturn

4. Whether or not cash flow will be sufficient to pay off financial debts

Business owners do not care about the price they could receive today for their business, or, if public, their current stock price. They care about their company's long-term fundamentals. Business valuations or stock prices will loosely correlate to these and other fundamental factors. In a perfectly efficient world, the link between fundamentals and price will fully correlate, but reality dictates otherwise.

Buffett, Graham, and many prominent graduates of the Columbia Business School think differently about risk. Business owners do not care about the stock price; they care about long-term fundamentals of their business. Fundamentally oriented value investors sip from the same chalice. Graham explained:

> So far I have been talking about the virtues of the value approach as if I had never heard of such newer discoveries as "the random walk," "the efficient portfolios," the Beta coefficient, and others such. I have heard about them, and I want to talk first for a moment about Beta. This is a more or less useful measure of past price fluctuations of common stocks. What bothers me is that authorities now equate the Beta idea with the concept of "risk." Price variability yes, risk no. Real investment risk is measured not by the percent that a stock may decline in price in relation to the general market in a given period, but by the danger of a loss of quality and earning power through economic changes or deterioration in management. ("Renaissance of Value," CFA Institute seminar, 1974)

Each company possesses risks that could materially affect its earnings power. By focusing on those structural risks, you establish a company's fundamental beta. A company whose structural long-term risk to-earnings power exceeds the market's has a fundamental beta greater than one. *Reasons to Pass* provides many examples of companies with high fundamental betas. Quite often these companies warrant exclusion from consideration because of their structural risks.

Buffett has laid out a general set of factors to help evaluate company-specific risk:

1. To what extent can the long-term economic characteristics of the business be evaluated?

2. With what certainty can management be evaluated both to realize the full potential of the business and to wisely employ its free cash flow?
3. With what certainty can management be counted on to channel flows to shareholders than to itself?
4. What is the purchase price of the business?

Diversify Appropriately: Prudently Yet Sparingly

It's not so bad to have one's money scattered over three wonderful investments. Suppose you were a real estate investor with a 1/3 interest in the best apartment complex in town, the best mall, and the best of another. Would you feel like a poor, undiversified investor? No! But as soon as you get into stocks, people feel this way.
—CHARLIE MUNGER, WESCO FINANCIAL ANNUAL MEETING, 2003

Not every type of strategy calls for an identically sized portfolio. The bookends of this spectrum are high and low diversification.

High Diversification: More Than 200 Names

A portfolio with high diversification is composed of many statistically cheap companies, with each facing some factor that makes valuation particularly compelling. Financial leverage might be high, business quality low, or growth prospects well below the market average. Many small- to micro-cap names may be illiquid and thus may allow only for limited investments, requiring greater diversification. Because the sheer mass of names makes depth of knowledge impractical, the need to know any name in detail is reduced. Any one name can plummet to zero without a meaningful impairment of capital. Diversify these names by industry and geography to limit risks of cross-correlation. This style of product is better suited for investors who are looking to turn the portfolio more actively. Individual names will converge toward intrinsic value, thus leading to sales. Many quants construct such portfolios.

Low Diversification

In the case of a portfolio with low diversification, you might uncover ten names, all high-quality franchises with limited risk to structural impairment of earnings power, and each exposed to different areas to reduce the risk of cross-correlations of underlying fundamentals. A deep dive into each name is necessary, with thorough due diligence and continuous monitoring. This effort is manageable given the small number of portfolio names. Margins of safety still need to exist but may be smaller and could be coupled with high odds of continued intrinsic value compounding over upcoming years. Engagement with management will be high to protect against imprudent capital allocation and to ensure the highest possible corporate governance standards. Individual investors likely will not have direct access to management. Thus, management quality and alignment with other investors is paramount. Margins of safety and high business quality protects the downside, while also providing a reasonable or substantial upside to provide excellent asymmetrical return-to-risk prospects. This approach is best suited to long-term investors looking to build a stable portfolio of businesses that compound wealth in a tax-efficient manner. Portfolio turnover will be slow. A ten-year average holding period is plausible.

Circle of Competence

Ted Williams, in *The Story of My Life*, explains why: "My argument is, to be a good hitter, you've got to get a good ball to hit. It's the first rule in the book. If I have to bite at stuff that is out of my happy zone, I'm not a .344 hitter. I might only be a .250 hitter."
—WARREN BUFFETT, BERKSHIRE HATHAWAY ANNUAL LETTER, 1994

Invest in what you know, Peter Lynch used to say. The Beardstown Ladies, a once-famous investment club, took that to heart, buying shares in well-known companies. Many memorable Berkshire quotes refer to their discipline of shunning fads, one-hit wonders, tech names, and other businesses too complex for them to understand. This advice applies to any investment, including bonds, real estate, equities, and options.

Can your circle of competence change shape, or expand? Of course, it can. Do you have a passion for semiconductors, or steel, or health care? Become a true student of that industry and build into a worthy capital allocator. Consider the many sources of information, including long-term demand and supply data, entrants, technology shifts, bankruptcies, supply risks, and the rest of Porter's five forces, as well as successful and unsuccessful case studies. Don't be intimidated by all this information. Rather, be a lifelong student and make it a goal to define and expand your circle. It's still important to know what you *don't* know. As Charlie Munger said:

> Confucius said that real knowledge is knowing the extent of one's ignorance. Aristotle and Socrates said the same thing. Is it a skill that can be taught or learned? It probably can, if you have enough of a stake riding on the outcome. Some people are extraordinarily good at knowing the limits of their knowledge, because they have to be. Think of somebody who's been a professional tightrope walker for 20 years—and has survived. He couldn't survive as a tightrope walker for 20 years unless he knows exactly what he knows and what he doesn't know. He's worked so hard at it, because he knows if he gets it wrong he won't survive. The survivors know. (Jason Zweig, interview, September 12, 2014)

As to the Beardstown Ladies, they wrote a successful book touting their high investment returns, only to discover later that capital inflows commingled with their investment returns. Their track record was redacted, but fortunately their lessons live on.

Treat Your Last Dollar Like Your First (Almost)

> Obviously you have to know a lot. But partly it's temperament. Partly it's deferred gratification, you have to be willing to wait. Good investing requires a weird combination of patience and aggression. Not many people have it.
> —CHARLIE MUNGER, CALTECH INTERVIEW, DECEMBER 14, 2020

I am a member of an angel investing group that raises a fund annually to invest in pre-seed and seed-stage investments. Angel groups have mediocre reputations because they generally like everything and rarely wait for the fat pitch. When the fund capital is spent, even excellent investments are passed over. It is no surprise that investment discipline increases as the fund's capital becomes scarce. Initial deals are almost rubber stamped during the due diligence process, whereas opportunities at the tail end are scrutinized. This particular fund must be invested within eighteen months or the capital is returned, which is similar to how special-purpose acquisition companies (SPACs) work. Again, it is not surprising that capital within angel funds and SPACs almost always ends up fully deployed.

At a 1994 University of Southern California speech, Munger explained: "When Warren lectures at business schools, he says, 'I could improve your ultimate financial welfare by giving you a ticket with only 20 slots in it so that you had 20 punches—representing all the investments that you got to make in a lifetime. And once you'd punched through the card, you couldn't make any more investments at all.' He says, 'Under those rules, you'd really think carefully about what you did and you'd be forced to load up on what you'd really thought about. So you'd do so much better'" ("A Lesson on Elementary Worldly Wisdom as It Relates to Investment Management").

An inordinate amount of patience is required to limit investments to the absolute best candidates, requiring extensive periods of inactivity. James Montier, a famed investor and one of the few Wall Street analysts worth listening to, created the concept of the action man. The goalkeeper in a football match must choose to dive right, left, or stay put. Statistically, the best decision is to stand tall and wide, like a spider. Yet keepers overwhelmingly dive because action is rewarded with cheers. No keeper desires the ire of European football fans. Action is celebrated, inaction detested. Yet inaction, equivalent to patience, is what's needed in investing to succeed in the long run. These patient periods spent gathering knowledge rather than hopping from one investment to the next is key to the success of Buffett and like-minded investors. Munger noted: "If you were an observer, you'd see that Warren did most of it sitting on his ass and reading. If you want to be an outlier in achievement, just sit on your ass and read most of your life. But they would fire you for that!" (Wesco Financial annual meeting, 2007).

Patience is an oft-neglected virtue, and it runs contrary to societal convention. Imagine a CEO who sits idly on their hands while competitors engage in large scale M&A, or the investor who rotates none of her portfolio this year. "Why are we paying you to do nothing?" What about the wealth adviser whose year-end portfolio review begins with "nothing's changed since last year, and here is my bill for my 1 percent fee." Societal pressure forces action. Don't let that dominate your investment activity. Treating each dollar like your last protects against disappointing outcomes when cash balances are high.

Personal Soul-Searching

Now it's your turn. Take some time to define your own investment principles. These principles will guide your decision-making, providing direction in an uncertain multivariate world. How patient are you? What is your risk tolerance? What is your level of confidence? What is your analytical sophistication? What are your long-term objectives? What is your own circle of competence, and how do your interests affect its evolving shape? There are many questions to ask, and truthfulness is key to drafting the principles you can live with. Any investment philosophy will be challenged by Mr. Market, giving you unexpected challenges. Stocks you thought were bulletproof investments will drop for temporary, or sometimes permanent, reasons. Economic conditions will turn unexpectedly and create anguish and uncertainty. Your investment principles are your lighthouse in stormy seas.

Some investors will forego the joys and potential upside of individual equities, instead outsourcing those responsibilities to industry professionals or simply indexing assets across asset classes in a prudent fashion. Stick with what you know. Remain in your wheelhouse. Stay within your current circle of core competency. There is no shame in lifecycle funds, simplistic rebalancing strategies, or passive options and low-cost strategies.

2

Main Street Versus Wall Street
A Rigged Market?

Wall Street analysts often play their part in this charade, too, parroting the phony, compensation-ignoring "earnings" figures fed them by managements. Maybe the offending analysts don't know any better. Or maybe they fear losing "access" to management. Or maybe they are cynical, telling themselves that since everyone else is playing the game, why shouldn't they go along with it. Whatever their reasoning, these analysts are guilty of propagating misleading numbers that can deceive investors.

—WARREN BUFFETT, BERKSHIRE HATHAWAY
ANNUAL LETTER, 2015

The investment world is highly competitive. Thousands of firms compete for a finite pool of assets: their professionals are steeped in education and experience. Individuals wonder, rightfully so, whether their efforts have any chance of being rewarded. Is the investment world rigged against them?

Wall Street firms are the remora to the shark, feeding off intermediary fees in symbiosis with the investment community. Their investment bankers pitch investment firms the latest hot initial public offerings (IPOs), their merger and acquisition (M&A) bankers reinforce a transactional deal-making culture, their capital markets teams syndicate bonds and follow on equity offerings to these same investors, their trading arms facilitate portfolio turnover among professional asset managers, and their sell-side analysts provide research to paying clients, encouraging capital rotation to more attractive areas. The more activity, the more fees. The more changes in recommendations, the more trading.

Wall Street's well publicized sell-side research spans the globe, and individual investors rarely receive access. Macroeconomic forecasts and company-specific projections guide investors, and prominent analysts' changes in recommendations can sometimes move markets in the short run. This sell-side research used to be incredibly well funded, with top analysts getting paid many millions of dollars to pontificate upon companies' future prospects. In recent years, however, declining commissions and regulatory restrictions have suppressed profitability of investment banks' equities businesses, leading to substantial cost cuts and resource reductions. The quality of sell-side research has declined, although interestingly not the quantity.

In a 1992 Berkshire Hathaway annual letter, Warren Buffett wrote: "We've long felt that the only value of stock forecasters is to make fortune tellers look good."

Forecasts drive the sell-side research business. Macro forecasts highlight even small changes in forward gross domestic product expectations, inflation, or small expected moves in foreign exchange rates. Company-specific research forecasts sales and earnings, typically providing at most a few years of historical financial information alongside extensive forward projections. Individual stock reports include buy, hold, or sell ratings, and twelve-month price targets. These projections, from some of the smartest graduates of prestigious Ivy League schools, are of dubious investment merit. The predictive power of these forecasts is low.

Large investment firms allocate extensive resources in the hopes of beating the index. Their efforts come in two forms. First, they hire investment professionals as economists, equity or fixed income analysts, and portfolio managers (PMs) who construct portfolios. Second, they pay commissions or annual fees to investment banks and other sell-side research providers to access their research. Investment banks pay their investment professionals with these fees. Wall Street pushes, or investment firms pull, thousands of research reports, hoping to gain an edge on the competition. These reports are not accessible to the public, seemingly placing individuals at a disadvantage.

Investment management professionals, including Wall Streeters, are hired because of their intellectual superiority and intense work ethic. They meet with managers, other analysts, industry experts, competitors, customers, research and development specialists or scientists, and suppliers to learn about the businesses. This scuttlebutt was made famous by the legendary Phil Fisher, the oft-acclaimed investor and author of *Common Stocks and Uncommon Profits* (1997).

At most investment firms, their analysts have too many names to cover and too many portfolios to feed. They constantly are pressed to provide new names to PMs and provide updates for even small moves in stock prices and after each quarterly earnings release. PMs, clients, subordinates, and senior firm executives all ask analysts to provide opinions (and investment solutions) to problems, exposures, and risks. How will this stock fare if the Japanese yen devalues? What is the likelihood of a crisis in the Eurozone and what is its impact on this stock? What will this company's earnings power be under an extended COVID lockdown? Which of these names will improve earnings the most in the next twelve months? Many demands placed on the investment professionals are in the "too hard" camp. They collect what data are available to substantiate their "hypotheses," although imperfect data and system complexity make these mostly loosely formulated guesses. Time allocations to these activities are material. The more demanding the PM or client is, the more effort will be required. The opportunity cost is substantial. These required justifications divert resources away from the more value-added activities that are consistent with long-term investing.

PMs then build investment portfolios after carefully distilling all available information. They may add quantitative overlays, momentum, or other technical factors to provide guidance on when to buy or sell. PMs are overachievers, eloquent communicators of their investment theories, with a knack for higher order persuasion. They generally are highly paid, held in high esteem, and expected to provide answers with conviction to many complex and interrelated risks and opportunities. "I don't know" is not a generally acceptable response. Like all humans, including Wall Street analysts, PMs face decision-making pressure that is both behavioral and institutional in nature.

Behavioral Biases Faced by Institutional Investors

Institutional investors face the following behavioral biases:

1. Conviction Bias—The pressure for answers is intense, and greater conviction comforts peers and clients. Studies have shown that conviction increases in relationship to hours invested, regardless

of the quality and relevance of data gathered. The act of conviction is circular. Presenting your investment case with conviction leads to greater conviction. You, quite likely, are the easiest person to persuade. Conviction runs contrary to reality. The world is awash in ambiguity. PMs demonstrate conviction with supersized allocations or excessive leverage. Both can prove to be financially fatal.

2. Confirmation Bias—Investors want to believe in their investments and will seek out information that reinforces their thesis. Greater data provide comfort to clients and justify investments made while providing cover if investments unfold unfavorably. Clients may read a changing investment thesis negatively, asking what the investment professional missed in their original thesis. Only when overwhelming information opposing an original thesis is revealed do most investors make an about-face. Confirmation bias leaves the wrong names in the portfolios too long.

3. Overconfidence—Highly confident of their intellectual aptitudes, PMs and analysts alike believe that they have the intellect necessary to prosper in the challenging investment markets. False precision in the calculation of intrinsic value, a common symptom of overconfidence, leads to decision-making without requiring the requisite margin of safety. This needlessly accelerates portfolio turnover as professionals make statistically insignificant decisions.

4. Complexity Bias—Most investment professionals are curious and intelligent creatures. They are drawn to complex issues because complex names are like puzzles begging to be solved. Many real-life investment problems do not have a defined solution, and initiatives to wade through this complexity are, at best, time drains and, at worst, the basis for conviction or confirmation bias. As Buffett wrote in his 1994 Berkshire Hathaway annual letter: "Investors should remember that their scorecard is not computed using Olympic-diving methods: Degree-of-difficulty doesn't count."

5. Narrative Fallacy—First proposed by Nassim Taleb, under the narrative fallacy, complex situations are inappropriately summarized into simple stories by our simple minds. The element of luck is disregarded, and the past becomes crystal clear. Clients and peers relish in these fallacies. Professionals with great narratives get hired and promoted and then are allocated increased assets under management (AUM). Hindsight bias results, disrupting lessons to be learned and reinforcing suboptimal decision-making in the future.

6. Herding—Decisions validated by many others feel superior to those made in isolation. Herding reduces career risk and client attrition. Bets gone bad are embarrassing and must be explained. It is better to fail conventionally. Although there is truly safety in numbers, in reality, great decisions are neither universally contrarian nor consensus. Looking at larger mutual fund portfolios in the United States, Microsoft, Apple, and Alphabet are staples. Most Wall Street recommendations herd closely together. No analyst will be fired for a strong buy on these stocks. These are excellent businesses with low incremental capital demands and a growth tailwind and have been solid performing consensus investments for many years running. Whether they belong in portfolios in 2021 is less clear.

7. Creativity Bias—The opposing impulse is the urge to build portfolios that are distinct from any other. Imagine a doctoral candidate presenting a not-so-creative thesis to the dissertation committee. Creative and distinct are not synonyms for correct or optimal when it comes to portfolio construction.

8. Fear-of-Missing-Out Syndrome (FOMOS)—Also called the barndoor closing effect, no one wants to miss a hot deal before the price gets too high. This is why professional investors seem foolish as they pile into successful names just before they turn down. Greed and his cousin envy weigh heavily in this behavioral bias. Seeing other professionals outperform your investment portfolio is frustrating and draws questions, ire, or worse from clients. Envy catalyzes greater risk taking in the hopes of catching up, and late-stage flooding of capital into ideas that previously offered excess returns. Underperformance from this behavior can be severe. Fortunately, individual investors and independently minded professionals can completely ignore the institutional pressures of FOMOS. If only envy was so easily ignored.

9. Sample Size Bias—Daniel Kahneman calls sample size bias the law of small numbers. Professional investors have access to countless investment reports, many of which are expensive but have limited circulation. The case study method, heavily used in business schools, provides anecdotes that aid decision-making. Empirical economists analyze specific countries, industries, and crises to make sense of the world. The problem with all of these approaches is that they are not statistically significant. Lessons learned from

small numbers may or may not apply to future decisions. These approaches facilitate lazy system 1 thinking and provide cover to investors should a decision work out poorly.

10. Myopic Loss Aversion (MLA)—The pain of loss is greater than the joy of gain. This aversion was well documented in early behavioral studies. Myopic loss aversion, identified in experiments conducted by Thaler, Tverksy, and Kahneman, proved that the more one looks at stock prices the more painful losses become. Greater pain leads to disadvantageous selling when asset prices are down. Institutional investors have constant access to Bloomberg and other real-time pricing sources that flash continuously on their desks. This makes them more likely to succumb to MLA than individual investors who have the ability to unplug, as needed.

Behavioral tendencies distort all of our thinking—professionals and amateurs alike. These biases are imprinted in our genes, and although they have served us well over the course of evolution, they present handicaps to optimal twenty-first-century decision-making. All investors face these behavioral pitfalls, but institutional pressures accentuate these core tendencies because of the intensity of the demands imposed. In addition, professional investors face additional limitations—that is, constraints imposed on them artificially by the nature of the money management industry. These impediments further handicap professionals' ability to outperform.

Structural Impediments to Institutional Outperformance

The following structural impediments prevent institutions from outperforming:

1. Fully Invested Mandates—Most consultants and many clients look for professional investors to fill a specific box, while the consultant or the client determines the higher-level asset allocations. They often don't appreciate managers who make tactical decisions that drive up cash balances or invest in unexpected assets. To protect against unexpected allocations, they also impose investment constraints. One common constraint is limiting cash to a maximum of 5 percent of a portfolio. Individuals face no constraints on cash balances or other constraints, and thus are free to focus on any assets within their area of competence, relying on a pure margin

of safety mindset. When investments become expensive and no viable alternatives are found, individuals are free to sell and sit in cash, regardless of cash weighting. This is an integral element of a disciplined investment process.

2. Allocation Constraints—Most consultants and even the Securities and Exchange Commission (SEC) place relatively tight constraints around portfolios hoping to protect investors from major adverse events. The rules are rather arbitrary and do not do the risk management process justice. Rather, they become operating constraints that keep managers from fully delivering on their highest conviction investments, thus dampening potential higher levels of outperformance. Nonsensically, these constraints treat all equities alike, while investors recognize that individual investments vary widely in their structural riskiness.

3. Short-Term Pressures—Clients and investors have become increasingly short-term oriented in recent years. Trading velocity is much higher. News intensity has been steadily increasing, while news quality is down as journalism budgets compress because of declining profitability. Trading costs have declined, reducing frictional costs of trading. Exchange-traded funds allow for intraday movements of funds because daily liquidity offered by mutual funds was considered inadequate. Cross-investor data availability is much higher, allowing for near-continuous monitoring of relative performance. Perhaps the advent of the smartphone has become an additional impediment because it has amplified the instant gratification gene. It is another irony of the industry that managers increasingly need to concern themselves with the short run to keep assets in the long run. Individual investors recognize that investing is a long-duration activity to increase lifetime well-being and are free to ignore short-term movements or underperformance in favor of accretive long-term decisions.

Managing portfolios to outperform over the long run is challenging. The greater the time period over which a manager is measured, the less likely it is that chance is involved in the assessment. A manager outperforming over twenty years is likely a statistically significant outperformer. Over a five-year measurement period, the element of chance starts to expand. Any manager measured quarterly (or even annually) demonstrates more noise than skill. Managers are apt to increase portfolio turnover hoping to compensate for recent underperformance and will lock in gains and the closet index all in an effort to reduce "risk" and stress.

4. Asset-Gathering Pressures—Declining fees, increased rotation into passive vehicles, higher regulatory costs, and the Markets in Financial Instruments Directive (MIFID II), which has forced most European managers to pay internally for Wall Street research, are driving up pressures on managers to gather assets. Asset management is a scale business with fixed costs, and necessary assets to cover fixed costs have risen substantially. Asset gathering is fine to a point, but few active strategies work with too much capital invested. Midsize private firms with good lean cost structures can still thrive in this environment, although small firms and those housed within public companies may force assets up beyond the logical limits of their strategies.

5. Minimum Liquidity Thresholds—Related to asset-gathering pressures, most institutions work with large AUM, or they build products that aspire to grow asset levels substantially. Only a focus toward large and liquid investments allows investment products to scale up as assets grow. Many managers and individuals generate excellent investment returns with small assets, only to struggle once size becomes an anchor. Individuals are well positioned to take advantage of excellent, low-liquidity investments.

Individual investors are immune from these structural constraints, while institutional managers can overcome these obstacles if they consciously structure their businesses correctly.

Conclusion

Individuals rarely gain access to Wall Street industry conferences. They will not be granted one-on-one meeting allocations with senior executives, be privy to cutting-edge research reports, or be given direct access to sell-side analysts. Although this presents some disadvantages, the net effect is not overarchingly negative. Wall Street research faces its own biases—pressures that individual investors are free to ignore.

Companies reviewed by Wall Street may react poorly to an analyst's negative recommendation, triggering less corporate access in the future or cancellation of attendance at the analyst's sponsored conference. Investment banking mandates are unlikely to be allocated to firms whose analysts portray the company negatively. These are lucrative activities for investment banks, and analyst compensation partially depends on these inputs. Therefore, Wall Street research is unjustifiably bullish, which translates directly to institutional investors, their customer base.

Wall Street is short-sighted, focusing on quarterly forecasts and twelve-month stock price targets. Institutional investors increasingly are measured by their short-term investment performance. Individual investors' lack of access to research and a pressure-free environment, however, insulates them from these short-term concerns, leaving them free to focus on what matters: long-run investment results.

It may be better for individuals to stay away from Wall Street and its many influences, focusing instead on names that can be understood without this seemingly value-added access. Certain names will prove too complex without access to research, and so a larger swath of investment candidates may end up in the too-hard pile. Alternatively, this type of focus may require digging up other supplemental sources of information to properly validate an investment thesis. Individual investors, and institutional investors structuring their businesses appropriately, are well placed to overcome behavioral and structural impediments to strong investment performance.

3

Fundamental Analysis in the Digital Age

The proliferation of artificial intelligence (AI) startups promises to tackle many of the world's largest problems. AI-imaging companies demonstrate superior diagnosis of radiology images relative to well-trained radiologists. One San Diego startup has amassed more than three million mammograms with an industry-leading track record in tumor recognition. AI agriculture companies reduce water waste and fertilizer usage. Retailers use their proprietary customer data to better predict purchase patterns, suggest product improvements to their vendors, and increasingly design improved private-label offerings. Data intensity is high and increasing, and the better and more comprehensive the data, the more capable AI analytical capabilities become.

Insurance actuaries are the quants in their space. Their job is to effectively price risks taken by insurance carriers. They review loss trends over time, ensuring that best estimates make their way into reserves and that pricing offers an adequate return for capital allocated. Although their efforts are noble and highly mathematical, blow-ups happen. Hurricane Andrew in 1992 was the largest storm loss to that time, catching actuarial models unaware because increasing coastal exposures had not been appropriately sized. Asbestos might have been the largest negative industry surprise, leading to many billions of dollars in adverse reserve development, loss costs, and bankruptcies when sympathetic courts began indiscriminately attributing blame to firms that, in some cases, had not produced asbestos insulation since the 1960s or earlier. The World Trade Center attack in 2001, lead paint litigation, flooding during Hurricane Katrina in 2005, and Thai floods in 2011 that froze the entire computer supply chain were all unexpected events in the sense that the mostly backward-looking actuarial models were not capable of pricing these risks because they were unaware of their presence and incapable of estimating their costs. A model developed in 1991 would have been ill equipped to deal with modern-day catastrophes, while current models have several generations more data and thus are better trained to deal with future surprises. Each generation becomes smarter, and actuarial models are no exception.

Investing faces a similar quantitative evolution. Credible U.S. databases track movements of the Dow Jones Industrial Average back to the 1920s, while certain academics have pushed back asset price movements into the 1800s. Databases covering individual stock performance and rudimentary fundamental information begin in the 1960s in the United States, and in the 1970s or 1980s in other countries. Databases originally included only high-level metrics, including consolidated revenues, operating profits, net income, common equity, total assets, and a handful of other data points. Database companies are working hard to backfill historical financial data, including more segment data, pension accounting, and other items previously available only in the footnotes or other sections of their annual reports. Outside the United States, databases are expanding, although they lag the United States in data capture. Financial data in many emerging markets, for example, is unavailable from before the 1980s.

The *Journal of Finance* was established in 1946, providing a platform to publish quantitative financial research. Harry Markowitz published his seminal paper, "Portfolio Selection," in 1952, setting the foundation for modern portfolio theory (MPT). Academic studies have proliferated since then, relying mostly on U.S. data (but increasingly on global data) to demonstrate market efficiency, then inefficiencies, and since the 1970s, behavioral biases demonstrating the world is less rational than predicted by MPT. Benjamin Graham, set apart from most professors by his twin passions as a practitioner and an academic, was perhaps the first to espouse financial data collection to thoroughly study the markets and opportunities presented to investors. He identified price to book as a noteworthy signal, along with low price to earnings. A groundbreaking academic study by Eugene Fama and Kenneth French quantified this value premium in 1992, finding that low price-to-book stocks outperformed over subsequent years. Professors Josef Lekonishok, Andrei Shleifer, and Robert Vishny, or LSV, in 1994 reinforced the value premium by confirming the alpha from low price to book, also adding low price to earnings and low price to cash flow as metrics of future outperformance over the subsequent three- to five-year period. Future studies confirmed that value signals outperformed in other countries and over most time periods, most notably over longer-run holding periods.

For many years, fundamental investors mostly ignored these sources of outperformance, preferring their status quo mental models to this broad-based academic rigor. This began to change in the 1990s and early 2000s as more quant firms started to incorporate value signals into their portfolios. Database quality has been improving in several ways, allowing greater analytical rigor in quants' processes:

1. Level of Detail—Segmental data began to become available, as were an increasing amount of other consolidated numbers and supplemental information previously available only by hand (i.e., analysts digging one at a time into publicly available disclosures).
2. Quality of Data—Many errors and omissions existed in the historical databases. There are a handful of publicly available database companies relied on most heavily by investors. These invested considerable effort in cleaning up their data quality.
3. Global Accounting Convergence—Many countries used their own version of Generally Accepted Accounting Principles (GAAP) until the late 1990s, leading to poor comparability of financial metrics, including book value, across countries. GAAP began its long road to convergence. Today, most companies across the world utilize the International Financial Reporting Standards (IFRS), or to a lesser degree US GAAP. Greater convergence has increased the accuracy of financial databases and aided cross-country comparisons.
4. Length of Data Series—A dataset lacking in consistency through the cycle data provides little basis on how to navigate the unpredictable cyclical pathway. Because each peak and trough are unique, multiple peaks and troughs are required when studying quant data for exploitable inefficiencies. The bull market of the late 1960s, the deep trough of 1974, the subsequent inflationary environment, various financial crises around the world over the past forty years, the 2006 and 2007 mega peak and the substantial 2008

global financial crisis, and arriving at COVID 2020 and the unexpectedly powerful recovery through 2021, each cycle improves the richness of the available financial dataset, making quant models better able to navigate future cycles, enhancing their predictive power in the process.

Beginning in the early 2000s quants started taking market share. Assets eventually rose to more than $3 trillion and are still rising. Quants employ many financial factors, the value tilt being just one of them. Momentum, growth, quality, a host of macroeconomic signals, and many other financial and other factors have made their way into their models and investment selection. A drawback of financial data is that its timing, while consistent, lags real-time application. Quarterly financials come out one to two months after the quarter end, whereas the more comprehensive annual reports are released up to three months after year end. Government data releases can lag by several weeks or more.

More recently, quants have built out capabilities to analyze nonfinancial data in the hopes of increasing the linkage with real-time economic changes and monetizing additional sources of alpha. Data are proliferating exponentially because the world has fully digitized. Every economic enterprise captures real-time data—airlines, hotels, credit card companies, Google, Expedia, Deere, Tesco, GPS location services, Wells Fargo, Minecraft, satellite imagery, and patent filings. Datasets are expanding and are becoming more comprehensive because companies have learned that this information provides them with competitive advantages. Much of this data is proprietary. Some data, however, do become available to investors—traditionally, quant investors, but increasingly, also fundamental analysts and even the general public. Some is accessible for free, whereas some are sold directly by the data producers and some are aggregated through data brokers. Data can arrive well-structured or unstructured, requiring additional competencies to analyze.

Much of the data that are becoming available to investors is called exhaust data. Sensors pick up select data, say, activity levels from mall security cameras, that are not helpful and that do not add value for the security company that owns the contract. They sell this data to a broker, who anonymizes the data and resells it to investors. Investors may receive it in an unstructured form, which requires them to process and convert it into usable information. Structured data fits more neatly into existing models. Unstructured data is cumbersome, of varying quality, and requires expertise to massage. Hospital invoices may be purchased from a broker, requiring natural language processing (NLP) capabilities to interpret and systematize. The dataset may be a time series, but inconsistencies across time make trend-based analysis almost impossible without imputing statistical estimates.

The business model of employing fundamental analysts to scour the investible universe looking for exploitable inefficiencies is not highly scalable. Analysts are expensive, and slow by quant standards. A single analyst may be able to dig into one name per day, or one per week at a deeper level. Only some fraction of these names will justify portfolio positions. Imagine a one-hundred-name portfolio with an average annual turnover of 100 percent. One analyst analyzes fifty names per year, and 10 percent of those justify an investment. That portfolio requires the support of twenty analysts and one portfolio manager, which is an expensive fixed cost that must be spread over enough assets to justify their compensation and some profits to the business owner. A $10 billion assets under management fund may earn fees of fifty basis points, equal to $50 million of annual revenues. Pay the twenty analysts $500,000 each, the portfolio manager $5 million, and the back office $5 million, and the investment firm generates a 60 percent margin. This fund has the necessary scale to survive. A $1 billion fund, still a sizeable portfolio, fails under these conditions.

The economics of a quant shop are better because big data by comparison is infinitely scalable once the models are built. Several quants working together can leverage their expertise, and, if needed, a small array of third-party vendors, to analyze every investible stock, evaluating them in real time using today's processing power. It is reasonable to ask whether fundamental portfolios, and human analysts generally, can still compete in investing.

Graham explained: "The moral seems to be that any approach to moneymaking in the stock market which can be easily described and followed by a lot of people is by its terms too simple and too easy to last. Spinoza's concluding remark applies to Wall Street as well as to philosophy: 'All things excellent are as difficult as they are rare'" (*The Intelligent Investor*, 1973, chap. 8).

Fundamental investors can outperform the quants. The following observations are relevant:

1. Simple-to-identify historical sources of alpha have disappeared likely because quant firms have closed the arbitrage. Low price to book, the quintessential value metric, was successfully used by a

generation of disciplined value investors. Buy low price-to-book stocks, companies unloved by the investors so structurally under-priced, while selling high price-to-book glamor stocks that the investment community has fallen in love with, and then sit back and wait for convergence. Although this arbitrage has behavioral justification, it has not generated excess returns in more than a decade, forcing value investors to look elsewhere for opportunities.

2. Quant strategies come in many forms, but many demonstrate high correlations among themselves. Inefficiencies found by one quant are highly likely to be identifiable by others because similar analytical techniques are used across the quant spectrum. Their analysts come from the same computer science programs and the same graduate schools and leverage some of the same datasets. Herding exists among quants the same way it exists among fundamental analysts. Some of the inefficiencies do not require an enormous amount of capital to arbitrage away, making any gains fleeting.

3. AI, a generic catchall for higher-order computer processes, is already commoditized. Amazon and Google have plug-ins that aid users in deploying cutting-edge AI. Third-party software has proliferated. Take proprietary data, a third-party platform, and voila, AI is embedded into your process. Even high-school students are pushing the boundaries of current generation AI. This is daunting to millennials and boomers, but it is no more than a school project for enterprising teenagers. Neural networks are attempting to better replicate the decision-making of the human brain. Traditional AI required large datasets to train software to make good decisions. Humans, meanwhile, process data differently, often requiring only small datasets and logic to arrive at statistically valid conclusions. One integral question, yet to be answered, is whether AI can evolve similarly without infusing the biases present in human processors.

4. Equities still provide an enormous amount of public disclosure that exceeds the volume of financial data provided by financial databases. The information in the footnotes is not well represented in the quants' numbers, whereas management discussion and analysis (MD&A) is a rich source of information that holds valuable insight into long-run economics. Most larger firms also provide supplements that dig into segmental data and presentations that clarify opaque GAAP disclosures. Discussions with management teams can provide strategic insight, appetite for risk, and other long-run

perspectives that can address the question of whether the future will look like the past. Some companies hold little debt on their own balance sheet, preferring to lever up their joint ventures that account for a material portion of their total assets. Land bank details offer a glimpse into real estate portfolios of homebuilders. Again, this type of insight is not captured by the databases.

Most quants are employing NLP, sifting through these disclosures in the hopes of extracting incremental data to increase the information content. Efforts to date leave much to be desired but undoubtedly will improve over time. Fundamental investors can benefit similarly in this regard. For example, third-party solutions leveraging NLP can scour all quarterly earnings transcripts simultaneously for positive or negative news items of note, providing almost real-time summary reports to analysts about the state of an industry's earnings.

5. Much of the data purchased by quant firms is bought from data brokers (i.e., resellers who monetize data collected by other companies). Other data are free and available to all or can be easily scraped off websites. A simple bot can track product prices over time, giving users information about companies' pricing power. Most purchased datasets have large holes. Time-series analysis is critical to fully understand data's value, and most data bought has a short history or is inconsistent or possibly unstructured with the nature of the information changing over time. Invoice layouts change frequently, even credit card statements face analytical challenges. The greatest challenge with unconventional data is that any exploitable value add quickly disappears once it becomes available to others.

6. Wall Street firms have invested heavily in quant, AI, and the exploitation of unconventional data. Investment firms are their customers, so these insights are broadly shared with investors and therefore are unlikely to offer repeatable or enduring alpha. Wall Street has the budget to rival resources committed by even large quant firms and will employ similar strategies to those used at quant shops. Once purely commoditized, the industry-wide benefit of AI will become no more valuable than the slew of fundamental reports produced by Wall Street analysts.

7. Accounting records are subject to occasional retroactive changes because of adjustments or acquisitions. Large acquisitions or mergers

lead to a restated beginning of period balance sheet and only a high-level proforma income statement. Cash flows and other material financial details get lost in translation. Fundamental analysts are used to dealing with these restatements, quants less so.

8. New accounting pronouncements can distort the databases and alter quant models. One recent example was an accounting change under both US GAAP and IFRS that brought operating leases on the balance sheet. The present value of leases was booked as a financial liability, like debt, whereas the same present value was booked as a long-term asset under property, plant, and equipment (PP&E). Retailers and others with longer-duration leases went from looking underleveraged to overleveraged overnight with no change in the underlying economics. Fundamental analysts were well equipped to deal with the change, but quants struggled.

9. Long-term investments on the balance sheet show up as one line item on the face of the balance sheet, while in-depth disclosure is provided only in the footnotes, the presentations, or possibly in the earnings transcripts. Many Japanese and Korean firms have large equity and bond investment portfolios, as do many publicly traded conglomerates around the world. Many of these firms have owned real estate for decades that were booked at cost but that now are worth significantly more. Investments in associates also are carried within the investments line, but the additional detail necessary to understand the economics, including leverage and profitability, is provided only in footnotes. This line item, if material, needs to be evaluated manually to understand a company's economics and credit worthiness.

10. Although IFRS and US GAAP are the predominant accounting regimes, Japanese GAAP is still used by most Japanese public companies, while Korean GAAP is commonplace as well. Canadian GAAP treats marks to market quite differently from US GAAP. These are significant parts of the global equity market, and differences between these and IFRS are varied but material. Quants struggle much more than fundamental investors to incorporate these accounting differences into their stock selection models.

11. Financials, mostly banks and insurers, still amount to 20 percent of the global market cap. Accounting differs meaningfully for these companies, and loan balances, investments, deposits, and policyholder liabilities are poorly disclosed in the face of the financial

statements and in databases. The risks and exposures present in these businesses need to be manually extracted by knowledgeable analysts.

12. Quants increasingly rely on unconventional data, really any data not produced from companies' financial records. These data are better suited to drive short-term conclusions. Satellite imagery counting automobiles in mall parking lots, although outdated, is the classic example of investors attempting to predict short-term, real-time, actionable factors, this one targeting the upcoming holiday season. Google searches for cruise offerings over time offer predictive value about short-term trends in bookings without much insight into long-term earnings power. Sentiment data gages short-term investor interest in an asset class or in specific names. Long-term investors will find little value in much of the unconventional data because of its relatively short shelf life.

13. AI is quickly becoming ubiquitous to the investment industry. Even the CFA exam added required readings in machine learning and deep learning as well as how to run big data projects to its Level II exam.

14. Perhaps most important, time horizons differ between quants and fundamental investors. Quants skew short term, with many averaging annual turnover well in excess of 100 percent. Fundamental investors do not directly compete with quants when targeting names desirable for long-term holding periods and can use the liquidity provided by quants to their advantage.

Other factors are also worth considering and will continue to weigh on quants' success over time. In his 1990 Berkshire Hathaway annual Letter, Warren Buffett cautioned: "Beware of past-performance 'proofs' in finance: If history books were the key to riches, the Forbes 400 would consist of librarians."

1. Data Mining and Overfitting—AI has a difficult time separating fundamentally justified inefficiencies from spurious and random historical patterns. Models can easily backfit data to arrive at "alpha-generating" opportunities, only to see them disappear on a forward-looking basis because no fundamental relationship underpinned the perceived opportunity. Many quants find historical databases too tempting to ignore, and AI can illuminate many

strategies that worked historically. Perhaps equity markets do better when the NFC wins the Super Bowl, or the S&P 500 outperforms when a U.S. model graces the cover of *Sports Illustrated*. Thousands of seemingly successful patterns can be uncovered that possess no economically rational foundation. Input any of these factors into an investment quant model and future returns will be no better than random.

2. Behavioral Biases—Quant models are built by people who remain vulnerable to the same cognitive errors that pollute fundamental investing. Quants can successfully program away some major cognitive errors, but other biases, including overconfidence, may become accentuated. LTCM, the failed 1990s quant shop that blew up spectacularly in 1998 after Russia defaulted on its government obligations, was run by a handful of Nobel Prize–winning academics who were convinced in the mastery of their financial models. Overconfidence runs amok.

3. High Turnover—New public disclosures are received from databases quarterly, whereas unconventional data can be provided in almost real time. Market prices move real time, and this temptation leads to high trading activity for most quants. Tax efficiency is poor.

4. Portfolio Leverage—Some quant products select quite conservative investments, and then overlay portfolio leverage to amplify returns. They may construct derivative overlays to further lever results. The math will be compelling, their efficient frontier optimization well justified, with judicious risk management, until some unexpected correlation breaks down, leading to unexpected fund volatility, higher than anticipated borrowing costs, and on occasion forced selling at low prices.

5. Cross-Correlations—Many quant funds' research efforts have uncovered and then deployed similar factors into their models. This creates greater correlations of the quant asset class than might be expected. Risk management initiatives face similar problems, leading to unpredictable distortions when models break or prices move unexpectedly. Derivatives, often used in risk management activities, face counterparty risk that is mostly ignored until a major counterparty faces capital stress. Results at that point become highly unstable. Buying a basket of quant funds offers only limited diversification.

6. Risk Management—Quants manage risk by changing net exposures and net leverage to protect against unlimited downside. Liquidity can dry up, sometimes spectacularly, just when portfolios are in the process of reducing net risk. High overlap with other quant products may further push down prices of broadly owned assets.

7. Trading Costs—Quant funds estimate trading costs for their vast holdings of credit, equity, and derivative exposures. Trading costs can spike unexpectedly when markets struggle or make certain hedges or other exposures unavailable at almost any price. The industry has grown materially since the Great Financial Crisis of 2008, and the next downturn might lead to some unexpected challenges.

Quants focus more intensively on the relationship between knowable factors in their databases and shorter-term price moves. In other words, they think about beta or stock volatility rather than structural risks to intrinsic value. These different mindsets have different time horizons. In addition, quants mostly build large portfolios that include many names to protect against the unsystematic risk of any one company behaving in a manner that is not predicted by their models.

The long run will see most investment firms incorporating more quant, AI, and machine learning into their core processes. Fundamental firms possess proprietary data from their intrinsic values, buy and sell prices, and levels of concentration, along with insights gleaned from discussions with management teams and site visits. These data can be easily studied using proprietary or third-party services for information content that regains a competitive edge against pure quants. NLP vendors can provide products that scour press releases and earnings transcripts for digestible conclusions or targeted questions for management discussions. Pure quant firms, meanwhile, may see fundamental sources of alpha as more sustainable and thus may seek out their versions of quantamental investing.

Quants will grow over time, and they will become smarter. Databases will continue to improve in quality and quantity, and unstructured data will become more standardized, with cleaner time series. Also, refinements to unstructured data analysis will simplify its use. All data will become conventional. In the very long run, thirty years or longer, all investors will incorporate this type of data into their decision-making. The trend line will be nonlinear, and some spectacular blow ups surely will occur for firms most reliant on data and most dependent on algorithmic decision-making. Models occasionally behave badly, and the laws of unintended consequences loom large when unchecked by human judgment!

Conclusion

Individuals also possess proprietary data, which comes in the form of their historical decisions. Look at a name and place it in the pass pile. Invest in the name, and it turns out well or poorly. Sell too soon or hold too long. Sell into downturns. Hundreds of decisions have been made over the years and across varying stages of economic cycles. Individuals and astute professional investors should capture and study this data, effectively becoming quants that better understand their decision-making tendencies. Much can be learned from a systematic compilation of data. Most professionals are too focused on the present to diligently study the past. Make this strategy part of your process, and your own algorithms will improve cycle over cycle.

When models behave badly, bottom-up fundamentalists who are mentally prepared for these market displacements, professional and individual investors alike, will profit handsomely from these occasional opportunities. Remember, a pure investment process requires only a handful of names to be successful. No new names in a given year? No problem. Do not rush to build a defensible, value-accretive portfolio. Finally, a long-term orientation will ensure minimal direct competition against the quants. Let them become Mr. Market, the erratic farmer calling out bid and ask prices, and then let your investment process benefit from their mercurial temperament.

4

Indexing
A Viable Option

Now let's talk about efficient market theory, a wonderful economic doctrine that had a long vogue in spite of the experience of Berkshire Hathaway. In fact one of the economists who won, he shared a Nobel Prize, and as he looked at Berkshire Hathaway year after year, which people would throw in his face as saying maybe the market isn't quite as efficient as you think, he said, "Well, it's a two-sigma event." And then he said we were a three-sigma event. And then he said we were a four-sigma event. And he finally got up to six sigmas, better to add a sigma than change a theory, just because the evidence comes in differently. And, of course, when this share of a Nobel Prize went into money management himself, he sank like a stone.

—CHARLIE MUNGER, "THE PSYCHOLOGY OF HUMAN MISJUDGMENT," HARVARD UNIVERSITY SPEECH, 1995

Popularized by Burton Malkiel, the efficient market hypothesis (EMH) asserts that free $100 bills do not just lie around for astute investors to pick up. There is no increase in return without taking additional risk. Rather, invest your assets in an index fund at a low cost. To a large extent, he stands correct. Indexing is good—good for clients, good for the system, and good for active investors.

Charlie Munger once quipped that between $200 billion and $300 billion of annual intermediary costs lower net returns to owners of investment assets. His number is likely conservative. Consider $20 trillion of managed assets × 1% = $200 billion. Globally, the number is much higher. Intermediation costs include asset management fees, investment banking fees, and trading costs including exchange fees and excess taxes on high-turnover portfolios. These fees pay for the highly talented and well-educated professional investors who generally command large wages. Many are in the top 1 percent of the income distribution, rivaling or exceeding doctors' wages.

High wages are warranted for specialized professions that add value to society. The problem with the investment management industry is that collective returns of those involved in active management have not bested the low-cost alternative of index funds in the short, medium, and long run. Roughly two-thirds of professionally managed portfolios underperform the "dumb" indices every year, and over the long run, this group of active managers underperforms by approximately the extent of their fees. Identifying, in advance, which funds are likely to outperform others is tough. Many institutional consultants screen managers on their three-year trailing track record, although little correlation exists between short-term trailing track record and future performance. The "law of small numbers" bias runs deep in the industry.

In this context, the continuing shift toward index funds, with their lower overall fee structures, makes sense. This phenomenon possesses both a structural and cyclical component.

Structural Elements Warranting Continued Shift into Indexing

The following structural elements warrant a shift into indexing:

1. Fees as a percent of assets were established by the industry many years ago when assets under management (AUM) were much lower, all funds were active, and index funds were not viable options. Fees of 1 percent were common and generally were held even as AUM ballooned many times over. Fees should have shrunk for competitive reasons but did not because nominal asset returns in the 1980s and 1990s were very good. Large returns made 1 percent fees seem trivial, which was the result of inappropriate anchoring. Hedge funds rose to prominence in the 1990s, charging 2 percent of assets and 20 percent of the profits, or carry. That made sense for small nimble hedge funds run by truly extraordinary investors, but future batches of funds generally did not earn the fees they charged.

Hedge fund assets swelled in the 2000s, as institutional stewards of capital, including pension funds and endowments, moved an increasing amount of assets into their "alternative" bucket in the hopes of raising their overall expected return. This kept large-scale fee pressures temporarily at bay.

2. Too many funds exist today that charge active fees but structurally are not likely to earn their fees. Many funds have lower active shares, meaning their exposures are more similar to the index to avoid large underperformance. Paying 1 percent or even 50 basis points for near indexing is outrageous. Many of these funds begin with index weights to industries, and then actively adjust up or down based on their perception of value. This framework, beginning with indexing as an anchor, is illogical.

3. Many of the most successful funds historically have grown quite large. The Vanguard Wellington Fund holds more than $100 billion in assets, and the T Rowe Price Blue Chip Growth Fund holds more than $60 billion. Many large funds invest in only the largest capitalization names, and they charge active style fees with too many names in their portfolios. The most successful hedge funds cannot help themselves any more than the long-only investors. Bridgewater and Renaissance Technologies manage in excess of $100 billion, and a handful of other funds manage more than $50 billion. Size is the enemy of performance.

Cyclical Elements Encouraging a Shift Toward Indexing

The following cyclical elements encourage a shift toward indexing:

1. Fee pressure intensifies during periods of lower investment returns. Poor returns in the 1970s partly catalyzed the deregulation of trading costs. Strong returns in the 1980s and 1990s kept fee pressures down, whereas more recent periods, including the 2008 financial crisis, have culminated in an extended period of lower investment returns.

2. Indexing has done relatively better over the past ten years. This compares to the 2000–2002 equity market decline in which active, fundamentally driven firms dominated with large outperformance.

The peak in March 2000 was led by a handful of mega-cap tech companies that traded at enormous premiums to their fundamentals. Indexes were heavily weighted to these companies and most of this group declined by more than 50 percent. Meanwhile, 70 percent of public companies were trading at low and compelling valuations. As their stock prices appreciated between 2000 and 2003, many value-oriented active managers generated excellent returns as a result.

A return to a bifurcated market, in which mega-caps outperform and reach high relative valuation levels with several names weighted above 4 percent in the S&P 500, as present at the end of 2021, may again provide an excellent opportunity for active investors to shine by underweighting these names. Apple, Microsoft, Alphabet, and Amazon have all grown to similar weights as the behemoths seen in late 1999. One difference, however, is that these incredibly profitable companies have durable moats around their businesses. Another difference is that they are less egregiously valued now based on their fundamentals. The future may or may not rhyme in this regard.

3. Rising correlations make active returns harder to come by. We have been stuck in an era of higher correlations among asset classes (specifically among equities). Older investment books talk about periods in which government debt did well while equities did poorly. Bond and stock returns began to become more correlated in the early 1980s when equity valuations were low and interest rates high. This almost forty-year trend of declining yields benefiting rising equity and long bond valuations may be coming to an end as rates hit rock bottom, portending a general lowering of correlations across asset classes. Shorter run breakdowns of correlations occur frequently, and future breakdowns will again provide opportunities for active managers.

Inflation has declined since the early 1980s alongside declining bond yields. Equities responded with their own tailwind, particularly given the low profitability and low valuations at that time. Today's equity valuations are high, and the same holds true for bond and real estate valuations. Equities and real estate likely will be seen as better inflation hedges than bonds, which could lead to declining bond prices and possibly further increasing equity prices if inflation takes root. Given the historically low bond yields, Jeremy Siegel, the famed market forecaster and Wharton professor, predicts that balanced portfolios will shift from a baseline 60/40 equity/bond split to 75/25. This could further stretch equity valuations. These are unknowable predictions and are too hard to call. The general message is that historically tight positive correlations may not be a prelude to the future, and astute active investors have an opportunity to outperform should these correlations break down further.

4. Asset flows over the past ten years have disproportionately gone into index funds. Excessive flows into index funds already have and increasingly will distort valuations for "in" index names. This may provide excellent opportunities to overweight out of index names as valuation spreads widen. Shrewd investors benefit from scouring through this large pool of "neglected" securities.

5. Corporate governance is an issue as indexing expands. In the United States, more than half of all large cap shares are now owned by investors who do not concern themselves with the fundamentals of the underlying businesses. These shares vote proxies, which is an important part of the capitalist ecosystem. They cannot understand the businesses in enough depth to ascertain whether the management and the board of directors is a good steward of the entrusted capital. Even index funds have begun to invest in corporate governance activities, but their efforts are formulaic at best. Active managers will find ways to arbitrage these robotic efforts both long and short. Corporate governance matters.

At the 2019 Daily Journal annual meeting, Charlie Munger explained:

It's happening in the world of stock picking where all this money and effort goes into it and trying to be rational is that we've had a really horrible thing happen. These index funds have come along and they basically beat everybody. And not only that they came out and beat everybody by roughly the amount of the cost of running the operation and changes in investments. So you have a whole profession [that] is basically being paid for accomplishing practically nothing. This is very peculiar. This is not the case with bowel surgery or even the criminal defense bar.

Indexing is great—up to a point. It is an efficient low-cost way to obtain equity exposure. Indexing has done investors a service by driving down fees in other parts of the ecosystem, particularly in sell-side equity business trading costs and in active management fees. It also has made portfolios more tax efficient because portfolio turnover is lower in index funds. Fee compression seen to date in active management likely is coming in other areas, including, notably, advisory fees among financial advisers. They still routinely charge 1 percent of assets in addition to underlying asset management fees. Roboadvisers will continue to make inroads as trust and sophistication in those platforms develops. Ultimately, investors will get better value for services provided.

Conclusion

> "In any sort of a contest—financial, mental, or physical—it's an enormous advantage to have opponents who have been taught that it's useless to even try. From a selfish point of view, Grahamites should probably endow chairs to ensure the perpetual teaching of EMT."
> —WARREN BUFFETT, 1988 BERKSHIRE LETTER TO SHAREHOLDERS

The problem arises when a good idea, such as indexing a portion of one's assets, goes too far. What exactly is too far will be identified by excess returns available to fundamentally long-term-oriented investors that exceed opportunities seen historically. Divergences between price and value will emerge, providing additional opportunities. Assets managed actively by fundamentally oriented investors have and are continuing to shrink, and may become smaller still, but the future of excess returns looks brighter as more of these assets move to indexed platforms. Fundamental investors focus heavily on risk-adjusted returns, considering the risk taken to generate those returns. Index funds make no distinction between the risk of Softbank, an enormous opaque Japanese mega-cap, and Toyota Motor, a similarly sized but much more conservative company with an incredibly strong balance sheet. Odds are that astute, independently minded, long-term-oriented active investors will earn satisfactory risk-adjusted returns, or better, in future cycles.

2

Reasons to Pass

Introduction

After 25 years of buying and supervising a great variety of businesses, Charlie and I have not learned how to solve difficult business problems. What we have learned is to avoid them. To the extent we have been successful, it is because we concentrated on identifying one-foot hurdles that we could step over rather than because we acquired any ability to clear seven-footers.

—WARREN BUFFETT, BERKSHIRE HATHAWAY
ANNUAL LETTER, 1989

The Goal: A Diversified Global Equity Portfolio of Twenty to Forty Names

When a company advertises on Facebook, Instagram, or Google, it pays the platform per impression. The top of the funnel for a digital ad campaign is the entire population base. It is not productive, however, to push ads to the entire population, as only a small percent will potentially be interested in your products. To save costs, the funnel narrows. A bubble gum manufacturer will aim to exclude all demographics unlikely to be interested—senior citizens with dentures, for example.

The New York Stock Exchange (NYSE) has 2,800 listings, NASDAQ has 3,300, and U.S. over-the-counter equities amount to roughly 10,000 at year-end 2021. The London Stock Exchange lists 2,600, Japan's stock market has more than 3,600 public companies, and Hong Kong SAR has 2,300.

The sum is well over twenty thousand publicly traded companies globally. Thousands of these public companies have issued corporate bonds. Real estate assets bought directly qualify as a component of your investment portfolio, as do the hundreds of listed real estate companies. Consider this overwhelming list the top of the funnel. The resulting portfolio, a small, manageable, and diversified portfolio, is the bottom of the funnel. Most investors, professional and amateur alike, frame the decision as follows:

"What Names Should I Buy?"

This is an overwhelming question. It requires a thorough review of many stocks, with hours allocated to each, or worse, it receives cursory and superficial examinations. Some investors use quantitative screens to filter the broad universe of possible candidates. Inevitably, too many candidates will pass their quantitative criteria, leaving these investors overburdened with an intimidating list of potential candidates. More still will sit at the cusp of acceptable quantitative criteria, leaving them to forever wonder whether the next big investment sits right beyond their screen's horizon.

Other investors forsake quantitative criteria, preferring the judgment embedded into their qualitative filters. For example, some will seek only the highest quality names with solid moats around their businesses. In today's world, quality as a factor is richly valued, forcing investors to pay well above a market multiple for names like Coca-Cola, Nestle, and SAP. Pay above intrinsic value, and risk increases. Yet even a quality filter results in an overwhelming candidate target list. Correlation among quality names will be high, as many quality screens rely on similar factors, such as high return on invested capital (ROIC), moderate leverage, and steadily growing earnings per share (EPS).

Still other investors will seek out a sector that offers value first and then will find the best investment among the group. This requires forming opinions on all or most names within that sector, which is an arduous ask that risks freezing the investment decision-making. Searching for the best investment in a wireless carrier will produce dozens around the world, each with positive and negative characteristics. Margins may be higher in the consolidated Canadian telco oligopoly, but so are valuation multiples.

Process matters. Asking "what name should I buy" forces one to build opinions on too many names. Human beings are simple creatures with limited bandwidth to process information. Overclocking one's processor leads to poor decision-making. A gaming PC dials back processing speed when overheating. It may slow down, but processing accuracy is maintained. Human processors treat overclocking differently. The mind looks for shortcuts, desperately seeking a pathway to catch up with the deluge of information and processing requirements. Mental shortcuts create errors of cognition. Behavior when overloaded with data is analogous to moments of crisis, in which higher-order system 2 thinking, detailed by Daniel Kahneman in *Thinking, Fast and Slow*, shuts down and is replaced by primitive fight or flight impulses. Kahneman calls this system 1, primitive and instinctual. These impulses work well for survival and immediate short-term binary decisions: Run or attack. Hide or surprise.

As Charlie Munger shared at the 2006 Berkshire Hathaway annual meeting, "If something is too hard, we move on to something else. What could be simpler than that?"

The goal of a successful investment methodology is to devise a strategy, a process, that protects the mind from overclocking. It must be simple enough not to overwhelm, frighten, intimidate, or result in mental fatigue. Preserve higher-order thinking! A famous Napa Valley winemaker, when asked about the simplicity of his winemaking process, uttered the phrase "simple is not easy."

Simple is not easy. It requires discipline and humility. Discipline to focus only on what truly matters, and humility to stay away from situations you don't understand well enough to know the odds. Keeping it simple will up your odds of outperforming the markets over time with less risk.

Value add from your investment process comes in two parts. The most important part is to stay away from investments that are too hard to call. Most names, in fact, are too hard to call. Devise your process to avoid these structurally risky names—the intrinsic range is too wide, the research process is too intensive or too challenging, the unknowables are too great, or the price is too high relative to the underlying fundamentals. The overarching goal of *Reasons to Pass* is this: Stay away from investments that are too hard to call and you will prosper.

The second part, selecting the actual investments, is the icing on top of an already delicious dessert. Exclusions provide the foundation of a robust investment methodology, protecting capital from harm that can set back financial goals or worse. Portfolio positions receive the glamor because they are seen as generating the returns, although they are mere representatives, the messengers, of an extensive process. Positions are the beneficiary of praise when investment returns prove fruitful and are blamed when performance suffers. This is an unfair characterization of an investment process.

In European football, the keeper, fullbacks, and midfielders are the core of a successful team. The striker receives the glory and the paycheck, but the rest of the team accords him or her the opportunity to shine. Now replace striker with investment, and the fullback with *Reasons to Pass*.

In business, the CEO is the striker, lavished with praise and large financial rewards. Many CEOs, perhaps most, do not earn their keep, and shareholders should revolt en masse rather than overpay these glorified strikers. CEOs are dependent on a team to deliver results. The head of marketing determines go-to market strategies, including methods of distribution, the head of research and development allocates scarce dollars, and so forth. One difference between a striker and a CEO is that other key positions report to the CEO. Consider the CEO a combination of coach and striker (i.e., more valuable than a striker but still a member of a team).

Index Investing

If you had simply invested in a global equity index over the past forty years you would have earned roughly a 10 percent return per year. A disciplined buy-and-hold strategy would have satisfied most every investor's goal of increasing future wealth. The power of compounding, once purportedly called the eighth wonder of the world by Albert Einstein, amplifies even small improvements to compound returns. If you invested $1,000 at 10 percent for thirty years, this would lead to a future value of $17,500. Raise your annual return to 11 percent and the future value increases to $22,900. Returns matter.

Based purely on statistics, generating higher-than-index returns is hard, very hard. Most investment professionals do not beat their relevant passive benchmarks over time. Indices are inherently low cost and do not carry the emotional toll of making active selections. Furthermore, fees and errors of judgment cost active managers, and individual investors, dearly.

Modified Index Investing

Indexes have their appeal, but on occasion, they can go far askew from the underlying fundamentals. The S&P 500 saw technology stocks reach

40 percent of the index weight in late 1999 at record-breaking valuations. Consider the following hypothetical investment process: Imagine investing all of your capital in a broad-based global equity index, including any additional flows, unless an obvious, statistically significant, high-conviction opportunity to stray from the index presents itself. Two types of deviations may occur, both of which are centered around the margin of safety. In the first, a large margin-of-safety opportunity emerges in some asset class, geographical region, or sector. In the second, market euphoria sends asset prices to extremes, warranting reduced exposure. Overpay for an index fund, and at best, forward returns will decline. At worst, you will face a structural risk of loss. It took NASDAQ fifteen years to regain its top seen in March 2000. As of 2021, the Nikkei 225 was still 25 percent below its December 1989 peak.

Most of the time, neither under- nor overvaluation is evident in a statistically relevant fashion. Strategists and Wall Street economists think otherwise because their job description requires frequent prophecies. Their projections mostly highlight statistically insignificant opportunities that do not in a major way benefit investors. "The Market will end the year 5 percent higher than the current level" is a typical forecast offered by these market watchers. Their careers depend on making frequent forecasts that can be sold to their clients. Predicting sixteen versus eighteen centimeters of rain next season does not help a farmer's well-being, but every once in a great while, a flood or drought comes along that can change that farmer's fate. Economists and strategists almost universally fall flat with these material predictions. The advice from *Reasons to Pass* is this: skip predictions until an obvious one comes along.

The following exercise attempts to create a mostly indexed portfolio that actively drifts from a passive allocation only when these obvious and material opportunities emerge. Creating a list of historical events around which excess returns existed is fraught with psychological risk. Hindsight bias is a powerful force elevating self-confidence. The wise and foolish both saw the collapse of the Soviet Union as imminent. Watch for this red-light alert: *disregarding the following analysis may be the wisest choice.*

A large number of historical, material events over the years would have lent themselves to incremental returns, but most were not obvious without the benefit of hindsight or unique insight. Was the rise of American industry after World War II an obvious outcome? Massive wartime stimulus that measured 50 percent of gross domestic product (GDP) kept the country afloat during the war. Wouldn't a return to the previous depressionary environment have been a reasonable projection once the stimulus was withdrawn? The Eurozone faced an existential crisis in 2012 when southern Europe came to the brink of collapse. Should the wealthy EU nations bail out more profligate spenders, and if so, to what extent? What would the consequences have been had the EU splintered? Was the rise of China to superpower status obvious in 1999, with its voracious appetite for commodities creating a supercycle in steel, copper, and other commodities? These were hard issues to understand, really hard, with too many moving parts, even though they seem obvious in hindsight. Overallocating capital to the southern countries, Greece and Italy in particular, or ten-year large allocations to iron ore companies in 1999, or big bets on American industry in the late 1940s all would have been massively accretive to portfolios. Unfortunately, the crystal balls were mostly low resolution.

Benjamin Graham once warned: "All my experience goes to show that most investment advisers take their opinions and measures of stock values from stock prices. In the stock market, value standards don't determine prices, prices determine value standards" ("Stock Market Warning: Danger Ahead!," University of California–Los Angeles speech, 1959).

A handful of events, however, would have been relatively easier to identify and exploit, yielding above-index returns with an overall reduction in risk. These areas were evident to many fundamental investors but less so to the markets at large, which became disconnected from the underlying fundamentals. Behaviorally, most investors really do anchor on price rather than on value.

Index investors face the obvious process limitation that they are overallocated to the most expensive parts of the market while they are underallocated to those with the largest margins of safety. This combination, although not deadly because of the high level of diversification inherent in a global index, still hampers return potential. Isolating just two or three of these more obvious opportunities as large over- or underallocations relative to pure index exposures would have enhanced annualized returns by 1 percent per year or more, providing a powerful boost to hard-earned savings and future values. Several examples of events that might have been foreseeable include the following:

1. Japanese Equity Market, 1985–1995: The Japanese equity market, the second largest globally during this timeframe, peaked in December 1989 at 39,000. Tokyo land prices rose 40 percent in 1985 and another 45 percent in 1986. Residential real estate prices

in Japan more than doubled between 1986 and 1990. Leverage expanded steadily and bank-fueled asset lending artificially pushed prices beyond their fundamentals. Optimism over Japan's economic inroads over the rest of the world began much earlier but built to a crescendo during this time period. Japan Inc. had been on fire, and many saw Japan making perpetual gains into tech, finance, industrials, and manufacturing. Equity valuations spiked during this timeframe. The late 1980s saw price-to-earnings (P/E) ratios stretch to 70x on inflated earnings well above midcycle levels. The Nikkei subsequently declined to below 17,000 by the end of 1992 with the market's P/E ratio dropping to 30x. The market eventually bottomed at 7,000 in March 2009. Real estate values halved by 1995, dropping another 50 percent by 2005. Although the optimal asset allocation strategy was to sell the market from 1989 to 2003, just staying away during the most obviously overvalued time would have added roughly 1 percent per year to your global equity index return.

2. Emerging Markets (EM) Crisis, 1997–1998: The early and mid-1990s led to increasing enthusiasm about the future of EMs. Growth expectations were high, sovereign and consumer leverage was low, and per capita incomes were but a small fraction of that of the industrial world but were rising quickly. Capital flows withdrew in 1997 and more dramatically in 1998 after the unexpected Russian sovereign debt default and the Brazilian currency devaluation. Valuations became compelling and many EM investment candidates with limited corporate debt, dominant businesses, and solid moats were found from Brazil to Korea. Buying a basket of high-quality EM names after the crisis with a ten-year holding period would have increased index returns by up to 1 percent per year.

3. Tech Bubble, 1998–2002: Valuations were disregarded for global and, in particular, for U.S. tech names during this period, and many of the largest names had valuations so obviously excessive that anyone fundamentally oriented would have easily identified them. The market typically sells at an EV per sales of two times, but high-tech mega caps during this timeframe were well over ten times and peaked at thirty times sales. Although the precise shape of the cycle was impossible to predict, just passing on names that obviously were overvalued would have added fifty basis points

annualized to global index performance. Having the fortitude to invest in the high-quality survivors in 2003 with the intent to hold on to them for the long term would have generated substantial additional alpha.

4. Global Financial Bubble, 2005–2008: This was a tougher cycle to call, although financials as a percent of the market peaked at around 30 percent of total market cap in the mid-2000s, with high returns on equity (ROE) versus history and low capital. These companies were highly leveraged. Underwriting risks were extreme with an increasing amount of interest-only, no-documentation (no doc) or low-doc loans, and enough subprime mortgage lending to provide an imprudent level of debt capital to the U.S. housing market. U.S. mortgages accounted for more than $10 trillion of exposure, which was material against $80 trillion in global GDP. Many financials further levered up on risky mortgage-backed securities. Much of the analysis was complex and not obvious, although simply framing the decision as staying away from financials with the potent combination of unusually high ROE and high leverage, followed by rebalancing toward financials once these risks became apparent, would have added fifty basis points to returns.

Sometimes investment decisions are easy and quick. Charlie Munger once noted that "Warren is amazingly quick to say both yes and no" (Wesco annual meeting, 2001). The highlighted periods did not require in-depth analysis, access to unique scuttlebutt, or inordinate wisdom or the ability to see around corners. A good idea is carried to excess as first envy, and then greed, trigger herding around a theme. Investing in individual equities is identical: a successful company expands its following to irrationality. Periods of excess are easy passes for investors and are focused on underlying fundamentals. Quite often, however, there is nothing obvious on the horizon. When nothing obvious exists, ambitious, self-confident investors will concoct elaborate investment theses with creative justifications. They will seek out corroborating data, which reinforces confidence. Unfortunately, more elaborate justifications are not directly correlated with improved odds of success. Our investment environment is cruel and unforgiving, and false proofs run deep: one part illusion of control, one part intellect-seeking challenges, and one part justification for high pay. Seeking out opportunities when little is to be done is dangerous. Astute investors recognize these risks and appreciate that almost all investments are too tough to call.

"What Names Should I Avoid?"

A successful investment process begins with this simple phrase. It liberates you from having to have an opinion on any one name. Instead, it allows you to pass, using only the justification that it is too hard to call. Munger might be credited with this innovation, along with other humble investors before him. Answer this question, and you can ruthlessly swipe left (or is it right?) most names that come across your desk as potential investment candidates. Most names can be eliminated in seconds or minutes. Don't worry if skipped names go up, as some invariably will. Do not let this alter your process.

As Munger cautioned: "We've probably made a significant decision every two years. But no one manages money this way. For one thing, clients won't pay you" (Wesco annual meeting, 2003).

Practice Makes Perfect

One way to practice your process of elimination skillset is by analyzing major indices. Select one that looks interesting, such as the Dow Jones Industrial Average (DJIA). Sort the names by market cap, and then begin your review from the top down. Evaluate each of the thirty companies independently, ruthlessly, based on the principles espoused in part 1 and the criteria that follow here in part 2. Measure the time it takes you to evaluate a business. Start with the business description, and then look at its historical financials. Can you determine in what pile it belongs: the yes pile, the maybe but needs more work pile, or the pass pile? Few people have tried this approach comprehensively within an index, even though the return on time invested is high. This is good practice for individual investors and illuminating for Wall Street strategists. This hypothetical elimination filter, rarely tried yet both time efficient and educational, works with any market. The key is to identify the appropriate filters to swiftly eliminate investment candidates that come across your desk.

A cursory review should be able to mostly evaluate the DJIA within a day. Your process, once honed, will eliminate 95 percent of names from investment consideration in short order. The maybes take a bit longer, requiring reviews of annual reports, other disclosures, and possibly further study. Don't let complexity bias enchant you; if the rabbit hole extends too deep too fast, slide the name over to the pass pile. Remember to stay within your personal circle of competence. The Hang Seng, Financial Times Stock Exchange (FTSE), Nikkei, CAC 40 (*Cotation Assistée en Continu*), and other major markets could be next. Once complete, names remaining in the maybe pile can be assessed in greater detail until the distillation process is complete. Few if any names will be immediately dropped into the yes pile. What will remain is a manageable portfolio. Most likely, simply indexing the few remaining names in an equal-weighted index will yield prosperous results.

The number of yes names will vary across time. The valuation filter will trigger many eliminations that do not provide a requisite margin of safety as the economic cycle approaches a peak level. Macro peaks will see fewer names fall into the yes pile. These periods often correlate with ballooning balance sheet leverage as management confidence rises. Other aggressive management actions consistent with peak behavior create additional unquantifiable risks. Rest assured that there is zero urgency to populate a portfolio immediately and that at least a handful of names will emerge in any economic climate. The goal is not to build a comprehensive fully invested portfolio on day one, and diversification across time is most always prudent. Rushed decisions equate to poor decisions. *Maintain your behavioral edge by keeping your investment process slow and deliberate.*

Lower stock prices accompany economic troughs, but so does declining profitability. These offer excellent corporate stress tests, providing visibility into a company's competitive position and a means to evaluate management prudence. Your short list of yes names will expand as troughs emerge, crest as economic stabilization sets in, and then shrink as a cyclical peak approaches.

Munger wrote: "It is counterproductive for a prey animal that is threatened by a predator to take a long time in deciding what to do" (*Poor Charlie's Almanack*, 2005).

To reiterate, build an investment process that minimizes the risk of becoming overwhelmed, preserving higher order thinking. Never allow mental faculties to become overloaded. Targeting too large a list for deeper analysis clogs scarce bandwidth, inevitably triggering an eruption of the self-preservation, fight-or-flight mechanism. Screen assets in a way that doesn't deluge your faculties with too many prospects. No one person can reasonably have an investment opinion on more than a small handful of potential investments. Accept that you will miss some outstanding names. Be satisfied that those will slip right by. To repeat, you need only a handful of names across time to be a successful investor. First and foremost, always remember that the goal of a successful investment process is to protect your faculties from overclocking.

The criteria highlighted in the remainder of part 2, our specific reasons to pass, are the foundation of a successful investment process. Criteria must be chosen carefully to protect against the risk of permanent loss. Find names that substantially lower the odds of permanent impairment, and solid investment results will follow. Market observers will call this risk management, but true investors consider it something much more foundational—a cornerstone embedded into their thinking.

The remainder of part 2 features the most relevant criteria leading to our reasons to pass. The criteria are intended to be strict, harsh, and unbending. They must be applied ruthlessly to adequately reduce your list of investment candidates to a manageable number of digestible names. Some of the criteria lend themselves to a quantitative filter, although a qualitative evaluation often will be required. These criteria apply equally to investments around the globe, and although primarily targeting equity investors, they apply to nonequity investments as well. Throughout part 2, case studies of U.S. and non-U.S. companies are provided for illustration.

5

Minimum Market Capitalization

These comparative results undoubtedly reflect the tendency of smaller issues of inferior quality to be relatively overvalued in bull markets, and not only to suffer more serious declines than the stronger issues in the ensuing price collapse, but also to delay their full recovery—in many cases indefinitely. The moral for the intelligent investor is, of course, to avoid second-quality issues in making up a portfolio, unless—for the enterprising investor—they are demonstrable bargains.

—BENJAMIN GRAHAM, *THE INTELLIGENT INVESTOR*,
1973, CHAP. 15

Reasons for a Large-Cap Bias

Publicly traded companies come in all sizes: micro-cap to mega-cap. The end of 2020 culminated with a handful of companies with market caps in excess of $1 trillion—Amazon, Microsoft, Alphabet, Saudi Aramco, and PetroChina. In 2021, three of these companies reached $2 trillion. Although the global definition of small caps varies, the Russell 2000, a U.S. small-cap proxy, has a median market cap of $900 million with a range of $150 million to $5 billion. Benjamin Graham addressed variances of size in *The Intelligent Investor*. His formulas may no longer work, but his principles stand. Larger companies possess some distinct advantages in the capital markets that lower the structural risks of an investment. In other words, the average large cap deserves a lower discount rate than the average small cap.

1. Cheaper access to capital—Banks, bond investors, and other debt capital providers are more willing to extend credit to large caps. Fewer terms and conditions apply, interest rates are lower, and maturities extended. Equity capital when required for expansions or recapitalizations is more readily available and at lower required investor returns. Vendors are more willing to extend terms of accounts payables, a source of cash, and landlords are more willing to offer temporary flexibility, if needed. Walmart is in a much stronger position to negotiate with capital providers than Macy's, which not long ago became a small cap, although it rebounded again in 2021.

2. Better management—Many small caps are run by founders or by people directly chosen by founders. Founders can be excellent managers, although many are better at starting companies than at growing them. The offspring of founders face higher odds of taking over family businesses with lower odds that they are best suited to run their business. Large caps employ significant resources to screen top management candidates and have the financial wherewithal to pay for professional best-in-class managers. They also have the resources to invest in a deep bench, training them to create smoother succession pathways.

3. Minimum level of diversification—Large caps rarely rely solely on one product or service. They operate in multiple segments with various profit streams and thus offer greater product and customer diversification. They also diversify their research and development (R&D) across multiple upside options, creating the next generation of revenues. They diversify regionally or globally with business operations that often span multiple countries, supply chains that can be flexed in different directions, and with many customers whose fortunes are somewhat less correlated. Regulatory and tax diversification can provide operating or financial flexibility.

4. Better access to capital if distressed—GE would have gone bankrupt many years ago if not for the generosity of the capital markets toward prominent companies. European companies in distress undertake rights issues instead of traditional stock issuances seen in the United States. Large caps have much easier access to rights issues at lesser discounts and the ready support of investment banks and their clients in the United States when overnight equity raises are needed. Small caps in need of rights offerings

sometimes struggle to secure an investment banking syndicate to underwrite their rights offerings or must do so under arduous circumstances. The most high-profile bankruptcies are well recognized large caps that fell from grace, think Enron in 2001, WorldCom in 2002, and Lehman Brothers and General Motors in 2008. These rare events are vivid financial traumas that investors systematically overweight. Most large-cap bankruptcies are U.S. companies—a function of a generous Chapter 11 bankruptcy filing that allows for great restructuring flexibility. Chapter 11 filings protect the enterprise value while rebalancing the capital structure from debt toward equity. Most other countries have no Chapter 11 equivalent and thus default to liquidation in bankruptcy. This heavily incentivizes companies outside the United States to (a) manage their businesses more conservatively, (b) keep debt balances lower, and (c) raise equity earlier to protect against the risk of insolvency.

5. Greater disclosure and investor communications—Spend one hour comparing a handful of investor relations (IR) websites of large and small companies. Many large companies attend investment bank conferences, dropping those presentations into their IR tabs. Annual reports are dense and comprehensive, with management discussion and analysis sections (MD&A) broken down by segment with deep granularity into their operations. Some large caps provide quarterly supplements with additional information. They host investor days to discuss specific segments. Well-versed investor relations personnel staff the phones and meet with investors, and when necessary, organize meetings with senior or divisional managers.

   Most small companies do things differently. They don't have the scale to support a large investor relations effort. They don't attend many (or any) conferences. Instead, calls to discuss their operations end up on the CFO's desk with uncertain odds of a call back. Company disclosures are sparse, and for foreign firms (particularly in Asia), English-language reports may not be available.

6. Other information availability—Do an information search on Cisco Systems, and you will find a treasure trove of analysis on its competitive position, management acumen, employee and customer satisfaction, and R&D initiatives. Search for information on Netgear, a small-cap competitor in certain product lines, and information is lacking. Investment banks publish dozens or even

hundreds of research reports on prominent large caps while mostly neglecting small caps. Relevant information can make a tremendous difference in investor conviction.

7. Trading liquidity—Many small companies particularly outside the United States still trade at wide bid-ask spreads, with trading by appointment the only way to keep costs down as purchase size increases. One Canadian small-cap stock held by my previous fund traded for $500 with a $100 bid-ask spread. Large-cap bid-ask spreads are often several basis points.

Reasons to Own Small Caps

If I were young and had a small amount of capital to invest, I would be looking in the small cap world.
—CHARLIE MUNGER, WESCO ANNUAL MEETING, 2010

Growth rates vary widely by industry and individual companies. Size is a factor, and small companies have generated a slightly higher average earnings per share growth than those seen among larger concerns. The law of large numbers affects growth prospects as firms grow. Growth rates decline once markets are saturated, while R&D, product innovation, brand extension, and new categories are less likely to be material as a percentage of revenues or earnings.

The book *Loonshots* (2019), by Safi Bahcall, highlights a structural problem with large-cap companies. Small-company employees focus intensively on the stakes of an initiative, because failure affects everyone associated with their team. Employees at large companies tend to focus, rationally, on their status and prestige within their organization. Any initiative, even if successful, will be immaterial to the overall organization, whereas a promotion within a large company can be personally material. This focus on the promotion rather than the initiative is why good teams at great companies kill great ideas. It's simply too risky. Small caps take the calculated risks that can lead to high returns.

Large companies face another structural disadvantage. Knowledge sharing within smaller companies works relatively well as fewer modes of operation mean less lost communication between staffers. Large companies with their diverse roles and plethora of committees means that cross-pollination of thoughts and ideas suffer. Occasionally, more nefarious intent, such as retaining information for the benefit of power, causes information to become siloed. The costs of these issues are not insignificant. Consider this a diseconomy of scale that large companies face.

Investing in small caps can be lucrative, as they are less well covered by Wall Street investment banks, get less press coverage, and have brands that are less familiar to investors. This makes small caps less efficiently priced and theoretically provides them with more opportunity for outperformance. Takeouts often occur at premium multiples that are still accretive to the large-cap acquirors. So why not invest in these companies exclusively?

Beware of Small Caps with Large Investor Relations Efforts

The challenge to finding solid long-term investment candidates in small-cap land is partly informational. Many small companies struggle to provide investors with enough information. Annual reports are too skinny, good comparable companies on which to benchmark operations are hard to find, and highly visible small caps often market themselves aggressively through investment conferences and media blitzes. These companies are just pitching their own stocks and thus are less credible. While acknowledging the inequity of punishing both small caps lacking in information and those who are heavily promotional, thoughtful investors will find some small caps that meet investment objectives.

Warren Buffett cautioned: "Here's a telling fact: of the ten non-oil companies having the largest market capitalization in 1965—titans such as GM, Sears, DuPont, and Eastman Kodak—only one made the 2006 list" (Berkshire Hathaway annual letter, 2006).

Borrowing from Graham, most small companies structurally are secondary companies. They could disappear tomorrow, and the world would not miss a beat. General Electric, with all its warts, is still a primary company, and its segments would be sorely missed by its customers and by the broader economy. Primary companies will come and go over the decades, and secondary companies will turn much faster. Primary companies' stock prices can be volatile but typically will trade closer to intrinsic value, whereas secondary companies trade up toward market multiples only near peaks and down to large discounts in troughs.

Tertiary companies, one step further removed from primary status, are grouped into the small-cap asset class. These even more insignificant companies exist to fill niches that easily may be overtaken by larger competitors. Odds of their eventual disappearance run high. Many are run by aggressive opportunists; the tenth initial public offering (IPO) in the nascent legalized marijuana market is one example. *Pass on all tertiary companies regardless of the sales pitch, growth prospects, or valuation!*

Country-specific factors also require consideration. The United States is the deepest market globally, and many companies are clearly secondary with $2 billion or greater market caps. That is, most market niches are sizable and can support multiple competitors, including one or two primary companies and one or more secondary companies. It is unusual in the United States to find primary companies in the small-cap arena. Meanwhile, tertiary companies may be valued at up to $1 billion. The United Kingdom has similar depth in its public markets, as do Japan and China. Many smaller countries, by contrast, have a handful of large caps and many small caps. Small caps in these countries can be primary or secondary companies. Embraer in Brazil is a small cap even though it is part of the world's oligopoly in commercial airplane manufacturing and thus meets the definition of a primary company. Compania Cervecerias Unidas (CCU) is Chile's dominant beverage company with a market share of almost 50 percent in both beer and nonalcoholic categories, and 20 percent market shares in other Latin American countries. With a market cap of less than $3 billion, it acts as a primary company while investment markets group it as a small cap. It is fully scaled with dominant distribution. Many smaller countries, including Chile, have limited to no tertiary companies available for investments, as their market caps would be insignificant.

One other country constraint relates to trading accessibility. U.S. retail investors cannot invest in locally listed companies in India, Korea, or other potentially attractive markets. Many large caps have American depository receipts (ADRs) that trade efficiently, although small caps rarely justify that added expense. Small caps that choose to invest limited resources to sponsor an ADR send a highly promotional warning signal. Small caps have limited revenues and scale to justify these added expenses, and most rational owners and managers would not be interested in paying the listing fees. Some international companies list exclusively in the United States because liquidity and valuations are higher. Small caps meeting this criteria may be reasonably viable investment candidates.

Finally, liquidity needs must be weighed against desired assets under management (AUM). Small caps outside the United States are inherently illiquid, while the disastrous performance of the Russell 2000 in early 2020 demonstrates just how quickly liquidity can evaporate for even U.S. small caps when economic prospects turn down. Even investment funds with small AUM, less than $100 million, can suffer from liquidity issues when targeting small company investments. Thus, greater diversification is required, and our goal of twenty to forty names may not be attainable should you choose a purely small-cap strategy.

Reasons to Pass

Even with so many reasons to pass, defining precise global constraints to minimum market capitalization is too challenging to call with precision. The goals are to pass on (1) tertiary companies; (2) the most illiquid; (3) companies for which lack of information impairs informed judgment; (4) companies with clearly incapable or overly aggressive management or mostly founders' descendants; and (5) single-product companies with R&D risk or those subject to market fads or fashion risks. Setting a hard global minimum market cap of $500 million is reasonable, and up to $1 billion is acceptable. Beyond that, adjusting limits by country can be helpful, such as minimums of $2 billion in the United States, $1 billion in the United Kingdom, and $500 million in Japan. These limits will ensure that most of the noted goals can be met while also providing access to a large number of excellent businesses, many of which are small cap for which the level of attention is low and the odds of outperformance are higher. Protect first and then seek opportunities. Remember: Simple is not easy.

6

Financial Leverage
The Ultimate Killer

We use debt sparingly. Many managers, it should be noted, will disagree with this policy, arguing that significant debt juices the returns for equity owners. And these more venturesome CEOs will be right most of the time. At rare and unpredictable intervals, however, credit vanishes and debt becomes financially fatal. A Russian roulette equation—usually win, occasionally die—may make financial sense for someone who gets a piece of a company's upside but does not share in its downside. But that strategy would be madness for Berkshire. Rational people don't risk what they have and need for what they don't have and don't need.

—WARREN BUFFETT, BERKSHIRE HATHAWAY
ANNUAL LETTER, 2018

A Firm's Optimal Capital Structure

Every business school student is taught to maximize firm value by optimizing the capital structure. The conventional academic mindset is that the cost of debt is lower than the cost of equity. Increase the amount of debt in the capital structure and magically lower the cost of capital, up to the point at which added financial risk to the enterprise overwhelms the benefit. In a discounted cash flow (DCF) analysis, this minimum cost of capital maximizes the present value of each year's free cash flow and results in a higher multiple of free cash flow in the terminal year. Presto, the DCF equity value is maximized.

Share buybacks funded by debt issuances seemingly make sense through this lens because they rebalance the capital structure toward lower cost debt. In 2018 and 2019, we saw record buybacks, annualized around $800 billion per year for the S&P 500. This drove up earnings per share (EPS), and higher EPS growth increased the earnings multiple. Record-low interest rates coupled with near-record-low credit spreads for corporate borrowers have allowed added leverage to exist without materially increasing companies' interest expense.

Interest coverage, operating profit divided by interest expense, is one of the credit metrics traditionally used by credit investors and equity investors that are interested in companies' credit worthiness. Declining interest rates, leading to ever-decreasing interest expense, increase interest coverage. Higher interest coverage justifies greater debt issuance, with debt capital going to fund either investments into capital projects that improve future earnings power, or into share buybacks. Looking back at 2019, interest coverage was strong and presented no alarm bells to the credit markets.

Net debt to earnings before interest, taxes, depreciation, and amortization (EBITDA), operating profit plus depreciation and amortization expense, has long been used as the other primary indicator of credit quality. The traditional threshold between investment-grade and non-investment-grade credits was three times, but this heuristic has drifted higher in recent years. This credit metric, more than interest coverage, has been predictive of future corporate distress. The more stable EBITDA is through the cycle, the higher the acceptable limit of net debt to EBITDA. Telecoms generate a more stable EBITDA and thus can apply more leverage. AT&T, for example, operates with a net debt-to-EBITDA ratio of approximately three times, as they have been quite acquisitive. For now, they are still investment grade but are reaching the high end of the acceptable range. Notably, they are one of the three largest barely investment-grade borrowers in the United States and thus are closely watched by the credit markets, as being downgraded to non-investment grade would be seismic for the junk bond market. Its recent announcement to spin off its media division to shareholders will result in its high debt load being distributed between the two entities, each of which will likely be heavily indebted in their own right.

Auto companies, by contrast, should quite plausibly be net cash at an operating level to avoid the painful dilution or risk of distress often seen by deep cyclicals. The last auto trough in 2008 was severe. Ford is one of the largest borrowers in the credit markets, although its debt is primarily related to its financing business and thus is offset by its loan book on the asset side. It lost its investment grade rating in 2020 during COVID concerns. It currently sits at BB+, which is less than ideal for such a large borrower.

EBITDA is not earnings. Many sell-side analysts, industry professionals, bankers, and amateurs value companies on an EV/EBITDA basis. As mentioned, EBITDA is a major indicator for credit investors. Ongoing expenses related to depreciation and amortization vary dramatically between companies and must be taken into consideration. This is why steel companies cannot leverage to four times EBITDA, but this also is why restaurant franchisers without any tangible assets to replace over time seemingly can. Beware of EBITDA: it offers information but is not earnings.

It is a simple process to uncover businesses whose earnings power should be relatively more stable over the cycle, and it is similarly easy to screen for names with low financial leverage. Combine the two, and the list is short indeed. Consumer staples, utilities, wireless telecoms, healthcare concerns, and other "defensive" operating businesses often load on additional debt. Business confidence runs high, with managers being optimistic about the future. Bankers and advisers who are well trained in business school valuation principles offer counsel. Aggressive investors taught by the same professors press for added leverage. Overlay a greater amount of financial debt onto a stable business and that equity investment quickly degrades to risk parity—that is, its structural riskiness to investors is no different than the deep cyclical that carries lower debt.

American Tower owns and operates almost two hundred thousand communications towers around the globe. Revenues and earnings have been annuity-like, growing annually even through the 2008 Great Financial Crisis (GFC). This is a desirable business with high barriers to entry. The balance sheet is less defensive, with $30 billion in total debt, $25 billion in net debt, which is covered by just $5 billion of EBITDA, and interest coverage of just three times. This is a defensive business offset by high debt.

In its defense, American Tower is structured as a real estate investment trust (REIT). REITs carry higher debt; between five and ten times EBITDA is the norm. The justification is that REITs should be capitalized more like private real estate concerns. A small multifamily property might be worth $1 million, have a $700,000 mortgage, and generate $70,000 in annual rents. The interest coverage on this property will be about two, and debt to EBITDA will be twelve times. Yet a 70 percent loan to value (LTV) seems conservative and would offer plenty of cushion to lenders should times turn tough. REITs need to be evaluated on a combination of rent stability, asset desirability, LTV, and net debt to EBITDA. On these metrics, American Tower appears strong, and hence it has a high valuation. Simon Property Group (SPG), the preeminent owner of Class A malls in the United States, is similarly levered at six times EBITDA. Because its rents are tied to a percentage of tenants' sales, the 2020 closure of malls because of coronavirus concerns materially depressed their sales. They are structurally at risk as consumers shift away from physical retail. A six times EBITDA for SPG is much riskier than six times EBITDA for American Tower.

Siemens is one of the strongest industrial companies, with high market shares and dominant businesses in a variety of industrial niches. This is a primary company, and the world would miss its products and services were it to disappear. Revenues and EBITDA are more stable than average, with earnings that grow cycle over cycle. Its financial performance through-out the GFC was impressive, with revenues barely down and EBITDA steady to growing. EBITDA peaked in 2019 at more than euro (EUR) 10 billion. Net debt unfortunately rose at a much higher rate, taking net debt to EBITDA from 0.7 times in 2006 to 2.4 times at year-end 2019. Leverage increased further in 2020, although EBITDA shrank to EUR 8 billion. A seemingly low-risk investment has become much riskier because of management overconfidence and an unexpected cyclical downturn. The risk of a Siemens insolvency is still low because, as a primary company with high-quality businesses, it is likely to be accorded access to necessary capital in any circumstance. Its financial flexibility has declined, however, leading to fewer accretive options for its management team.

British American Tobacco (BAT) is one of a handful of mega-cap tobacco companies. Revenues and margins have been stable, and the addic-tive nature of their products makes them somewhat immune to recession-ary forces. This stability has led to high confidence, and it is no surprise that management has driven up leverage. It trades at nine times its 2020 earnings, which is a discount to the market but probably is fair given its low growth and future structural decline rate as volumes slowly decline and pricing power flatlines. Its dividend, however, might unexpectedly come under pressure given its more than four times net debt-to-EBITDA lever-age ratio. *High-quality stable yet slowly declining earnings in future years, accompanied by high debt: Pass.*

Enbridge, the Canadian pipeline company, is one of many midstream energy companies seen as toll operators making money on the throughput regardless of underlying commodity prices. This reliability makes them less sensitive to economic variability and commodity cycles. These companies are seen as excellent businesses. Buffett himself has allocated capital to this space. The temptation to lever up this stable earnings stream is powerful, and even conservative managers are pressured by aggressive investors to force debt higher. Going into 2021, Enbridge had a debt of Canadian dollars (CAD) 68 billion versus a market cap of CAD 90 billion and EBITDA of CAD 12 billion, giving it a five times net debt-to-EBITDA leverage. Continuing COVID concerns and unexpectedly large reductions in energy demand are sure to pressure earnings and may lead to a reduction in its 7 percent dividend or, at worst, a forced debt restructuring.

Buffett gave this advice: "My suggestion: Before even discussing repurchases, a CEO and his or her Board should stand, join hands and in unison declare, 'What is smart at one price is stupid at another'" (Berkshire Hathaway annual letter, 2016).

Corporate profit margins influence companies' decisions around capital structure. Margins ebb and flow over time in tune with the business cycle, industry microeconomics, and individual company performance. Assessing credit risk using 2019 EBITDA gives investors a false sense of security as EBITDA was near peak levels for many companies. Confidence to take on additional debt is highest near cyclical peaks. Share buybacks, a primary use of capital when confidence is high, peaked in the 1998–2000 peak environment, and again between 2005 and 2007, and most recently between 2017 and 2019. Billions of dollars of capital were wasted because companies borrowed to buy back shares above intrinsic value.

Investors need to look at the structural risk of unexpected earnings declines that can place companies at risk. HP Inc. generates 60 percent of its revenues from desktop PCs, which until recently faced structural decline in demand as digital solutions replaced paper. Xerox faces an even more precarious downward slope. Tobacco companies have forestalled structural declines with aggressive pricing actions, but per unit prices are becoming prohibitively expensive particularly when taxation trends are also on the rise. 3M Group, an otherwise high-quality industrial and consumer-branded company, faces a potential litigation overhang that may reach $50 billion in a downside scenario. It produced PFAS (per- and polyfluoroalkyl substances) materials that offer broad applications, including as fire retardants and insulating properties. A consequence is that these materials biodegrade very slowly and have been identified as cancer-causing substances that reportedly have seeped into a third of the U.S. drinking supplies. Its market cap of just under $100 billion might survive the onslaught, but at a substantial cost. DuPont also has been linked to this litigation. The higher the risk of structural declines or risk, the stronger the balance sheet must be to protect investors.

Economic peaks see strong revenue growth, high gross and operating margins, and high-capacity utilization leading to greater asset turns. Return on invested capital (ROIC) hits new highs. Overconfidence does not just incite investors to make irrational choices, C-suite personnel also are driven by the same impulses. Strong results translate to high management compensation, which drives greater overconfidence. Strong results also inflate the EBITDA, optically driving down debt to EBITDA. High return on equity (ROE) often is a component of incentive compensation, and there is no easier way to temporarily increase ROE than by reducing equity. In a peak, all signs point to increasing leverage beyond prudent levels.

This scenario is precisely what the system has seen in recent years. Net debt to EBITDA for U.S. nonfinancial companies averaged around one and a half times for investment-grade borrowers between 2003 and 2015, with a temporary blip in 2008 and 2009 when EBITDA declined. Recent years have seen an unprecedented corporate debt expansion, rising to two times in 2017 and close to two and a half times by year-end 2019. Remember, year-end 2019 EBITDA was potentially near peak level. In a downturn, EBITDA declines abruptly while debt lingers painfully. The consequences are severe.

Walt Disney Versus Six Flags at Year-End 2008

Disney historically has operated with a conservative balance sheet. Its net debt at year-end 2008 of $12 billion compared favorably to that year's peak EBITDA of $10 billion. For such a durable and well-diversified business, 1.2 times is fairly conservative. Disney used its strong cash flow in 2009, a recession year, to pay down $2 billion in debt against EBITDA, which declined 30 percent year over year. This was obviously a survivor and worthy investment candidate at that time.

Six Flags also runs theme parks, although its business mix is not diversified. It was highly acquisitive during the 2000s and managed its balance sheet aggressively. By year-end 2008, its $2.2 billion net debt equaled nine times its 2008 peak EBITDA of $275 million. EBITDA declined in 2009 as the GFC hit demand, and Six Flags declared bankruptcy as necessary liquidity could no longer be obtained.

Returning to Disney, its fate today faces a different risk profile. Its core business is still strong, with a solid moat around most of its businesses, although its ESPN franchise faces a declining moat over time because of changing viewership. It stretched its balance sheet in 2019 when it purchased Fox for $71 billion, and net debt to EBITDA stood close to three times at year-end 2019. This is near-peak EBITDA, which is heavily dependent on advertising revenues and park attendance. The risk of financial distress shifted from below average during 2009 to an average, or slightly above average, level. Disney magic will endure given its strong franchise, though financial flexibility has declined.

Buffett noted: "We will always be prepared for the thousand-year flood; in fact, if it occurs we will be selling life jackets to the unprepared" (Berkshire Hathaway annual letter, 2014).

The conservatively leveraged company benefits in multiple ways in the face of a revenue decline and an economic trough environment. These benefits can add to intrinsic value and offer solid downside protection.

1. Earnings before taxes (EBT) will remain more stable because interest expense, a fixed cost in the short run, is lower. Interest coverage will remain stronger because of smaller interest expense, the denominator. This gives banks and capital providers greater certainty of eventual repayment. Interest expense is also a component of free cash flow, and free cash flow is highly valued during downturns.

2. It will have greater financial flexibility to fund its operations if the macro environment remains depressed. The deeper the downturn, the more valuable flexibility becomes. Cash burn during downturns is common. Having spare debt capacity to fund cash burn can distinguish winners from losers.

3. Total debt capacity will be measured by bankers—the same lot who previously espoused optimal capital structures. The amount of room, total debt capacity less debt outstanding, determines whether access to incremental debt is granted.

4. Cost of debt capital will remain lower. The aggressively run company will need to pay higher interest rates to the banks or credit investors to access additional debt capital, with tougher terms and conditions. The conservative company will continue to obtain debt capital at reasonable prices.

5. Debt capital may not be available as needed in a deep recession because capital markets have frozen. The conservative company may burn less cash or have more cash and liquid assets available to finance cash burn.

6. Equity raises at distressed prices are to be expected of aggressively financed companies with no liquidity buffers. They will be forced to issue new equity at a very high cost of equity capital. In other words, they face substantial dilution that impairs existing shareholders. AIG required a government backstop in 2008 that placed more than 80 percent of the value of the equity temporarily into the hands of the federal government. The dilution to shareholders was massive, permanently impairing their equity positions.

7. In lieu of raising expensive capital, the aggressive business may be forced to divest assets at a discounted price to raise capital. Often, these divestments are the crown jewels of the business, not the most poorly performing segments that management would most like to divest. Distress will attract opportunistic capital providers, selling life vests at expensive prices. The conservative company will stand ready to bid on these assets at fire-sale prices well below intrinsic value, enriching their own shareholders.

8. Market share gains often accrue to conservative companies in downturns. Customers prefer to deal with solvent companies that are guaranteed to be around when orders materialize and that are available to service their products as needed. Natural shifts in market share occur during recessions, with stronger companies benefiting.

9. Quite often, distressed companies end up selling themselves at large discounts to their intrinsic value, permanently impairing equity holders. In the worst case, bankruptcies wipe out shareholders while converting bondholders at deep discounts into the next generation of shareholders.

Investors should always ask the question of why one company was able to build its business without resorting to leverage whereas another company was not. The answer is often rooted in underlying quality. McDonald's built its franchise patiently over several decades, allowing it to invest its industry-leading profit margin in purchasing the land beneath most of its outlets. Krispy Kreme, by contrast, grew quickly and aggressively by leasing its outlets. Each company looked to be highly profitable, justifying premium multiples. Each experienced a temporary impairment of revenues for competitive reasons, which proved temporary for McDonalds and almost lethal for Krispy Kreme.

To fully account for leverage, it is necessary to aggregate short-term debt, long-term debt, the operating leases and pension, and other post-employment benefits, including health-care commitments to retirees. Companies that began their existence after 1980 are unlikely to have post-retirement obligations. Conversely, most companies beginning operations in the early to mid-twentieth century face material postretirement liabilities. This factor holds true in the United States and abroad, although many countries other than the United States have little in the way of health-care obligations because health care is covered by the state. *Read the footnotes carefully and pass on names with large postretirement promises relative to the size of their operations!*

The U.S. and international auto industry and most auto parts suppliers became dominant companies after World War I. Union negotiations increasingly expanded retirement benefits through the twentieth century, and managements preferred expansions of these commitments to salary increases because they were entirely off-balance sheet until the 1980s. This flattered operating results. Once liabilities went on balance sheets, it became clear how material these obligations were, and the industry has struggled to overcome them. Cash commitments to fund these heavily underfunded plans continue to this day, reminding investors that these liabilities are almost identical burdens to financial debt, just less prominently displayed.

Another factor that heavily influences the level of financial riskiness of an equity investment is the company's debt maturity schedule. Companies with large maturities in the next twelve to twenty-four months face additional scrutiny by the capital markets. If cash and other liquid assets cannot cover impending maturities, and business earnings are volatile, unstable, or declining, capital markets may extract additional punishment. A benefit of the loose debt capital markets seen over 2019–2021 is that most companies, even secondary, tertiary, and over-leveraged enterprises, were able to term out their debt maturity schedules. Looking at assorted companies at year-end 2019 and 2020, large-scale principal repayments are not forthcoming until 2022 and more materially in 2023. This may limit the extent of distress seen in the short run, because nothing scares the credit markets more than impending maturities during an earnings downturn. This is one of the great ironies of life: bankers prefer to extend credit to those who demonstrate no need. *Protection is key. Just pass on companies with more than average debt outstanding of which a sizeable portion is due within two years.*

Buffett explained: "And as we all learned in third grade—and some relearned in 2008—any series of positive numbers, however impressive the numbers may be, evaporates when multiplied by a single zero. History tells us that leverage all too often produces zeroes, even when it is employed by very smart people" (Berkshire Hathaway annual letter, 2010).

A general rule is that better businesses with better management have less need for leverage. Data suggest that companies with higher payout ratios, in the form of dividends, are better businesses. Logic corroborates this premise, as high-quality companies have less intense cash flow needs and thus generate more free cash flow, allowing for ongoing investments and better dividend payouts. Screening for low-leverage, high-dividend payers can produce excellent results.

Reasons to Pass

Assessing probabilistic outcomes of highly leveraged companies is complex and uncertain. Many leveraged situations are speculative, with wide possible outcomes for equity holders. Large gains are possible, as are large losses, and professional and amateur investors alike struggle to calculate accurate odds that prove actionable—the higher the leverage, the smaller the equity component, and the greater the intrinsic value variability. *This is one of the most powerful and effective reasons to pass!*

Low odds of disastrous outcomes because of financial leverage are not worth making, as Buffett cautioned:

> Even in 1965, perhaps we could have judged there to be a 99 percent probability that higher leverage would lead to nothing but good. Correspondingly, we might have seen only a 1 percent chance that some shock factor, external or internal, would cause a conventional debt ratio to produce a result falling somewhere between temporary anguish and default. We wouldn't have liked those 99:1 odds—and never will. A small chance of distress or disgrace cannot, in our view, be offset by a large chance of extra returns. If your actions are sensible, you are certain to get good results. (Berkshire Hathaway annual letter, 1989)

The majority of companies carry debt, and a large percentage of those companies carry too much debt in today's environment. The economic prospects have been favorable, and low interest rates exacerbate the temptation to increase leverage. Most equity investment candidates can be excluded in the current debt-seeking environment. Other asset classes require nuanced analysis. As a general rule, high leverage on the underlying common equity translates to less cushion to creditors in other parts of the capital structure. Less cushion increases the risk of permanent impairment. When variability is too high, just pass.

7

High–Fixed Cost Businesses

Online selling (relative to traditional retailing) is a scale business characterized by high fixed costs and relatively low variable costs. This makes it difficult to be a medium-sized e-commerce company. With a long enough financing runway, Pets.com and living.com may have been able to acquire enough customers to achieve the needed scale. But when the capital markets closed the door on financing Internet companies, these companies simply had no choice but to close their doors. As painful as that was, the alternative—investing more of our own capital in these companies to keep them afloat—would have been an even bigger mistake.

—JEFF BEZOS, AMAZON ANNUAL LETTER, 2000

Every business has fixed costs. Rent, labor, factory expenses, and insurance are payable no matter how many units a company produces. Unit volumes vary depending on company success as well as microeconomic and macroeconomic factors. Spreading fixed costs over fewer units depresses operating profits and margins.

No industry better demonstrates this principle than the airline industry. High fixed costs burden airlines at two levels. First, its administrative structure, reservation system, some airport fees, and general and administrative (G&A) expenses require substantial units of air travel to adequately cover. Second, individual flight costs are fixed. Gate fees, depreciation, labor costs, and fuel do not change based on the load factor. Airlines' breakeven load factor varies by time and by airline but is more than 50 percent. In other words, more than 50 percent of seats have to be sold just to cover the fixed cost of a flight. The marginal cost of any one ticket sold on a plane is near zero. This incentivizes airlines to price tickets to ensure 100 percent occupancy no matter what the price, which is a primary competitive reason why the airline business has been so mediocre over its history. Cruiselines face much the same economics and fares are priced down toward marginal costs. Airlines lose units in downturns and flight prices decline, whereas cruiselines manage a full load factor by pricing down aggressively toward marginal cost. Either path leads to sharp and material losses in downturns.

Warren Buffett shared this: "When Richard Branson, the wealthy owner of Virgin Atlantic Airways, was asked how to become a millionaire, he had a quick answer: "There's really nothing to it. Start as a billionaire and then buy an airline'" (Berkshire Hathaway annual letter, 1996).

Most industries do not face such inferior economics. Railroads operate with enormous fixed costs and thus faced the same risks as airlines, but large-scale consolidation over the last couple of cycles into its current oligopoly has tempered price wars, as did higher land scarcity, which made new entry impossible. Add to that higher fuel prices, which make rail shipments that much more competitive against substitutes, namely trucking, and the economics of rails have improved substantially.

The trucking industry is also deeply cyclical with wild swings in revenues and profits. It carries some G&A at its headquarters and its network of owned trucks that produces some fixed expenses. Its primary expense burden, however, comes from depreciation, fuel, and labor. These expenses are mostly variable in the short run—stop truck runs and the costs disappear. Not to minimize the wild swings seen by trucking firms, and plenty of trucking companies go bankrupt in difficult times, but operating flexibility is greater than that seen with airlines and cruiselines.

Software companies are often seen as excellent defensive companies with more stable than average earnings and low fixed costs. Oracle, the global leader in enterprise software, invests heavily in new software, say, a major product launch for cloud security, and then follows that up with repeated updates. Programming expense is a fixed cost and is necessary no matter what the unit sales. The contribution margin of a new sale is near 100 percent because almost no direct costs are associated with software. The reason software companies are seen as defensive is not because of low fixed costs. Rather, margins on software are high because differentiation is substantial, and switching costs are high, which provides greater pricing power. In other words, think of software companies as high–fixed cost businesses with high and sticky margins that protect the franchises during downturns. Oracle, for example, has 80 percent gross margins and 40 percent operating margins, giving it financial flexibility to cover its large fixed costs.

Pharmaceutical companies face similar economics because of high research and development (R&D) expenses relative to sales. These are fixed costs that must be covered by a large amount of units, or possibly a lesser number of units selling at very high prices. Gilead's drug Sovaldi costs $30,000 in 2021 and still requires a drug cocktail with two other drugs to cure hepatitis C. The manufacturing costs are minimal and gross margins are very high, but they must be to fully offset ongoing R&D expenses and allow for a reasonable return. Development expense for software can run at levels similar to drug R&D (i.e., up to 20 percent of sales or higher). These business models work only when high gross margins are available to cover high fixed costs.

Revenues less cost of goods sold (COGS) equal gross profit, and gross profits divided by revenues equal gross margin. A general rule is that COGS is reflective of direct variable costs tied to sales, whereas sales, general, and administrative (SG&A), or at least G&A, are more representative of fixed costs. Businesses with high COGS and small SG&A are likely more variable cost based, whereas high SG&A companies have more fixed expenses. SG&A includes R&D and IT development costs, headquarters and administrative expenses, many sales expenses, and advertising costs. COGS includes direct costs of sales, including those required to build units, steel, labor, and so forth. It possibly includes some depreciation charge from assets directly used to manufacture the inventory. These general rules must be further dissected before the determination of fixed cost intensity can be evaluated.

Distributors fit the classic profile of low–fixed cost companies. Gross margins are low (e.g., 10 percent to 20 percent), with the cost of goods sold consisting of the prices that distributors pay for goods versus sales prices. Drug distributors, grocery distributors, restaurant distributors, and medical supply distributors all sell different products even though they operate with similar underlying economics. These are low–fixed cost businesses and thus possess greater operating flexibility in downturns and are less likely to generate large operating losses.

Physical retailers are similar to distributors in that their gross margins are relatively low and consist primarily of the spread between inventory purchase prices and sales prices. Grocers, Walmart, and Costco operate at just slightly higher gross margins than most distributors. Costco's gross margin is south of 20 percent, which is the average level it marks up its products in its retail stores and online. Retailers face one fixed cost burden that is not shared by distributors—that is, expensive leases and other operating costs related to storefronts. These fixed costs can become heavy anchors in tough times, and many retailers have gone bankrupt because of burdensome fixed lease expenses that declining unit sales could not adequately cover.

Online retailers such as Amazon, however, have a different relationship with fixed costs, especially in the growth phase. Jeff Bezos said as much in the early years: "Since we expect to keep our fixed costs largely fixed, even at significantly higher unit volumes, we believe Amazon.com is poised over the coming years to generate meaningful, sustained, free cash flow. Our goal for 2002 reflects just that" (Amazon annual letter, 2001).

Growth companies with high fixed costs face two opposing forces: one beneficial for shareholders and one for customers. Fixed costs remain relatively stable as volumes change. Startup companies in their early years often generate losses because units sold do not cover fixed costs. Investors forecast an expected time period to break even, to operating profitability, and to positive cash flow generation. More mature growth companies may be generating average levels of profitability today with expectations of excess profitability in future years when fixed costs are even better covered against higher unit volumes.

Amazon is currently in this phase. Units continue to grow well above market, spreading fixed costs over a larger and larger revenue base. The debate on Amazon is principally about whether expanding margins will pass to shareholders or customers. The historical distribution has been decidedly in favor of customers, and the future is unclear. Currently, a third constituency, labor, is extracting a greater share because of COVID-related payouts and societal pressures. Amazon also faces a fourth constituency, investment in growth options, that historically has taken a large share of its ever-expanding profitability. How the pie will eventually be split among stakeholders is unknown and is too hard to call. *When it's too hard, just pass.*

This heuristic does not quite do justice to an incredible business like Amazon. Digging into Amazon's cash flow statement, Bezos proved prophetic in his 2001 annual letter, as every year thereafter generated, and continues to generate, positive and growing free cash flow. Historical review of the financials would have missed this inflection point. Free cash flow burn, though modest, was seen each year before 2002. Peak free cash flow burn was seen in 1999 (–$377 million), followed by 2000 (–$265 million), and

2001 (−$170 million). These were challenging times for dot-coms. Capital dried up overnight and equity valuations plummeted. Amazon navigated this environment well, reaching positive free cash flow in 2002 (+$133 million) and 2003 (+$347 million), then never looked back. Free cash flow in 2019 increased again to $20 billion and ticked up massively to $26 billion in 2020. Revenues have grown steadily, including the difficult early 2000s. Revenues grew 169 percent in 1999, 68 percent in 2000, 13 percent in 2001, and 26 percent in 2002. This last burst adequately spread fixed costs across necessary volumes to generate positive free cash. Free cash, of course, is heavily influenced by discretionary capex and investment decisions. Operating margins in Amazon's case trended similarly, from −10 percent in 1999 to −2 percent in 2001 to 3 percent in 2002.

Many excellent businesses do not burn material amounts of cash during their high-growth spurts. Amazon is one such example. Its revenues grew from $609 million in 1999 to $3.9 billion in 2002. Measured against its cumulative cash burn of −$679 million over that period, this is an impressive feat, indeed, particularly compared with the current batch of startups that have gone public and burn cash like capital possesses no cost.

Time Value of Fixed Costs

No costs are fixed into perpetuity. Expensive headquarters; large-scale manufacturing facilities in the wrong locations; an oversupply of airplanes, trucks, and warehouses; a bloated office staff or excessive CEO compensation; an oversupply of airport gates; an inefficient or overly expensive labor pool; loss-making subsidiaries; and high R&D expense, advertising costs, and obsolete inventory all eventually can be rightsized by a restructuring-oriented management team.

The challenge with fixed cost adjustments is one of time. Expensive inventory in a high-inventory-turn business may flush out in weeks or months, causing only small losses before costs are rightsized. Large excess manufacturing facilities or those mis-located may run for one to two years or longer before capacity adjustments are fully reflected in the cost structure. Bloated administrative staff may reluctantly take small compensation hits in year one, followed by eventual layoffs and deeper rightsizing of staff.

Companies often are loath to make large adjustments to fixed costs. Most managers are optimists, and cutting fixed costs often results in a reduction of capacity. Silly is the manager who cuts capacity right before a rebound, losing the benefit of an upward participation in the next recovery. Managers suffer from confirmation bias just like investors, and their inherent belief in their business requires multiple pieces of contrary evidence before a new reality sets in. Managers mostly believe in the cost structure they themselves designed.

Case Study: Travis Perkins Versus Stora Enso

Travis Perkins, a UK-based distributor of building materials, and Stora Enso, the Swedish paper manufacturer, are both deeply cyclical. Revenues and earnings vary materially through the cycle, although both are long-term survivors and solid competitors in their industries. Each has financial characteristics that stand out, providing evidence as to their fixed cost intensity, which in turn offers clues about expected financial performance in a deep trough.

Travis Perkins (TP) has a flexible business model. COGS averages 71 percent of sales over the past five years, consisting primarily of its purchase costs for various products to be distributed to its customers. Its gross margin should be more stable over the cycle, flexing with changes in sales because of changing UK housing construction conditions. Depreciation expense averages less than 2 percent of sales because property, plant, and equipment (PP&E) is only 20 percent of tangible assets, about the same as the inventory level. Operating margins average 5 percent over the past five years and fixed costs amount to about 15 percent of sales. TP may lose money in a downturn, mostly because of lower inventory turns at lower than expected spread versus purchase price, but operations are quite flexible.

Stora Enso is a manufacturing-intensive business. COGS averages 60 percent of sales over the past five years, consisting of various input costs, including raw materials and labor, a heavier component of the cost structure. Its gross margin will fluctuate more over the cycle. Depreciation expense averages 5 percent of sales. PP&E is 67 percent of tangible assets and inventory is 10 percent. High PP&E is a telltale sign of a high–fixed cost business. Operating margins averaged 9 percent over the past five years. Higher margins are required when PP&E is too large to cover firms' cost of capital. According to my estimate, fixed costs amount to 30–40 percent of sales, providing much less flexibility in the event of a deep unexpected downturn. Higher restructuring expenses often are incurred with more capital-intensive businesses because exit costs to shrink capacity are greater.

This was the case with Stora Enso during the financial crisis, when it took multiple restructuring charges to rightsize their production.

Reasons to Pass

Midcycle environments will see many businesses of varying degrees of fixed costs earning similar overall margins, profits, and return on invested capital. Peaks will see revenue expansion across all cyclical companies, with margins benefiting high–fixed cost businesses disproportionately. Deep economic troughs are when the highest fixed cost businesses suffer the most notable effects. Operating losses initially will be severe, leading to large free cash flow burn and leverage expansion. Prudent managements will run these businesses with conservative financial leverage, particularly near peaks, understanding that an eventual trough is inevitable. Institutional and behavioral reasons, including most prominently recency bias and overconfidence, leads to a truncated cyclical outlook and excessive optimism. It is rare for high–fixed cost businesses to have adequately prepared their balance sheets for the next major downturn.

Adding insult to injury, major restructuring initiatives in the middle of downturns to downsize capacity and lower fixed costs are expensive. This use of capital will have to compete with companies' need to fund operating losses and debt paydowns. Flexibility declines, leading to material intrinsic value destruction. Bankruptcy and a complete wipeout for equity investors is not out of the question.

To summarize, predicting the cycle of any industry is hard, too hard. Once a downturn commences, those with high fixed costs that did not adequately reduce leverage during the peak when cash flows were strong will face unpredictable challenges. Demonstrating a compelling investment case will be difficult. *Businesses with high fixed costs in the latter stages of an economic expansion should mostly be avoided.*

Once an economic trough has stabilized, high–fixed cost businesses that successfully navigated through this challenged environment should be considered for investment. Most likely, these companies will continue to sell at a discounted price for some time as many investors desire "clear visibility" of the improving cycle before investing. *Predicting the timing of any downturn is a fool's game filled with false promises. Don't try it; it's too hard. Predicting the subsequent rise is equally challenging, although the asymmetry of low downside and unpredictable upside provide strong risk-adjusted return potential.*

8

Accounting

When Charlie and I read (annual) reports, we have no
interest in pictures of personnel, plants or products. References to EBITDA make us shudder, does management
think the tooth fairy pays for capital expenditures? We're
very suspicious of accounting methodology that is vague
or unclear, since too often that means management
wishes to hide something. And we don't want to read
messages that a public relations department or consultant
has turned out. Instead, we expect a company's CEO to
explain in his or her own words what's happening.

—WARREN BUFFETT, BERKSHIRE HATHAWAY
ANNUAL LETTER, 2000

The Wayward Machine

As a former certified public accountant (CPA), value-added accounting
sleuthing reached its crescendo in the 1990s with U.S. Generally Accepted
Accounting Principles (GAAP), UK GAAP, German GAAP, Brazilian
GAAP, Korean GAAP, Canadian GAAP, Japanese GAAP, and so forth. Each
had its own nuances, and astute analysts could make a living by converting
various accounting standards back into U.S. GAAP, and ideally, into better
representations of economic reality.

Differences among the various GAAPs were substantial. Some marked
assets at cost, some at market; revenue recognition varied; and merger
accounting, provisioning, and even share count calculations differed. German
GAAP, consistent with conservative Germanic principles, was notorious

for its special provisions, rainy-day reserves. Without any bad events, these reserves slowly transferred into shareholders' equity and belonged to the shareholders. Brazilian GAAP relied heavily on its version of inflation accounting, given its high historical inflation rate. Depreciation rates for similar assets varied wildly, and amortization of intangibles, and especially the treatment of goodwill, hugely influenced book values and earnings.

Even U.S. GAAP had historical issues. Pension fund liabilities were completely off-balance sheet until the 1980s, while unfunded health-care liabilities were finally required to be included as liabilities in 1992. It's little wonder that U.S. unions had a relatively easier time negotiating better benefits than hourly wage increases, given that wage bumps hit profitability but future post-retirement promises did not.

A material change to U.S. GAAP occurred in the early 2000s with merger accounting. Previously, any acquirer could follow either pooling of interests or traditional purchase accounting. Pooling of interest allowed for combined assets to be shown at book value without the creation of new goodwill. This increased postmerger return on equity and kept goodwill amortization off the income statement. Traditional purchase accounting grossed up assets to market value for the acquired company, generated large amounts of goodwill, and inflated shareholder equity. Many mergers took place right before the pooling window closed to take advantage of the more favorable accounting. Subsequently, goodwill amortization disappeared, keeping it on the balance sheet perpetually. Analysts could invest many hours converting industry competitors' financials into a like-for-like analysis while cleaning up historical comparisons.

Today

Accounting is still the language of business, and accounting records need to be carefully scoured if the goal is to become an effective fundamental equity analyst. The world's accounting platform unfortunately has become vastly more efficient. Generally speaking, only two accounting standards remain: U.S. GAAP and International Financial Reporting Standards (IFRS).

Accountants have dreamed of global accounting convergence for decades. U.S. GAAP is obviously utilized exclusively in the United States, but also is implemented around the world. Switzerland, for example, with many globally significant public companies, allows its enterprises to utilize either IFRS or U.S. GAAP. Most prominent Chinese initial public offerings (IPOs) in recent years utilize U.S. GAAP for their accounting.

A convergence between U.S. GAAP and IFRS also has been occurring. IFRS is based more on principles, giving companies more discretion in how to record their financial records. U.S. GAAP issues principles as well as more specific guidance, affording managers less flexibility. IFRS, for example, allows real estate assets to be booked at either cost or market value, whereas U.S. GAAP requires all real estate to be booked at cost. Real estate investment trusts outside the United States tend to mark their real estate assets at market value, and so their book value per share is representative of a true net asset value (NAV). When running a global real estate screen, U.S. real estate investment trusts (REITs) will trade at multiples of their book value, whereas most international REITs will trade around their book value. Other companies with significant real estate, insurance companies, for instance, may keep these assets at cost but then include a footnote highlighting the difference between cost and market value. U.S. REITs are required to show their real estate assets at cost, but they may include a non-GAAP NAV somewhere else in their disclosures. The NAV is obviously a much more important number for investors than a book value based on historical cost. This general convergence should be expected to continue, and in future years, differences likely will continue to shrink, further reducing the value add of a CPA in the investment industry.

The long-term investments account is worth mentioning. Some companies carry large long-term investments portfolios. Two-year treasuries, money good in most countries, reside in this category, as do publicly traded equity portfolios. Japanese companies continue to carry cross-shareholdings with their suppliers and customers. These equity positions are valuable assets. Many companies also carry equity interests—that is, ownership stakes of 20 to 50 percent, that allow them to influence but not control an investment's operations. These significant influence investments are booked at cost and are adjusted for proportionate retained earnings each year. Analysts need to understand these investments to determine how much credit to give these in their valuations.

Buffett noted: "In any business, insurance or otherwise, 'except for' should be excised from the lexicon. If you are going to play the game, you must count the runs scored against you in all nine innings. Any manager who consistently says 'except for' and then reports on the lessons he has learned from his mistakes may be missing the only important lesson—namely, that the real mistake is not the act, but the actor" (Berkshire Hathaway annual letter, 1985).

Non-GAAP disclosures can be included in companies' financial statements. Earnings before interest and taxes (EBITDA) is presented by most companies, although that is strictly speaking a non-GAAP metric. Operating earnings is the most significant non-GAAP disclosure made by most firms. It begins with GAAP net income and adjusts for line items that the management considers to be nonrecurring. Restructuring expenses are added back, even for companies that restructure regularly. Early extinguishment of debt may force companies to pay a premium over par, with these losses added back. Investment gains and losses often are added back, as are certain hedging costs. Problems exist with this specific non-GAAP disclosure. First, no standardized definition of operating earnings makes cross-company comparison more difficult. Second, companies are not required to abide by a consistent definition of operating earnings. Definitional changes occur frequently, most often to companies' benefit. High-quality companies typically will include fewer adjustments to net income, although many companies, good and bad, utilize this practice. Berkshire Hathaway adjusts net income for realized and unrealized gains and losses that run through the income statement to provide readers a better representation of underlying earnings. Oracle, a high-quality company by most accounts, still excludes the costs of options grants in its operating earnings, despite indisputable logic that these are economic expenses.

Charlie Munger explained: "So people who have loose accounting standards are just inviting perfectly horrible behavior in other people. And it's a sin, it's an absolute sin. If you carry bushel baskets full of money through the ghetto, and made it easy to steal, that would be a considerable human sin, because you'd be causing a lot of bad behavior, and the bad behavior would spread. Similarly an institution that gets sloppy accounting commits a real human sin, and it's also a dumb way to do business, as Westinghouse has so wonderfully proved" ("The Psychology of Human Misjudgment," Harvard University speech, 1995).

Analytical Considerations

A book on the intersection of accounting and investing is a worthy project best saved for a future effort. The following considerations, however, offer notable highlights in the current global investing environment:

1. All public companies globally present annual reports. The depth of disclosure varies dramatically. Many large caps globally provide

annual reports that are two hundred pages or more. AIG's 2019 10-K clocks in at more than three hundred and fifty pages. Global small caps in certain countries may provide only a twenty-page English-language annual report with limited to no footnotes. Accounting methodologies might be unclear, hidden assets and liabilities undetectable, and adjustments necessary to arrive at impossible economic earnings. When it comes to reading annual reports, practice makes perfect. Are accounting records and management goals consistent over time? Have definitions of operating income changed? These changes send red flags to an analyst.

2. Differences between US GAAP and IFRS still exist. Don't forget to peruse the footnotes to discern material investment considerations. If you cannot understand the accounting from the company under review, try disclosures from larger peers. They often are better and may treat issues similarly. Occasionally, footnotes befuddle even the most seasoned investors. Derivative footnotes are notoriously horrific, providing little insight into exposures and risk buckets.

3. Accounting is not intended to be representative of economic considerations. In some ways accounting tilts toward the balance sheet, meaning that accountants' goal is to show the true economic snapshot of a company's financial condition at period end. In other ways, accounting standards tilt toward the income statement. Occasionally these goals are mutually exclusive. Berkshire Hathaway several years ago was forced by its accountants to mark all of its investment positions to market quarterly, with gains and losses running through its income statement. This has produced tremendous volatility in its reported earnings but places book value a bit closer to economic value.

Case Study: Enron

Enron, the world's largest accounting scandal, brought a Fortune 100 business to its deathbed in 2001, destroying its formerly reputable auditing firm Arthur Andersen in the process. It had a $70 billion market cap at its peak, crumbling to zero in a matter of months. It owned energy plants and pipelines that physically distributed 15 percent of U.S. gas supplies. This segment was a real business with real assets. Segment disclosures in the year 2000 listed $7.5 billion in assets and $732 million in operating profit. The trading business, called its Wholesale Services (WS) business, became the star. This was extremely high growth, expanding assets from $12 billion in 1998 to $44 billion at year-end 2000, while profits more than doubled to $2.3 billion. WS matched buyers and sellers in gas, power, and other commodities, keeping a spread. Many contracts extended years into the future, requiring estimates for both revenue and profit recognition. The accounting was similar to percentage of completion, in which case margin estimates held until evidence to the contrary materialized. Margins were thin, with less than 5 percent gross margins, leaving little room for error. The most egregious activities occurred within their equity interests. Footnote disclosure indicated that their "unconsolidated equity affiliates" amounted to $5.3 billion at year-end 2000. Total assets were much higher, $34 billion, against consolidated Enron assets of $66 billion. The equity interests were run mostly by Enron executives, with many related party transactions going back and forth, and carried debt of $10 billion. Some of the debt was guaranteed by Enron Corp., making its recourse to Enron shareholders. About half of these equity interests were marked to market, which is highly unusual. Enron stuffed its worst assets here, collateralizing much with stock in Enron rather than cash. The revenue recognition was poorly disclosed and thus quite possibly not an obvious red flag, although the material, quickly growing equity interests with recourse to the parent were enough to warrant a pass regardless of how compelling the valuation appeared shortly before its bankruptcy in December 2001.

Case Study: Parmalat

While Enron's rise and fall took only fifteen years, Parmalat was a third-generation family business producing dairy products headquartered in Parma, Italy, the birthplace of parmesan cheese. It created the market for nonrefrigerated milk, gaining large market shares in most of Europe and many emerging markets. This was a real business with legitimate sales. Its downfall began with an out-of-footprint acquisition spree in the late 1990s that increased total assets from 6 billion Italian lira (ITL) at year-end 1996 to ITL 17 billion at year-end 2001, while revenues increased from ITL 5.6 billion to ITL 11 billion. These acquisitions were debt funded, overpriced, and led to losses that became difficult to navigate. Gross debt ballooned from ITL 1.9 billion to ITL 7.5 billion, although net debt rose by a much smaller ITL 1.5 billion because of its ever-growing cash balance. The year-end 2001 balance sheet listed ITL 5.5 billion cash and ITL 17 billion total assets against ITL 7.5 billion total debt. The cash flow statement poorly disclosed how cash increased so much without equity issuances. The primary red flags were to (1) understand the cash flow statement, (2) remain skeptical of the very quickly growing asset base, (3) question the competency of large out-of-footprint companies, and (4) be wary of large cash balances that offset large debt balances.

Reasons to Pass

> Three suggestions for investors: First, beware of companies displaying weak accounting. If a company still does not expense options, or if its pension assumptions are fanciful, watch out. When managements take the low road in aspects that are visible, it is likely they are following a similar path behind the scenes. There is seldom just one cockroach in the kitchen. . . . Second, unintelligible footnotes usually indicate untrustworthy management. . . . Finally, be suspicious of companies that trumpet earnings projections and growth expectations.
> —WARREN BUFFETT, BERKSHIRE HATHAWAY ANNUAL LETTER, 2002

Once complete, your accounting review should be able to answer some key questions about the quality of the business, and the quality of management, and the forthrightness of their communications. Generally, high-quality companies' accounting records will be easier to understand, include less noise and ambiguity, be more consistent over time, and be less likely to trumpet future growth. This may affect your bottom-up company valuation, and in certain situations, it will warrant enough skepticism to place a company in the too-hard pile. Over the years, I have read hundreds of annual reports, and these red flags would have been sound to avoid.

Intentional Obfuscation

Accounting is not inherently complex. Large transactions have debits and credits that equal, allowing the balance sheet to balance. Understand which accounts large transactions hit, and you can understand reasonableness. I frequently utilized T accounts, pounded into me during accounting classes, even asking CFOs to walk me through T accounts in complex situations. Enron was an egregious example of obfuscation. Management descriptions of transactions were confusing at best, most likely deceptive, and fraudulent at worst. *If you can't understand the accounting, either in the face of the financials or in the footnotes, just pass.*

Segment Disclosures and Reclassifications

Companies globally, under all accounting standards, are required to present segment information. Typical minimum requirements for any material segment are (1) revenues; (2) some measure of profit like EBIT, EBITDA, or net income; and (3) and some allocation of assets, typically total assets by segment. Most public companies have multiple segments that need to be analyzed and understood before you can reach an understanding of intrinsic value. Straightforward management teams will present segmental detail that allows investors to understand the economics of those businesses. Frequently seen additional segment disclosures include capital expenditures, depreciation and amortization, interest expense, and allocated financial debt and shareholders' equity. Management may provide segmental detail in three places. First, their annual reports will have a required segment footnote. Second, each annual report will present a management discussion and analysis (MD&A), which typically is broken out by segment. Third, they may present additional non-GAAP segmental detail in company presentations or supplements. Look to all three for a comprehensive viewpoint.

Ideally, segments remain consistent over many years, allowing the analyst to assess performance through the cycle. Some managements, however, regroup segments frequently, for the following reasons:

1. Acquisitions or divestments
2. Large-scale changes in business strategy
3. Desire to emphasize multiple businesses (e.g., recurring revenue streams like software as a service, streaming segments (Disney) and cloud platforms (Amazon))
4. Hiding loss-making businesses
5. Making poor performance tougher to pinpoint
6. Shifting bad management decisions

Reasons range from legitimate efforts to better communicate firmwide economics, to nefarious deception. *If frequent segment reclassifications can't be explained rationally, just pass.*

Percentage of Completion Accounting

Some companies enter into multiyear construction contracts—including, for example, civil engineering firms or defense contractors, whose projects may span three years or longer. This type of accounting leads to a large amount of management discretion, as they estimate profits on an interim basis for contracts that have fixed commitments with unknown future economics. *If the percentage of completion revenues are material, just pass.*

Early years of revenue and profit estimates are just guesses, and lifetime contract profitability is impossible to ascertain. Only when overruns become material and persistent are companies forced to change their estimates. Cost overruns are typical in large-scale extended contracts, and often the construction firms end up bearing the brunt. Seemingly profitable contracts in years one and two can end up being disastrously loss making. *This is too hard for public investors to adequately evaluate. Pass.*

Derivatives Disclosure

Companies with notable derivatives exposures provide a footnote and risk management disclosures. Unfortunately, derivatives come in such a large variety of flavors and structures that summary disclosures are mostly meaningless. Many companies utilize derivatives. Auto companies may hedge palladium and steel input costs, airlines hedge fuel, copper producers hedge their output, and financials lower net exposures each day through the use of derivatives. *When derivatives exposure is higher than justified for a given industry, and operational rationale dubious, don't just pass, run.*

Value at Risk

Value at risk (VaR) is a somewhat recent disclosure that is attempting to create certainty around volatility, particularly for financial firms. This model-based approach offers limited insight to analysts estimating downside risk as inputs are not standardized across companies and variable across time. Increasingly, regulatory metrics have incorporated adverse loss scenarios similar to VaR. Inputs are more standardized and scrutinized by the regulators and thus are worth deeper assessment. *The worst performers in adverse scenarios for regulatory stress tests for highly leveraged financials are red lights. Pass.*

Conclusion

Beware of companies who aggressively define operating earnings, net income less adjustments. Operating earnings have some merit in specific situations in which GAAP requires nonsensical adjustments. Non-GAAP operating earnings can better present underlying economic earnings. Wall Street analysts almost always rely on these adjusted earnings to assess earnings per share and support their valuations. Some companies abuse this opportunity to present overly flattering results. On occasion, companies will change their operating earnings definition over time, usually in ways that present an "even better" representation of their economics. In these cases, management is manipulating results, or the business is too complex to understand. *When the sum of five years of operating earnings does not correlate to the sum of five years of net income, and large differences cannot be adequately explained, pass.*

9

Regulatory Uncertainties

Many years ago Ben Franklin counseled, "Keep thy shop, and thy shop will keep thee." Translating this to our regulated businesses, he might today say, "Take care of your customer, and the regulator—your customer's representative—will take care of you." Good behavior by each party begets good behavior in return.

—WARREN BUFFETT, BERKSHIRE HATHAWAY
ANNUAL LETTER, 2011

Regulation is like death and taxes. Boeing/Airbus, airlines, transportation companies, utilities, media companies, and most other industries are touched by regulation. Regulations can protect the earnings power of incumbents by restricting new entry or can limit earnings power and growth in governments' zest to protect consumers.

Strong businesses with natural moats around their earnings power prefer less or no regulation because they can compete effectively without artificially created barriers. Occasionally, large businesses benefit from regulation as the complexities and costs keep new entrants at bay. Big tech stocks, particularly Meta (formerly Facebook) and Alphabet, fit this profile, as many startup digital competitors cannot bear the emerging costs of regulatory burdens. Regulation exists on a sliding scale. It generally is not a variable that warrants exclusion from investment consideration, except in its extreme application.

Regulation is not static across time. It swings like a pendulum, often correlated to the larger political environment. Understanding these natural swings and progressions prepares investors for possible risks and opportunities. Cycles are long, many years on average, and the pendulum swings slowly.

The U.S. banking system is an example of this regulatory pendulum at work. Banking was unregulated through the 1920s and early 1930s. The 1930s saw nine thousand banks fail as the Great Depression took hold, with four thousand of those failing in 1933. Panicked depositors triggered many of these failures as they attempted to withdraw their savings en masse. The Glass-Steagall Act responded to this crisis, establishing the FDIC and deposit insurance and also restricting commercial banks from engaging in investment banking activities. Investment banking activities were more speculative in nature and led to massive losses when capital markets imploded. The equity market dropped almost 90 percent from its highs in 1929. Subsequently, U.S. banking morphed into a utility-style return with 10 percent return on equities (ROEs) and little variation across time. Even deposit rates were regulated to avoid cutthroat competition that could jeopardize banks' financial well-being. This began to change in the 1970s, after forty years of stability when banks were again allowed to make commercial loans; in 1978, when banks were permitted to make out-of-state loans; and most important in 1980, when deposit rates were deregulated. Competitive intensity skyrocketed and loan book quality deteriorated, leading to the savings-and-loan crisis in the early 1990s. In 1999, Glass-Steagall was repealed fully, and aggressive management seized the opportunity to juice earnings, improving ROE to the mid to high teens by the mid-2000s. In 2008, we experienced the worst banking crisis since the 1930s as poor loan quality and high leverage led to bank failures, massive equity dilution for surviving institutions, and large-scale reregulation of the industry. Large failures included Bear Stearns and Lehman Brothers, two formerly preeminent investment banks. Washington Mutual ($300 billion assets), IndiMac ($32 billion), Downey Savings ($12 billion), BankUnited ($12 billion), and Colonial Bank ($25 billion) all failed. Other large banks close to failure were forced to merge with stronger competitors. Wachovia, Merrill Lynch, and even Countrywide with its 20 percent market share of the residential mortgage market were bought at highly discounted prices. Fannie Mae and Freddie Mac, lynchpins of the U.S. mortgage market, were nationalized. Reactionary regulations enacted after 2008 included forced capital raises and permanently increasing FDIC deposit guarantees. Passage of the Dodd–Frank Act in 2010 massively reregulated the banking system, undoing a good portion of deregulatory efforts over the previous fifty years. It forced greater equity capital into the system, annual stress tests, and limited dividends and share repurchases. It also forced banks to increase balance sheet liquidity, capped mergers above a certain size to reduce too-big-to-fail risks, and restricted riskier asset exposures and proprietary trading activities. These changes had, and continue to have, a negative impact on industry ROE.

One hundred years of U.S. banking history demonstrates some valuable lessons. Regulations have a material impact on profitability and downside risk. Regulations change slowly, and then change abruptly after a crisis materializes. Years of subsequent prosperity and stability begin the process of unwinding regulations. Also, regulations ebb and flow with the political winds. A left-leaning majority tends to increase regulations as faith in government increases. Prosperity relaxes regulatory zeal.

Legislation that relaxes regulations is the equivalent of a starting gun in a race to the bottom. Many similarly equipped competitors enter simultaneously, each vying for greater market share and profits. Banks in 1980 quickly raised deposit pricing to lure in depositors after restrictions on deposit rates were lifted. They needed higher asset yields to justify the higher deposit rates and thus expanded lending efforts across state lines and even across country lines, lending increasingly to emerging markets and other risky borrowers out of footprint where banks had no underwriting expertise. What seemed like rational decisions, growing profits, led to greater risk taking without higher returns. Conservative managements have no place here, and the most aggressive prosper. Initial response in the equity market is euphoria—rising future profits elevate equity values. The sugar high wears off after greater risk taking becomes apparent, and stock prices begin to spiral downward. As a general rule, stock prices drop when regulations intensify and rally during periods of deregulation, often beyond justified intrinsic values, offering valuation-oriented investors entry and exit opportunities. Beware of favorable regulatory relief over the medium run. Quite often excess profits are quickly competed away.

Warren Buffett explained: "If voters insist that auto insurance be priced below cost, it eventually must be sold by government. Stockholders can subsidize policyholders for a short period, but only taxpayers can subsidize them over the long term" (Berkshire Hathaway annual letter, 1988).

This high-level mindset regarding the nature of regulation provides long-term-oriented investors a distinct edge relative to short-term investors because they consider longer-term implications of regulation and regulatory changes. Most investors are inherently short-term oriented. The idea of dead money is unpalatable, as is the risk of continued price declines after an equity purchase, or the risk of missing out on a lucrative upswing. Utilities are an obvious area in which one witnesses the dichotomy between short- and long-term investors. Short-term investors see utilities as a hiding place rather than a place to invest for the long run because earnings power is relatively stable. Utilities become attractive to short-term investors when (1) global uncertainty rises and (2) when interest rates are low, as dividend yields are typically above the overall market. Long-term investors think differently about how to invest in utilities, because they think about multiples of expected earnings power. Impending regulatory shifts may materially shift the earnings power over time, which affects the intrinsic value per share.

Several factors influence odds of regulatory intervention, which inevitably affects future earnings power. Regulatory action is often seen as a black swan–type event, impossible to predict in advance. Although sympathetic to this viewpoint, industry and company characteristics make companies more likely to face increasing regulations. Considering these elements tilts long-term odds to your favor.

1. Barriers to entry—Low barriers to entry allow new entrants to emerge if incumbents treat consumers poorly. High barriers to entry more permanently restrict consumer choice and allow incumbents to aggressively raise prices. Industries with high barriers to entry are more likely to be considered for regulatory intervention. Amazon is often talked about as a candidate for greater regulation given its behemoth influence on the retail markets. Ten years ago, risks were negligible, but Amazon has worked hard to increase its moat, and with it, its pricing power.

    No event better illustrates the perils of low barriers to entry than the dot-com bubble of the late 1990s. Those years saw hundreds of online retailers emerge. None possessed pricing power, and consumers benefited, although eventually that wave of entrants overwhelmed consumer demand and washed away most sandcastles of prosperity.

    The difference today is distribution. Amazon's distribution advantage is the moat around their castle, tough to replicate and providing a valuable consumer service that differentiates them from every other online competitor. Anyone can set out a virtual retail shingle, packaging and shipping a product from their garage. Yet only Amazon can offer overnight delivery at a reasonable price because their distribution centers reign supreme. A handful of competitors are investing in similar infrastructure, such as Walmart and Target, and likely they will have the scale necessary to make their online initiatives work. They now both offer third-party procurement, a key complaint against Amazon. This may demonstrate enough competition to keep the regulators at bay, although continued retailing inroads will jeopardize that unregulated position.

2. Organic verses acquisitive growth—Few companies are prone to regulatory intervention if they build up their business organically over time. Microsoft built its near-monopoly position in operating systems organically and is an exception to the rule because of its highly unusual level of success. Case studies otherwise are devoid of companies who grow into a 90 percent market share organically in a large market, sustaining that position over several decades. Heavily acquisitive industries trending toward oligopoly, oil in the early 1900s, wireless carriers in the 2000s, large case insurance brokerage over the past thirty years, see greater risks of future regulatory action.

3. Customer satisfaction—High customer satisfaction lowers the odds of regulatory action. Amazon provides excellent service at a reasonable price. Consumer trust is high, and when that trust is violated, quick action through refunds quickly appeases frustrated customers. Third-party vendors are less satisfied, and Amazon is proving to be a double-edged sword as it both allows access to otherwise inaccessible customers and quickly launches private-label products when vendors demonstrate success.

4. Margins—Industries with structurally low margins and ROIC are less prone to regulation irrespective of their market position. Amazon has low margins and charges only small markups on products sold through their site. Retailing generally is not a high-margin business. Less excess profits means that there is less fat available for regulators to redistribute to consumers. Distribute too much and regulators jeopardize the industry's long-term ability to provide these services, insurance being a primary example of a service that must be priced appropriately over time.

5. Essential service designation—Goods and services seen as essential are more likely to be subject to heavy-handed regulation. Given recent events surrounding COVID-19, Amazon has become more of an essential service. This is an especially sensitive time for Amazon, and other retailers, including Costco, face similar risks. Upset consumers resulting from price gouging, or preferential distribution, and future regulatory action increase.

Vaccine development efforts underway by a host of biotechs and pharmaceuticals may determine the regulatory fate of these critical service providers. Price a successful vaccine too high or misallocate availability, and the regulatory pendulum will swing quickly to rein them in.

Following are industry-specific thoughts that may assist in better defining the regulatory filter, sorted from most to least affected by regulations.

Utilities

The majority of utilities globally are heavily regulated. They often are monopoly providers of electricity, water, gas, fixed-line telecom, and trash in their regions. Regulators define the asset base used in production and distribution of the product or service and define an allowable return on that asset base. Quite often regulatory environments are stable and predictable, but they can become politically entwined during strong shifts from left-leaning to right-leaning environments. Politicians may call for reprieve from high power prices by usurping regulatory panels, instilling lower allowable price increases. They also may allow greater unregulated activities to flourish. Utility deregulation has multiple examples globally of new unregulated power capacity overwhelming the natural demand, forcing down power prices and leading to impairments or insolvencies of unregulated subsidiaries with related distress upon regulated entities. Some emerging markets, Argentina and Brazil, for example, have experienced bouts of high inflation in past cycles. Politicians may suppress required increases in utility power prices to subdue inflationary pressures. These pressures reduce earnings power and may permanently impair intrinsic values of publicly traded utilities. One universal truth, regulate profits down too far and essential services, including utilities, underinvest in their networks, creating future shortages and market stress. Regulators do have an incentive to act rationally enough to ensure that necessary capacity makes its way to their customer base, because customers' frustrations will translate to political change. Buffett noted that the UK utilities market is a fitting example:

> Here's a tidbit for fans of free enterprise. On March 31, 1990, the day electric utilities in the U.K. were denationalized, Northern and Yorkshire had 6,800 employees in functions these companies

continue today to perform. Now they employ 2,539. Yet the companies are serving about the same number of customers as when they were government owned and are distributing more electricity. This is not, it should be noted, a triumph of deregulation. Prices and earnings continue to be regulated in a fair manner by the government, just as they should be. It is a victory, however, for those who believe that profit-motivated managers, even though they recognize that the benefits will largely flow to customers, will find efficiencies that government never will. (Berkshire Hathaway annual letter, 2003)

Banking and Insurance

Banking and insurance are two of the most heavily regulated industries. Both are essential parts of a country's economy, and major losses of industry capital trigger economic stress or even collapse. Also, both business models are heavily leveraged, as total assets are ten times equity capital or higher. Both purchase large amounts of securities issued by governments and corporates, and banks provide loans that fuel countries' growth. Small changes in the values of their assets can materially hurt equity capital, and weak capital restricts lending. Regulation here makes sense. The 2008 Great Financial Crisis (GFC) presented a firsthand encounter of regulatory swings, as heavy government intervention took hold over even sound institutions. Many investors in global financial stocks—yes, the 2008 GFC was a global phenomenon—underestimated how forcefully governments and, specifically, regulators would intervene. U.S. regulators forced banks to issue more than $200 billion in new equity capital through the Troubled Asset Relief Program (TARP). No price sensitivity existed in these equity raises, providing an excellent entry point for value-driven investors. *Investing in banks and insurers after the passage of tough regulatory restrictions has often proved profitable, as did selling positions after periods of deregulation.*

Health Care

Roughly one-third of total health-care expenditures in the United States is paid by the government, and this number will rise in the future as baby boomers continue to retire by the millions and the government increases those eligible for coverage. Health-care spending as a percent of gross domestic product (GDP) has continued its ascent around the globe at a rate well in excess of inflation. The United States is the most profligate spender globally with 18 percent of GDP allocated to health care. This compares to the low teens for most other industrial countries. Ironically, U.S. health-care outcomes are not notably better than countries who spend less, and according to some measurements, are worse. The burden is becoming more unsustainable with each passing year and may soon begin the process of rightsizing. Much of the reform might be regulatory driven if the free market does not come to the rescue. Price caps are a tempting regulatory fix as is reducing access. A full takeover of the U.S. health-care system, a Medicare-for-all solution, increases with each passing year unless costs are brought under control. Controlling pricing becomes easier when customer power increases.

At the 2017 Berkshire Hathaway annual meeting, Charlie Munger commented: "And a lot of it is deeply immoral. If you have a group of hospital people and doctors that are feasting like a bunch of jackals on the carcass of some dying person, it's not a pretty sight."

And at its 2018 Berkshire Hathaway annual meeting, he noted: "When democrats control both houses and the White House, we will get single payer healthcare, and it won't be friendly to PBM's, and I won't miss them."

It is possible that market forces will come to the rescue in the United States. What is needed is greater transparency, which allows consumers to bring more of a shopper's mindset to the health-care purchasing decision. Imagine a world in which one needs a hip replacement. Empowered consumers might obtain disclosures about local, regional, or even national facilities who do the most volume of that particular hip replacement procedure. Statistics detailing success along many measures would be available, allowing decisions as to which facilities and doctors were most appealing to the patient. Importantly, transparent pricing would be available, with knowledge about how much each facility would require in total and out-of-pocket expenses based on insurance coverage. Informed consumers could then compare and determine what was best for them.

If this sounds miles away from our current system, welcome to the club. Government intervention has focused on provider reimbursement rates, pushing some doctors to cease taking Medicare or Medicaid patients. Veteran Affairs (VA) hospitals suffer from their own inefficiencies. Consumers motivated to gather information to make informed decisions are mostly stymied in their quest.

Future costs must stabilize as government resources are increasingly constrained by high debt levels. The current laissez-faire approach guarantees continued upward drift in health-care expenditures, making some form of U.S. government intervention likely. Timing is unpredictable. Large-scale structural reforms of health care are complex and time consuming, while price controls are easier political decisions. The uncertainty surrounds all aspects of health care, from pharmaceutical companies to publicly traded hospital chains to device manufacturers, distributors, and beyond. Industry margins are robust relative to most other industries, and compensation for health-care professionals is high, making regulatory action more defensible to politicians. Finally, a continued emphasis on Medicare for all or some other form of a one-payer system heightens risks further. The health-care industry prefers the status quo, although this seems unrealistic as spending continues to rise.

As Munger recommended:

I think you have to change the incentives. I think there are places in America that are very admirable that don't do a lot of unnecessary stuff, and other places that do. And I think we're going to have to change the system. If you take the medical system of Singapore, it costs 20 percent of what ours costs and it has better statistics. And it's not opaque, it's open. We have a whole industry that tries to make the payment things opaque so they can take advantage of people. And they think it's free enterprise. I think it's stealing. (Daily Journal annual meeting, 2020)

Restricting price or access of health-care services will reduce industry revenues, margins, and ROE. This pain will be widely shared, and the system may soon begin to feel the effects. The pie seems likely to shrink, leaving well-healed competitors fighting for the spoils. Many subsectors exist within health care—for example, medical device companies' economics may evolve differently from pharmaceuticals. Determining which subsectors are relative winners, and which companies are likely to suffer less, are incredibly hard calls to make. Will drug distributors be insulated because of their very low 1 percent margins? Will biotechs be the winners because of goodwill created from their COVID-19 successes? Begin with the current state of the industry, namely, that margins and ROE are at the high end of any industry globally. Fade rates are uncertain, and revenue paths and governmental interference are near impossible to predict. *When a system is too multivariate and hard to figure out, like health care, just pass.*

Telecoms and Cable

AT&T was a telecom until 1977 in the United States, when forced deregulation split this inefficient behemoth into the Baby Bells. Several buyouts and mergers have rebuilt telecoms into the U.S. oligopoly we see today. Telecoms, both fixed and wireless, are heavily capital intensive, making entry challenging. No rational competitor would attempt to replicate Verizon's wireless network today. It would crush the market for all competitors and returns on newly invested capital would be low. The telecom industry is an excellent example of the regulatory pendulum at work. Complete regulation gives way to free-market economics, only to realize that some regulation is necessary even as cable and satellite, emerging entrants, began to encroach on incumbents' activities. Telecoms have self-structured into an oligopoly in most countries, with two to four primary competitors. The top-three wireless Canadian carriers have 90 percent market share. Japan's NTT Docomo has 40 percent, with the top three possessing 75 percent market share. China Mobile controls 60 percent of the Chinese wireless market, while the top three have more than 90 percent market share. Some oligopolies are quite stable and generate high margins. The Canadian providers fall into this bucket. Others see one dominant competitor generating most of the profits, with upstarts looking to disrupt. China falls into this category. Country regulations can restrict mergers, entry, pricing, and capital allocation. A long-term perspective and an astute eye toward regulatory changes can help, as can a natural skepticism toward regulatory stability. The high margins generated by the Canadian telecoms possibly are a medium-run risk. Thus, lower multiples are warranted. China Mobile is likely to invest heavily into 5G no matter what the returns on capital and also is likely to face continued regulatory pressure to suppress pricing. These risks far outweigh natural competitive forces at work. If various pathways all lead to profits, apply a conservative multiple to base-case earnings and ideally purchase nearer to a downside earnings scenario. *If, however, it's too hard to figure out the pathway with any confidence, just pass.*

Technology

Historically unregulated, the tech space in its modern sense began to spring to life with the advent of the IBM PC, and later, the emergence of Apple. Microsoft created the IBM PC operating system, and then expanded its client roster to Compaq and other PC clones. This created natural competition in the PC market, which eventually forced IBM out of the consumer PC market. Excess returns existed for Microsoft and Intel, who monopolized their segments, but consumers kept seeing better products at lower prices. Satisfied consumers make regulation difficult to justify. The late 1990s saw the first calls for some regulatory oversight of Microsoft given its monopoly position, and the 2000s led to small hand slaps by the European Union but nothing of note in the United States.

Calls to regulate Meta have intensified, as the United States and European Union grapple with appropriate guidelines surrounding digital property rights. Facebook grew from zero to two billion users in a decade. Impressively, it achieved this phenomenal growth organically rather than through acquisition, and globally, there are few examples in which regulators place the hammer down on organically grown companies. Typical regulatory reaction comes from anticompetitive acquisitions, and it seems unlikely that Facebook would have faced such governmental wrath had they focused exclusively on their Facebook social network.

Facebook, however, made two shrewd acquisitions: Instagram for $1 billion in 2012, and WhatsApp for $16 billion in 2014. Both have experienced substantial growth. In 2019, Facebook had 2.4 billion users, Instagram had 1 billion, and WhatsApp had 1.5 billion. In total, Facebook collects data on roughly three billion people, almost the entirety of the global online population. Still, had Facebook taken a conservative approach to their data collection and analysis, they might have been offered a regulatory reprieve. Management instead decided to aggressively mine private data to generate greater advertising potency in their quest to raise profits. The European Union and United Kingdom have already enacted much tougher privacy rights standards, and the United States continues to contemplate some type of material action. Some espouse the breakup of Facebook, with forced sales or spinouts of its two major acquisitions. Either way, this is a major overhang that could materially impair earnings in an adverse outcome. Earnings are likely to be strong in any reasonable scenario even though profit dispersion is wide. This example is not quite a pass. Instead, be conservative about earnings and multiples, attempting to buy to structurally protect against impairment by lowering the buy price, while letting the various upside scenarios dictate a sell strategy.

Few heavily regulated businesses go bankrupt. This consideration makes them more likely to be buyable at some price rather than an automatic reason to pass. They are integral to society. Otherwise, why bother regulating them? A bankruptcy could result in an unanticipated inter-ruption of service and thus is a cause for concern. No regulator wants an unhappy constituency. When faced with distress in cases in which compa-nies no longer allocate capital to supporting services, regulators eventually will allow a combination of price increases, allow access to additional lever-age, or force equity issuances to keep services.

Case Study: PG&E

PG&E filed for Chapter 11 bankruptcy protection in January 2019 in what was called a defensive bankruptcy filing. It faced more than $30 billion in litigation claims arising from California fires that even the utility acknowl-edges probably started because of their power lines. New credit and equity commitments have been made since, and a $21 billion state fund has been created to help utilities cover these losses. The state regulator will likely allow some price increases over time to help cover losses. Existing equity holders will not be wiped out here, although huge uncertainty exists, which makes this situation almost unanalyzable. The recent emergence from bankruptcy dilutes shareholders but reduces risk materially though has not eliminated the prospect of further payouts. This is a more analyzable situa-tion today given its more certain profile, but at the time of the bankruptcy, this was too hard. A pass was a good call.

Reasons to Pass

Normal regulatory shifts are manageable for long-term investors, as the odds of large permanent impairment of capital is low. Investors focused on the long run can find interesting opportunities in the regulated space given the importance of those businesses to society and frequently low expectations of excess returns. In some circumstances, uncertainty is too large, and investors need to choose between two options. First, lower your intrinsic value by assuming some earnings impairment from regulation, and invest only at a sufficient margin of safety. Second, pass when regula-tory uncertainty is too great.

10

Corporate Governance

Imagine that four sisters open a restaurant. Each contributes one-fourth of the equity capital, but one claims she should receive greater power because the business was her idea and she is the most responsible partner. She proposes super-voting shares, which give her four times the vote for her equity stake, giving her four-sevenths of the total votes. In addition, she receives veto power over material transactions, including whether or not to sell the business.

Now imagine that this restaurant has grown into a large chain, with ownership dispersed among one hundred owners. The owners, led by the one sister, agree to hire a manager to oversee day-to-day operations and select her daughter, who commits to doing what is necessary to grow profits. She conducts a personnel review, deciding to replace the head chef with her husband, who is a seasoned chef. She performs a vendor review and determines that fruits and vegetables from her family's farm are superior, and so she replaces those vendors. Several restaurant locations are determined to be suboptimal, and so she moves them to better locations that happen to be owned by a real estate partnership controlled by a former business associate, of which her family has an interest.

The chain goes public, retaining current leadership and formalizing its board of directors. Board members represent the owners' interests and increasingly are staffed by knowledgeable outside experts whom she has suggested. Boards have various committees, including a compensation committee, and her chosen "outside directors" staff the compensation committee. Profits do increase over time, and the compensation committee determines that her performance warrants a large raise. She also receives an additional ownership stake in the restaurant that is struck in the form of an option: no downside but a large upside if results grow.

The message is simple. Nothing can siphon away more value from minority shareholders than poor corporate governance culminating from conflicts of interest.

Alphabet has three classes of shares. Class A shares trade publicly under the ticker GOOG.L, each with one vote. GOOG, the class C shares, have no voting rights, whereas the class B shares are privately held by insiders with ten votes per share. Most investors own GOOG, which allows them to share in the economic rights proportionately but does not give them the ability to influence the board of directors. Other notable companies with multiple classes of shares with unequal voting rights are Artisan Partners, CBS, Dell Technologies, Expedia, and of course Meta (formerly Facebook), whose class B shares receive ten times the votes of the class A shares. The intent of these arrangements is to insulate the founders from minority investors' potential agitations.

Charlie Munger once suggested the following: "When I was an officer in the military, we had a rule called Conduct Unbecoming an Officer. It was not specific, but it said there were certain ways to behave as an example for others. I don't see why we shouldn't have this for our corporate executives" (Wesco annual meeting, 2004).

Most public company top executives have multifaceted pay structures. They receive a salary, cash bonuses worth three to five times salary, and equity grants mostly through options, which are time or performance vested. Elon Musk, the controversial CEO of Tesla and SpaceX, had his board structure one of the most unconventional compensation plans. He receives minimum wage, never cashing those checks, no cash bonuses, and an enormous options package. The options grant in 2018 was worth up to one hundred million shares (i.e., 10 percent of shares outstanding), if over the next ten years he (1) increases the market cap above $100 billion; (2) generates more than $20 billion in sales or $1.5 billion earnings before interest, taxes, depreciation, and amortization (EBITDA); and (3) remains CEO of Tesla. A second set of milestones requires $35 billion of sales and $3 billion of EBITDA.

Touted as being shareholder friendly and perfectly aligned with shareholders, much is wrong with the Tesla pay plan. Options provide no downside with enormous upside and thus are not at all comparable to shareholder exposures. When options performance targets are not met, new grants inevitably arrive, thus providing another opportunity for management wealth creation at the expense of shareholders. The new strike price will again be "at market," the difference being that the firm's value is now lower. Second, his options metrics included market capitalization, which is more easily reached than value per share because new shares can always be issued. This is precisely what Tesla has done multiple times: raise new equity in the market. Third, its performance metrics are unambitious. Consider that 2019 revenues and EBITDA came in at $25 billion and $2.2 billion, easily meeting the first set of ten-year milestones in year one. The second set of milestones has now been reached in less than one year, COVID-19 and electric vehicle market buzz notwithstanding. Easily achievable financial hurdles speak to a compromised board of directors heavily influenced by a charismatic leader. Warren Buffett wrote:

> Over the years, Charlie and I have seen all sorts of bad corporate behavior, both accounting and operational, induced by the desire of management to meet Wall Street expectations. What starts as an "innocent" fudge in order to not disappoint "the Street"—say, trade-loading at quarter-end, turning a blind eye to rising insurance losses, or drawing down a "cookie-jar" reserve—can become the first step toward full-fledged fraud. Playing with the numbers "just this once" may well be the CEO's intent; it's seldom the end result. And if it's okay for the boss to cheat a little, it's easy for subordinates to rationalize similar behavior. (Berkshire Hathaway annual letter, 2018)

Corporate governance concerns encompass any compromised decisions that affect a company's ability to provide the best possible financial outcome for minority investors. An investment in a startup is obviously entrusting capital and decision-making to a founder who is looking to build a business. A trustworthy founder ensures that decisions are being made that look out for the best interests of all shareholders, including minority investors, to maximize returns on all capital deployed.

An investment in a common equity is a less obvious but identical decision. You purchase a share of stock from another partial owner of a business or from the company directly when they issue equity. Either way, your equity capital is in the hands of the company's management team and the board of directors. They decide how to run the business, where to invest the profits, whether to raise new equity to expand operations, and when to sell the company. Managed optimally, the value of your ownership stake grows and is reflected in a rising share price. Managed poorly, the equity price declines as the value of the company deteriorates. The safety of your capital and future returns depend on their decisions. No factor discussed in this book is more integral over the long run to protecting your investment and helping it compound positively than corporate governance.

Corporate governance acts as the checks and balances that protect management from themselves. Managers make thousands of decisions over the course of their stewardships that contribute to the profit maximization process. Decisions such as major investments of capital, large-scale divestitures, and the degree of leverage to employ can meaningfully swing firm value over an extended holding period.

The perfect CEO does not require any corporate governance checks. Every decision they make will be for the benefit of all shareholders. Boards of directors have a fiduciary responsibility to oversee corporate decision-making, but a perfect CEO requires no supervision. Management compensation will be fair, capital allocation will be properly focused on long-run profitability, and balance sheet management will be appropriately conservative. Super-voting authority, which you see quite often in family-run businesses or those still run by founders, does not affect decision-making, because the perfect CEO will find no objections from minority investors. When they offer input that differs, it will be taken into advisement.

The parallel within a government stands clear. The perfect prime minister, chancellor, or president requires no legislative or judicial oversight to protect the populace from nefarious decision-making. There is no risk of self-enrichment, or undesired power transfer, to our collective detriment, when the perfect leader is in charge. The task then for shareholders and citizens is simple: just hire or elect the perfect leaders and give them broad-based discretion over operations.

This idealized scenario has two major problems: identification and power transfer. First, how does one identify ideal candidates to fill the CEO or president's role? Track record is important: find candidates with irrefutable qualifications. Information flow is not perfect, however, and decision-makers may be missing blemishes that could compromise candidates' decision-making ability. Also, leaders with ideal track records evolve unexpectedly. Power can corrupt in unpredictable ways. The second and equally important issue, power transfer, becomes tougher on a sliding scale the more power the current management or executive team has. Those in charge may not want to relinquish that power, even as their faculties decline. Eventually, they pass away or acquiesce, designating a successor. Too many CEOs have held onto their position of power too long, and too many have passed the torch on to inferior next-generation leaders.

Most decisions in life can be reduced to an upside or a downside analysis—that is, risk versus reward. Corporate governance is no different. The upside of robust standards is long-term protection of shareholders' rights. Excellent managers will make excellent decisions well justified and explainable to shareholders and the board. Solid corporate governance practices do not alter the decisions made by excellent managers. Those managers may have to work harder to communicate their decision-making to shareholders, but their decisions will be well received by investors. Be wary of managers who look to reduce corporate governance protections or to resist improved checks and balances. These are flashing red lights to investors. In other words, the upside in a robust corporate governance environment is identical to one in which the perfect CEO rules without checks and balances.

The downside of a poor CEO ruling in a weak corporate governance environment may cost minority investors dearly. Capital allocation could be disastrous, balance sheet management could be too risk seeking, and management compensation could redirect significant value away from investors. Calls for change may go unheeded, and the market valuation becomes impaired without recourse to alter direction.

Limitations exist when it comes to assessing the robustness of a company's corporate governance controls. To get a sense of where in the spectrum a company lies, focus on these primary variables, in absolute terms and relative to global best practices.

CEO Compensation

Well I think I've been in the top 5 percent of my age cohort all my life in understanding the power of incentives, and all my life I've underestimated it. And never a year passes, but I get some surprise that pushes my limit a little farther.
—CHARLIE MUNGER, "THE PSYCHOLOGY OF HUMAN MISJUDGMENT," HARVARD UNIVERSITY SPEECH, 1995

Total compensation is the most readily definable indicator of corporate governance. It is the responsibility of the board of directors, and specifically the compensation committee, to determine appropriate compensation for CEOs and top management. Boards of large companies rely heavily on competitive analysis provided by compensation consultants. Every company wants to ensure their CEO earns above the median level for good performance. It is no surprise then that the CEO pay continues to escalate, as not everyone can be north of median. This circularity has impaired the credibility of compensation consultants and directors alike. Smaller companies will take their cue from larger peers less some discount. Compensation is divided into categories. Most parts of the world have a fixed component, a variable cash component, and an equity grant.

Structure of CEO compensation has changed over time, from more heavily fixed to more heavily variable and equity driven. In the United States, 80 percent of total compensation or more is composed of incentive awards that must be earned. They will vest only if certain future metrics are met. These metrics vary but often are a combination of revenue growth, earning per share (EPS) growth, minimum return on equity hurdles, and stock price movements versus a select peer group. Market cap thresholds, like the one seen at Tesla, are highly unusual.

> Munger explained this approach to incentives: "An example of a
> really responsible system is the system the Romans used when
> they built an arch. The guy who created the arch stood under it
> as the scaffolding was removed. It's like packing your own para-
> chute" (Berkshire Hathaway annual meeting, 1993).

The problem with incentives is that they incent certain specific behaviors. Revenues can be driven upward by poor pricing or aggressive sales practices or even through bad acquisitions. Return on equity (ROE) can be increased by lowering noncash charges like depreciation or amortization, shrinking research and developing (R&D) or ad costs, or by writing off equity accounts. Operating earnings, often used in compensation plans because they measure underlying profits, are subject to manipulation. Share prices are tougher to directly manipulate over a multiyear period. Some companies, however, will invest heavily in investor relations (IR), hiring articulate, persuasive even sometimes good-looking IR directors to meet with potential investors. C-suite personnel were promoted to their positions of power in part because of their persuasive abilities, and promotional firms will provide extensive access to investors in charm offensives. Investment banks and their analysts are accidentally complicit, subject to C-suite charms and eager to invite managers to their investment banking conferences. There are hundreds of these around the world, many attended by investors representing billions in assets under management. Some companies invest heavily in slick presentations, posting them on their IR sites, or invite analysts to remote locations to showcase emerging businesses, which are their growth options. Sometimes one sees small-cap companies whose IR efforts resemble those of Boeing. These efforts are expensive and are illogical for small companies with limited scale. These misallocated efforts promoting a company as opposed to running a company may boost stock prices yet do little to increase intrinsic value—but management still gets paid.

Incentives matter. Buffett earns $100,000, and Jeff Bezos made $81,840 per year for the past two decades until his retirement in 2021. Neither has ever taken an equity grant nor an option grant, and their equity stakes are perfectly aligned with shareholders because they own the same shares with the same rights as minorities. They experience perfect alignment because they feel the proportionate ups and downs in the share price identically to minority shareholders. Both built businesses from the ground up and have been excellent partners to shareholders. These are extremes, obviously, but they get to a larger point. Namely, does the CEO offer good value for money?

The theoretically correct question is whether other equally talented managers are available to run that business who command less in total compensation? It is a tough ask for an investor to make this determination, so some other questions answerable mostly from the annual proxy statement or annual reports should help.

1. *Are senior managers required to hold some multiple of their salary in company stock?* Convention in many countries, including the United States, is that a CEO should hold three years' worth of salary, or more, in the form of direct share ownership of the company. Many Japanese CEOs, by contrast, own little directly in their companies. Direct ownership, more than option grants or cash rewards, incent prudent behavior by CEOs, because the symmetry experienced in their shareholdings mirror the gains and losses faced by ordinary shareholders. The multiple of salary is not important, as

much as the exposure relative to a CEO's net worth. A CEO with a material portion of their net worth in direct company ownership is most likely to behave like an owner—that is, someone who will benefit minority shareholders.

2. *Did they purchase these shares with their own savings, or were they granted through equity grants?* High-quality CEOs will make large equity purchases immediately after accepting their position that are material to their own financial circumstance. This raises the odds of direct alignment with other shareholders.

3. *Do they continue to get large equity grants, severely diluting existing shareholders over time?* Some companies, even larger ones, have employee options grants outstanding that total 10 percent or more of shares outstanding. This may be fine for an early lifecycle company with an enormous growth ramp ahead but with limited cash flow to properly incent personnel. Unfortunately, many later-stage companies have adopted similar policies. They often pay market cash compensation supplemented by options grants to mid-level employees alongside upper management. This is egregious. U.S. companies are the worst culprits in this regard, and it is not unusual to see even large caps granting 1 percent of shares outstanding annually for equity comp, with 10 percent of outstanding shares previously issued. International companies are typically less generous with equity awards. HSBC, the global megabank dual listed in London and Hong Kong SAR, has only 3 percent of outstanding stock issued in options.

4. *Are incentive metrics long-term oriented enough to represent a normal business cycle of that company's business?* Some companies, such as poultry producers and fish hatcheries, operate around business cycles that last one to two years. That is the duration typically required to correct production peaks and troughs. The aerospace cycle, by contrast, may last ten years or longer. Some insurance company liabilities average a two-year duration, some with large, long-tailed lines of policies like worker's compensation and general liability are longer, seven to ten years. The decisions made by a CEO and her team at an auto insurance company will prove themselves out in less than three years. Incentive compensation can be measured, and that compensation can be vested, over a shorter timeframe. Meanwhile, the CEO and team at Boeing will

make decisions whose success will not be evident for ten years. A three-year vesting schedule at Boeing is grossly inadequate. HSBC uses a three-year vesting and subsequent five-year payout with clawback features, aligning plan duration with its operations and making long-term thinking more likely among its managers.

5. *Is the CEO and senior manager pay properly correlated to the economic cycle?* Corporate profits increase during economic expansions and decline during downturns. CEO pay tends to be correlated, as does employee compensation generally. This is logical within certain brackets as more profitable companies have more resources to pay employees. Also, financially strong employers are more likely to bid higher for talent, forcing incumbent employers to raise wages to keep their own talent in house. The extremes, specifically for senior managers, is where investors should become concerned.

Banks globally faced large losses on their mid-2000's loan originations during the 2008 Great Financial Crisis (GFC). Many banks ran aggressively with too little equity capital, forcing them to raise large amounts of new capital at highly dilutive share prices. Prudent banks did relatively better, Wells Fargo, for example. In a perfect corporate governance world, management pay would drop in relation to the level of distress and overall dilution faced by investors. The worst would have been immediately replaced with more prudent stewards. In reality, management pay did drop, although most failed this acid test of corporate governance. PNC's CEO, James Rohr, received $19 million in total compensation for full year 2007, $12 million in 2008, and back to $18 million in 2009. PNC was a relative winner throughout the GFC and management deserved a better than average outcome, yet such a small drop in CEO compensation in the worst banking crisis since the Great Depression sent a poor corporate governance signal. Roughly two-thirds of Rohr's total compensation came in the form of equity grants and options. Grant dates include the 2008 grants made based on the stock price as of February 12, 2009. This was near the absolute low stock price and enormously below intrinsic value. The fair value of these grants was at least two to three times the accounting value, further enriching the CEO.

6. *Can you identify a fleet of jets, ritzy offices, or other lavish perks?* Does the CEO live a flamboyant lifestyle? Although not directly

related to incentive compensation, CEOs with lavish personal lives don't often check their spending excesses at the front door of company headquarters. Dennis Kozlowski was once seen as the archetype of the perfect CEO, building the conglomerate Tyco into a multibillion dollar powerhouse. His personal excesses were well documented, including an infamous Greek-style toga party on the island of Sardinia, a $2 million affair funded by Tyco's shareholders. It eventually became clear that his proclivity for personal excess translated to his management style. Returning to PNC, the company disclosed that it allowed its executives to travel on a private plane, and until 2009, it allowed up to $50,000 per year in personal flights. This sends a poor signal to employees, which may explain why policies were eventually tightened. As Peter Lynch said: "The extravagance of any corporate office is directly proportional to management's reluctance to reward shareholders."

The shareholder holds the power of the proxy vote. Exercise it. Compensation packages should align managers as closely as possible to shareholders. That is, they should feel pain or gain proportionate to the shareholders. Poor alignment should be voted against. In most countries, the proxy vote on executive compensation is legally binding. Companies work hard to lobby for their pay packages, engaging large shareholders and consultants to build a package that is likely to be well received. In the United States, proxy votes surrounding compensation are advisory in nature, but a near-majority vote or better against will be enough to force changes going forward. We live in a world in which more than half of the shares are owned by passive vehicles. These investors are poorly informed and are not well equipped to make good decisions surrounding compensation, which requires a bottom-up analysis by informed investors. Nevertheless, exercise your vote. It matters.

Board of Directors Analysis

Why have intelligent and decent directors failed so miserably? The answer lies not in inadequate laws—it's always been clear that directors are obligated to represent the interests of shareholders—but rather in what I'd call "boardroom atmosphere." It's almost impossible, for example, in a boardroom populated by well-mannered people, to raise the question of whether the CEO should be replaced. It's equally awkward to question a proposed acquisition that has been endorsed by the CEO, particularly when his inside staff and outside advisors are present and unanimously support his decision. (They wouldn't be in the room if they didn't.) Finally, when the compensation committee—armed, as always, with support from a high-paid consultant—reports on a mega-grant of options to the CEO, it would be like belching at the dinner table for a director to suggest that the committee reconsider.

—WARREN BUFFETT, BERKSHIRE HATHAWAY
ANNUAL LETTER, 2002

The board holds a fiduciary duty to shareholders. The proxy is the most comprehensive source of information for the board, and it should be scoured carefully for the following:

1. How many directors sit on the board? A small board, say five to ten members, will be more engaged and more individually accountable. The tendency is for board size to increase with market cap. In many countries, labor has a seat at the table. Shareholders should push back when management is recommending an increase in board size because management likely will offer input into new members, and as the group expands, CEO control tends to expand alongside.

2. What are the backgrounds of the board members? The majority of members should house deep industry experience, and connections that help expand sales or product reach. Biotechs should include scientists but also those with contacts to larger pharmaceuticals or distributors. Theranos, the disgraced diagnostics startup, loaded up its board with heavy-weight politicians who added credibility but were easily fooled by its dubious science.

3. Is board compensation reasonable? Board members of public firms receive an annual stipend, maybe $50,000 for small caps and $200,000 or more for large caps. Private company directors may receive only equity because most earlier stage companies are cash starved. Become concerned when compensation levels are too high for directors, as self-preservation may override optimal decision-making. Option grants should be avoided, because options contain asymmetrical outcomes, and if stock prices decline, members will

get additional grants, and the upsides are potentially huge. Directors will be better aligned if they own shares on the same terms as
shareholders.

4. Direct share ownership is ideal. Are board members owners of
   shares outright rather than simply option grants? Is ownership
   likely material to their net worth? Directors with skin in the game,
   better aligned with shareholders, will act more like a true fiduciary.

5. How often are directors reelected? Ideally, shareholders vote to
   elect all board members annually. In many parts of the world,
   boards are staggered, with three-year terms.

Buffett explained:

> Is it any wonder that a non-wealthy director ("NWD") now hopes—
> or even yearns—to be asked to join a second board, thereby vault-
> ing into the $500,000–600,000 class? To achieve this goal, the
> NWD will need help. The CEO of a company searching for board
> members will almost certainly check with the NWD's current CEO
> as to whether NWD is a "good" director. "Good," of course, is
> a code word. If the NWD has seriously challenged his/her pres-
> ent CEO's compensation or acquisition dreams, his or her candi-
> dacy will silently die. When seeking directors, CEOs don't look for
> pit bulls. It's the cocker spaniel that gets taken home. (Berkshire
> Hathaway annual letter, 2019)

The power to vote for directors is the shareholder's greatest power.
Read the proxy carefully for clues as to whether directors act independently
or in their own self-interest. If the compensation package for the CEO is
inappropriate, vote against all members sitting on the compensation committee. If management candidates are unsuitable for office, vote against
all members of the nomination committee. If financial reporting is overly
aggressive, lacks transparency, or creates operating issues, vote against the
entire audit committee.

Case Study: Berkshire Hathaway

Berkshire Hathaway has performed brilliantly for investors in spite of its
board governance. Its fourteen members in 2021 include five insiders and
nine outsiders. Buffett is both chair and CEO. The outsiders, including Bill

Gates (who recently stepped down to focus on philanthropy), were hand selected by Buffett. Their independence is lacking. Two of the fourteen have media backgrounds, which is of questionable utility to the Berkshire Hathaway conglomerate of today. Each is independently wealthy and owns shares of Berkshire outright. Buffett's son is on the board. Being on Berkshire's board is not an enrichment vehicle as average compensation is only $5,000 per year. The median age of directors is seventy-eight years old, which is older than some boards' mandatory retirement age of sixty-five. One notable difference is that board members are not provided with any directors and officers insurance, placing them personally liable if the company is sued. This crazy structure surely will be adjusted to market norms once the next generation rises to power.

Buffett wrote: "Another of my 1956 Ground Rules remains applicable: I cannot promise results to partners. But Charlie and I can promise that your economic result from Berkshire will parallel ours during the period of your ownership: We will not take cash compensation, restricted stock or option grants that would make our results superior to yours" (Berkshire Hathaway annual letter, 2001).

Berkshire Hathaway is a great example of a company operating with a benevolent CEO who operates in the shareholders' interest without robust corporate governance constraints. His message is one of fairness. His desire is that Berkshire always trades around intrinsic value so that entering and exiting partners are treated equally. Most management teams do their best to talk their stock prices higher, thinking that higher is better. Beneficial to their paychecks, yes, but not beneficial to newly entering shareholders.

Historical Capital Allocation

Most management teams and boards have been at the helm for at least a few years, and CEOs have a documented track record of success. Evaluating track records provides clues about how shareholder-friendly managers might be in future cycles. During this analysis, focus on the following:

Has capital allocation been prudent? Review the cash flow statement for clues.

1. Capex—Study capital expenditures (capex). Was it far above depreciation expense? Did high capex lead to growth in revenues or improvements in efficiency? Many industrial Japanese companies

have underspent capex versus depreciation for many years, harvesting their operations to protect cash in what has been an extended downturn now in its twentieth year. Did capex investments taper off near peaks as it is reasonable to expect or did management double down at the wrong time?

2. Acquisitions—Intrinsic value can compound through disciplined acquisitions, made at prices below the fair value of assets acquired. Google bought YouTube in 2006 for $1.65 billion, versus an estimated value today well in excess of $100 billion. Statistically speaking, however, acquirors are more likely to overpay rather than underpay, as information asymmetry makes for smarter sellers than buyers. Often, incented sellers dress up their companies for sale, pushing forward sales or temporarily slashing expenses. Also, the heat of bidding wars can lead to irrational anchoring of price.

Buffett offered this explanation: "Many CEO's attain their positions in part because they possess an abundance of animal spirits and ego. . . . When such a CEO is encouraged by his advisors to make deals, he responds much as would a teenage boy who is encouraged by his father to have a normal sex life" (Berkshire Hathaway annual letter, 1994).

Think of a $10 billion acquisition, in which a $1 billion increase might be material to the bidder but amounts to only a 10 percent increase in price paid. GE's CEO Jeffrey Immelt oversaw a large number of acquisitions during his almost twenty-year tenure, many made at premiums to intrinsic value at the wrong points of the cycle. Alstom was one such example, as GE bought a power generation company near the peak of the cycle in 2014. Initially the bid was $13 billion, but that bid was raised to $17 billion before the deal concluded.

The timing of large acquisitions speaks to management discipline. Do they chase fads, like Immelt buying Alstom near the peak of the energy cycle? Franklin bought Legg Mason at what may prove to be near-peak market conditions, announcing the transaction in January 2020. Ideally, management has set aside dry powder for a rainy day, purchasing competitors, or expanding its footprint only when attractive opportunities present themselves. Managers require the appropriate and unusual blend of patience and discipline to be successful in the mergers and acquisitions game. Study a manager's acquisition history carefully.

3. Changes in leverage—Check the financing section of the cash flow statement to see gross issuances and repayments of financial debt. Is management using its free cash flow to pay down debt if they are over-levered? If they are under-levered, is management increasing dividends, making prudent investments, or otherwise being smart in how they deploy capital? A cyclical company should create a rainy-day fund near economic peaks, decreasing net debt as profits soar. The airlines were printing money in 2019, yet few took the opportunity to materially pay down debt. Instead, they repurchased shares at what appeared to be inexpensive valuations. Deep cyclicals should be heavily net cash by the time a market cycle turns down, providing a financial cushion through which to manage future losses in the next downturn.

Ideally, companies lever up for good investments made at attractive prices. The Alstom transaction, valued at $17 billion, raised debt levels at GE. GE would love to have that capital available today to help it manage down its still very large debt repayment plan. How a management maneuvers its balance sheet across time is one of the most critical aspects of corporate governance. Certain managements are aggressive, shooting for high returns with a high-risk strategy. Managers tend to remain consistent in this regard.

4. Free cash flow dividend policy—Many companies want to raise cash dividends year over year, using this as marketing fodder for potential investors. Realty Income in San Diego even has a slogan, "The Monthly Dividend Company," prominently advertising its ninety consecutive quarterly dividend increases. High-growth companies with many places to invest their capital should pay no dividends, whereas more mature stable businesses, especially those that are less capital intensive, should pay out 50 percent to 100 percent of earnings or free cash flow. Companies approaching cycle troughs should consider eliminating their dividends to free up capital to pay down debt or buy back highly discounted stock.

Evaluating the discipline of management surrounding dividend policy speaks volumes about corporate governance. The 2020 COVID-related oil downturn witnessed sub-$20 oil, which severely depressed Chevron's first-quarter 2020 earnings. The CFO made it clear on the call that preserving the dividend was the company's number-one priority, and it cut capex by 30 percent in the process. This prudent behavior may partly explain Chevron's premium valuation.

5. Share buybacks—In the late 1990s the U.S. auto industry spent billions of dollars to repurchase shares. Ford repurchased shares at an average price of $23 in 1998 near its all-time peak stock price of $34 in 1999. The stock sits at $10 as of mid-2021. These billions of dollars were mostly wasted for two reasons. First, they paid above intrinsic value at the time to buy back these shares. That net difference equates to capital wasted, earnings that did not accrue to shareholders. Second, the billions spent would have come in handy in subsequent recessions as Ford became desperately short on capital because of its high debt load and large operating losses generated in the recessions of the early 2000s and 2007–2009. They raised large amounts of equity during the GFC at low prices. Management bought high and sold low, which is a primary way to destroy value.

Buffett cautioned: "When CEOs or boards are buying a small part of their own company, though, they all too often seem oblivious to price. Would they behave similarly if they were managing a private company with just a few owners and were evaluating the wisdom of buying out one of them? Of course not" (Berkshire Hathaway annual letter, 2016).

Ford, however, is a company that seems to have learned some lessons since the late 1990s. It was deeply distressed in the 2008 GFC, yet it navigated through the crisis with the distinction as the only U.S. auto company not resorting to a government bailout. It is fiercely determined to outperform this time around. Time will tell.

Capital Allocation Guidance

Consider a semiconductor company with $100 million in equity and a 15 percent normalized return on equity. The current management team therefore will be allocating a total of $75 million of newly generated equity capital over the next five years, an amount almost equal to its current equity base. Trust in management to properly allocate this equity is paramount. Forward-looking guidance often is provided on how earnings will be allocated. Management may state that they would like, for example, to reduce debt from three times net debt to EBITDA to two and a half times, or that its capex will rise 50 percent next year to invest in a next-generation plant.

Guidance sends a clear message of management priorities and their overall level of aggressiveness or prudence.

Cohesiveness and Consistency of Corporate Strategy

Corporate strategies come in many flavors. Does management have a clearly laid out vision of its company? How do they define their competitive advantage? Are they a low-cost producer, or do they operate with a premium price strategy? Are major decisions consistent with their corporate identity? Are growth strategies reasonably likely to materialize given the level of commitment made and competitive advantages the company brings to the growth initiative?

Read the financial reports, listen to transcripts, and, when needed and accessible, speak to managers and competitors. Watch year-to-year capital allocation for clues. A good estimate of this vital signaling factor will emerge. It may not obviously seem like a corporate governance issue, but few items affect an intrinsic value as much as corporate strategy, which to a large degree are guided by management motivations.

Poor Expense Management

The customer-experience path we've chosen requires us to have an efficient cost structure. The good news for shareowners is that we see much opportunity for improvement in that regard. Everywhere we look (and we all look), we find what experienced Japanese manufacturers would call "muda" or waste. I find this incredibly energizing.
—JEFF BEZOS, AMAZON ANNUAL LETTER, 2008

Always focus on the most material factors important to an investment decision. Many expense issues are seemingly immaterial. A corporate jet, for example, or a guaranteed pension plan only for senior managers, or a lavish new headquarters are small as a percent of operating profits. They do affect, however, culture, morale, ethics, and other spending decisions. Why shouldn't an employee justify a lavish client dinner while in London rather than an equally productive office visit when the CEO spends opulently? These immaterial signals have material consequences.

Accounting Transparency and Communications

Accounting records are the primary means of communications between the management team and shareholders. These communications should be simple to understand and should be as comprehensive as needed to understand the economics of their businesses. CEOs receive daily and monthly summaries by segment, business line, or other groupings important to help them manage their business. These are similar metrics that management teams should make available to shareholders. Anything less ranges from incompetent neglect to intentional obfuscation.

Accounting governance issues range from egregious to simply suspicious. The most extreme violations justify a quick pass, whereas others might affect your assessment of intrinsic value or influence your initial entry price. Frequently seen accounting concerns include the following:

1. Adverse audit opinion: Public companies are audited at least annually by mostly the four large accounting firms. Adverse opinions are often too little too late, but a continuing holder should run when seeing this opinion. A qualified opinion is a lesser but still significant concern that requires deep thought.
2. Accounting restatements: These historical adjustments occur more frequently and vary in materiality. Minimal restatements may offer a buying opportunity even if negative, whereas major restatements can influence intrinsic value by, for example, lowering the historical margin used to assess forward looking profitability.
3. Segment information: Managements often change their definitions of segments. Perhaps they bought a new business, or divested a material asset, or justified their changes in some other way. Advice to management: it is fine to add segments but highly suspicious if historical segments cannot be easily linked to new segment breakdowns.
4. Aggressive assumptions: High-quality managements maintain conservative assumptions. Portfolios are well served for avoiding firms that utilize aggressive accounting assumptions, as they typically reflect stretched behavior in other areas. Examples include high assumed returns in pension assets, unusually long depreciable lives, or operating earnings through the cycle that materially exceeds generally accepted accounting principles net income. Allianz, the German insurance giant, consistently embeds conservative

assumptions and prudent reserves into its financial records, helping to explain its often premium valuation.

See part 2, chapter 8, "Accounting," for more detail. This is material
stuff.

Ethics

> Warren told the story of the opportunity to buy Conwood, the #2
> maker of chewing tobacco. I never saw a better deal, and chew-
> ing tobacco doesn't create the same health risks as smoking. . . .
> Warren and I sat down, said we're never going to see a better
> deal . . . but we're not going to do it. Another fellow did and
> made a couple of billion easy dollars. But I don't have an ounce of
> regret. I think there are a lot of things you shouldn't do because
> it's beneath you.
> —CHARLIE MUNGER, WESCO ANNUAL MEETING, 2007

A company should make products and services that offer value for consumers. Southwest has built its well-earned reputation by offering complete
transparency around its pricing. It does not have change fees or baggage
fees, and it follows a lower cost strategy with a win–win outcome. Compare
that to Match.com. It does not have fees to start, but it practices deceitful
push communications and restricted access with the allure of promising
excellent outcomes only once costly monthly subscriptions begin. Or imagine a search engine that actively pushes banner and other ads to maximize
monetization versus a second that operates with a more restrained strategy.
Certain life insurance companies aggressively market high-cost products
that offer little value for customers, while timeshare companies pay 60 percent of proceeds out in sales commissions, understanding that only high-
pressure tactics close deals.

As Graham wrote: "My point is, that from the standpoint of national
policy, 'good ethics is good economics.' The same is no doubt true for an
individual business" (*The Ethics of American Capitalism*, 1956).

Invest in companies that make products or provide services needed or
wanted by customers. Limit your investment quest to companies offering
win–win propositions to their customers. *Companies that charge fair prices
for good products have more durable businesses. Pass on the rest.*

ESG

Environmental, social, and governance (ESG) has become increasingly prominent in recent years. The concept was first introduced to global markets in 2004 by the United Nations, followed up with an in-depth compact in 2005 cosponsored by the United Nations and the Swiss Federal Department of Foreign Affairs and was endorsed by many of the world's largest financial institutions. It encouraged investors to consider these three categories of company behavior as relevant to societal aims and as adding improved returns over the longer run. Astute ESG investors might foresee, for example, toughening regulatory standards through a more thorough analysis of a company's environmental footprint.

ESG, endorsed first by European investors, has expanded its prominence worldwide. Today, more than $20 trillion in managed assets explicitly utilizes an ESG overlay. The UN Principles for Responsible Investment (PRI) has grown from the fifty original signatories to more than two thousand in 2021. These firms represent more than $70 trillion in assets. These firms commit to abiding by a series of six principles that include ESG considerations.

Labels aside, ESG always has been an analytical cornerstone for long-term-oriented investors. Environment liabilities can be substantial, and industrial companies with long operating histories are more likely to be faced with fines or other remediation costs. Astute investors will consider these costs in their valuations. Social policies affecting employees, suppliers, customers, and other stakeholders will influence long-term cost competitiveness and durable advantages. What economic impact did Nike suffer when accusations began to fly regarding its supplier labor policies? Lost sales and forced supply chain changes affected financials and might have been seen as short-sighted decisions made by aggressive managers. JUUL, the vaping company, delivers nicotine through an innovative design accompanied by delightful flavors like watermelon and mango. This group faced little regulation until recently and marketed aggressively to minors, designing products that specifically appealed to those under eighteen. Long-term investors embedded these risks into their assessments irrespective of a formal ESG framework. *Egregious ESG lapses warrant a pass. Either long-term earnings power is too difficult to ascertain, or costs of remediation are too uncertain. Similarly, companies that make products without obvious win-win characteristics should be avoided.*

Family Founders and Operators

Company founders come in two varieties. The first hands off power either voluntarily or involuntarily after a company reaches a certain point of maturity. They accept or are made to see their limitations. Quite often they possess a technical background necessary for innovation and development, but not the people or operational or marketing skills to take their business to the next level. They will either retain their ownership stake, slowly divest it over time, or be diluted into obscurity as the company raises fresh equity to continue its growth ramp. Large continuing ownership may justify a seat on the board or other continuing involvement. Otherwise, their influence will wane.

The second situation finds a founder who successfully transitions from inventor to operator, continuing their presence as CEO. She or he will have sold none or little of their holdings, and their stake will constitute almost the entirety of their net worth. Reliance on dividends is seen, as are other senior management positions held by family members.

The goal of long-term investors is to find managers who think like true business owners, those focused on the business as a perpetuity. Ask yourself, how would I run this business for the long run? How would I maximize per share value? Founders can be uniquely qualified in that regard. They built the business on their vision, defined the ideal culture reflective of their personality, and have pride in their creation. They want to see their business succeed. Given its materiality to their net worth, they are heavily incented not to do anything stupid. This incentive can lead to prudent management, or it can paralyze growth initiatives because of the founder's concern of principal preservation. Long-term investors need to understand founders' motives, ensuring that they run their businesses prudently but opportunistically.

Case Study: Persimmon Plc

Persimmon Plc is a UK home builder. Home builders are deeply cyclical. The UK real estate cycle mirrored the U.S. cycle with a deep trough in 2008 followed by a strong rebound. Persimmon is the largest UK builder and performed relatively better both in the downturn and subsequent recovery, although it did lose money in 2009 and net debt was elevated versus compressed EBITDA. Jeff Fairburn joined the group in 1989, running smaller divisions before becoming CEO from 2013 through 2018 until he resigned because of a highly controversial pay package that would have made him the most highly compensated UK CEO of all time. The board chair, responsible for negotiating the package, resigned a year earlier amid intense pressure.

The pay package, negotiated at the beginning of his CEO tenure, called for 10 percent of shares to be allotted to managers over ten years. Directors claimed that this reward was for past efforts, not future efforts. Performance conditions were minimal, requiring only a 10 percent stock price increase from the 2012 issuance date to fully vest. A rising tide for all UK home builders easily led to full vesting, which would have paid the management team GBP 500 million in incentive options. The board must have been feeling generous as even the retiring CEO in 2013 was allowed to keep twice the options he was contractually entitled to. Fairburn personally would have been paid out GBP 125 million, but with the uproar, he voluntarily returned GBP 25 million to the company and committed that another GBP 25 million would be donated to charity. Looking back over his track record, he had been a director of more than three hundred companies, an obvious red flag. Two of the board members from that era are still on the board.

In summary, Persimmon blends a solid track record with disastrous corporate governance. Board oversight was minimal and value transfer to employees was substantial. This strong misalignment could justifiably have caused prudent investors to pass irrespective of valuation. *You only need a handful of names, so why bother with one in which management or the board is working against you?* Alternatively, another approach could be to use a higher discount rate, lower earnings power or future growth, or a combination to attempt to factor in these variables into an intrinsic value. Purchase Persimmon at a nice discount to this beaten-down down intrinsic estimate, in which case the downside is limited with a possible upside if corporate governance eventually straightens out.

Fast forward to 2017, and a new tougher incentive compensation scheme was implemented that, at year-end 2019, gave no awards under the 2017 Performance Share Plan. This in spite of solid financial performance and still industry-leading metrics. Even bad companies can change.

Controlling Insiders

Occasionally, public companies are majority owned or controlled by parent companies. A number of European, Canadian, and Asian publicly traded holding companies own controlling positions in other companies.

Corporate governance at these subsidiary companies is only as good as (1) structural protections accorded to minorities and (2) the integrity of management at the parent. You are essentially a silent partner in their business with proportionate rights to the earnings power.

Case Study: Ambev

Ambev is the dominant brewer in Brazil with strong positions in other countries in the Americas. It checks a lot of boxes for a desirable publicly traded investment. It has a dominant franchise, is net cash, and has a history of conservative balance sheet management. It currently trades at a reasonable multiple of earnings while paying a 4 percent dividend yield. A series of transactions over the past ten years led to Ambev being 61.8 percent owned by Inbev, the world's largest brewer. Inbev is the product of mergers, most notably the acquisition of Anheuser Busch in 2008 for $52 billion cash. This transaction levered up Inbev's balance sheet. It continues to be levered, with $83 billion net debt at year-end 2020 versus EBITDA of $17 billion.

A levered parent and a net cash subsidiary can lead to potential problems. The parent could potentially drive down the share price of the subsidiary and then seek a take-under. The parent could force a large, extraordinary dividend beyond what is prudent for the subsidiary's long-term prospects. It could force underinvestment in the franchise and then raise the dividend or have Ambev extend a loan at "reasonable" terms to the parent. Alternatively, Inbev could become a forced seller of large blocks of shares, driving down prices. This has no bearing on Ambev's intrinsic value and conceivably could be an excellent buying opportunity unless these stakes are sold to another even less benevolent parent.

Most countries including Brazil have some minority rights protections that can protect against unwanted take-unders and outright pilfering of assets. Some parent subsidiary relationships involve multiple classes of shares. Fortunately for Ambev, only one share class exists. The risks to Ambev seem manageable overall and an investment in Ambev viable at the right price.

Reasons to Pass

Few firms around the globe meet the most stringent criteria for excellent corporate governance. Given that only a small number of companies are required to build an outstanding portfolio, excluding all names with even small blemishes is a reasonable decision. This may eliminate even more names than those filtered out with a leverage screen.

Corporate governance malfeasance comes in distinct shades of gray. Materiality matters, and an unbending corporate governance criterion may leave some viable and attractive investments in the pass pile. Egregious violators should be immediately passed over in any circumstance as well as those with multiple concerns of an intermediate nature. Smaller infractions may warrant investment either at a discounted price, or if truly immaterial, without application of any price discount. Either case requires ongoing monitoring for future changes, as corporate governance rarely remains static.

11

Asset Liability Mismatch

A business obtains the best financial results possible by managing both sides of its balance sheet well. This means obtaining the highest-possible return on assets and the lowest-possible cost on liabilities. It would be convenient if opportunities for intelligent action on both fronts coincided. However, reason tells us that just the opposite is likely to be the case.

—WARREN BUFFETT, BERKSHIRE HATHAWAY
ANNUAL LETTER, 1987

A business begins with the right-hand side of the balance sheet. Equity, debt, accounts payable, and other liabilities fund assets on the left-hand side that produce the revenues. Assets can include tangible assets, such as inventory and property, plant, and equipment (PP&E), which are booked on the balance sheet, or assets can be intangible, such as software development or drug research and development (R&D), which are expensed but are just as important to the generation of revenues.

Asset durations vary widely. Short-term assets, including inventory and accounts receivable, turn every few months, whereas PP&E, booked intangibles, and off-balance sheet assets, such as the useful life of R&D, vary widely. Steel company PP&E will last thirty years or more, whereas software development investments may last five to ten years. The nature of the company's business is the most important determinant of asset duration. To understand the business, you need to understand the asset durations.

Is a Company's Funding Profile Consistent with Its Business?

The liability profile, the right-hand side of the balance sheet, is critical in understanding potential downside risks of companies. The hypothetical company that is purely equity-funded faces duration mismatch because its asset durations are shorter than its perpetual equity duration. Yet solvency risk is low because no company goes bankrupt without some type of liability. We are less concerned about a duration mismatch in which equity purely funds a shorter duration asset base because risks are low.

Companies rarely fund their businesses entirely with equity capital. Financial debt, both short term and long term, and other liabilities complete the funding profile. Short-term liabilities, due in the next twelve months, often are matched against current assets and thus are not a material source of concern for most. If materially different, this mismatch should be investigated. The largest duration mismatches occur with long-term liabilities, as corporate debt mostly matures within the next five or ten years, while operating assets last longer. There are no thirty-year corporate bonds. For most businesses, it is impossible to appropriately match long-term asset durations against their funding profile.

Banks collect demand deposits and short-term debt, investing them in longer-term loans and investment securities. Manufacturers borrow money to build long-lived factories, while pharmaceuticals borrow money to invest in R&D that may take a decade or longer to convert to profits. Real estate investment trusts (REITs) borrow money to purchase income-producing properties.

Short-term funding is less expensive than long-term funding. In fiscal year 2021, the U.S. government actively reduced the duration of its sovereign debt borrowings to lower interest expense, to 5.5 years. Aggressive companies do the same thing, shortening liability duration to artificially expand profits. Conservative companies, and typically higher quality companies by contrast, tend to seek longer-term funding sources in spite of the higher associated cost.

Warren Buffett wrote: "As house prices fall, a huge amount of financial folly is being exposed. You only learn who has been swimming naked when the tide goes out—and what we are witnessing at some of our largest financial institutions is an ugly sight" (Berkshire Hathaway annual letter, 2007).

Why does a mismatch matter? Although the risk seems purely academic, few risks cause greater consternation for investors than major duration mismatches:

1. Rollover Risk—Debt maturities must be paid off or rolled over. Few companies have enough extra cash on the balance sheet to completely pay off maturing debt. This creates rollover risk because companies are forced to issue new debt to replace maturities. Weak companies operationally and the most levered financially face the greatest rollover risk, and these companies usually have the toughest time with large refinancings. Holding assets of equal duration as liabilities allows for the greatest balance sheet flexibility. Rental car companies, for example, borrow to buy car rental fleets on a relatively matched basis. Assets are sold when debts become due. This duration match lowers financial risk by increasing financial flexibility.

2. Economic Cycle—Debt rolls in midcycle environments typically can be managed when the environment is benign and access to capital plentiful. During economic peaks, such as the one seen in 2005–2007, credit spreads were tight and terms and lending conditions were loose, allowing for even the weakest credits to roll over their debt. In 2008 and 2009, weak companies with large debt rolls were unduly punished, which proved challenging. Rental car companies may be mostly matched on a duration basis, though the value of their used car fleet varies through the cycle, creating unexpected mismatches.

3. Credit Spreads—Credit spreads are highly correlated to both the economic cycle and company-specific issues. An operationally struggling company faces wide credit spreads, forcing them to pay more interest when large refinancings materialize. This scenario can hurt interest coverage when companies can least afford it.

4. Fleeting Liquidity—During the 2008 Great Financial Crisis (GFC), liquidity temporarily dried up for the weakest borrowers. No yield seemed sufficient to allow certain weaker companies to refinance. Equity raises in lieu of debt refinancings at very low equity prices hugely diluted existing shareholders. The cost of this capital was enormous and led to massive intrinsic value impairments. The worst-hit companies were unable to raise equity at any price,

forcing them into bankruptcy. In bankruptcy, equity holders are most often wiped out. The Federal Reserve worked hard to eliminate this risk through the COVID crisis, offering to be the buyer of last resort for corporate credit. This triggered a massive refinancing boom as companies took advantage of guaranteed liquidity. Companies good and bad retained access to credit in 2020, although future cycles may unfold differently.

5. Economic Equity Fluctuations—Large shifts in interest rates cause the economic values of assets and liabilities to move. Assets generating a fixed stream of income are worth less when interest rates rise as the opportunity cost of holding those assets versus owning risk-free treasuries increases. When long-term rates move up 1 percent with a ten-year asset duration and a five-year liability duration, the asset values decline twice as much as the liabilities. This is a major issue with most banks and insurers, as even moderate moves can affect the value of their economic equity. This translates to real income lost because assets earn 1 percent below what the market provides today, whereas they will pay an additional 1 percent interest on its new debt issued in five years.

A simple illustration demonstrates the financial impact of an asset liability mismatch. Destructible Insurance Co. carries a mismatch (table 11.1), while Indestructible Insurance Inc. matched its asset and liability duration (table 11.2). Notice the economic impact to shareholders' equity when interest rates rise 1 percent. Equity value is impaired at Destructible but remains stable at Indestructible.

Table 11.1
Destructible Insurance Co.

Base Case			
Cash	100	Debt, 5-year duration	900
Investments, 10-year duration	900	Equity	100
Total Assets and Liability	1,000		1,000
Interest Rates Increase 1%			
Cash	100	Debt, 5-year duration	855
Investments, 1-year duration	810	Equity	55
Total Assets and Liability	910		910
		Equity (% change)	−45%

Table 11.2
Indestructible Insurance Inc.

Base Case			
Cash	100	Debt, 7-year duration	900
Investments, 7-year duration	900	Equity	100
Total Assets and Liability	1,000		1,000
Interest Rates Increase 1%			
Cash	100	Debt, 7-year duration	837
Investments, 7-year duration	837	Equity	100
Total Assets and Liability	937		937
		Equity (% change)	0%

6. Management Prudence—Asset and liability durations are an excellent indicator of how conservatively management teams steward their businesses. The yield curve is typically upward sloping. Companies pay higher rates of interest for longer maturities and receive higher levels of income for longer durations. Aggressive management teams focused on short-term benefits may borrow short term and invest long term to temporarily supercharge profits. Well-intended compensation plans create these perverse incentives. Negative consequences materialize only when rates rise rapidly, reducing low-cost access to liquidity or worse. Aggressive managements may indeed swim naked when these follies are exposed.

Covenants can alter a firm's liability duration. Bank lines and even bonds can contain covenants that force premature repayment if covenants are violated. Typical covenants will cap net debt to earnings before interest, taxes, depreciation, and amortization (EBITDA) or define a minimum interest coverage. Covenants may restrict further borrowings to protect debtholders. Rarely will covenants trigger premature repayment, as most lenders accommodate covenant waivers for additional fees and higher interest rates. Capital markets behave poorly and unpredictably, however, when borrowers come near covenant restrictions as the duration uncertainty introduces another unknown into a business that is likely already facing obstacles. A worst-case scenario forces premature repayment of debt, skewing asset liability durations unpredictably. Duration matters.

Note that companies and investors prefer fixed interest rates to variable rates. Stronger companies mostly structure their debt with fixed rates because the slightly higher cost of borrowing is not material to their operations and interest expense is more predictable and thus can be better managed. Weaker companies, aggressive management teams, and even decent quality emerging market companies choose to, or are forced to, borrow mostly at variable rates. A variable rate balance sheet introduces an additional element of risk and should be appropriately stress-tested against higher interest rates. Fixed rate assets versus variable rate borrowings introduces an equally toxic mismatch when rates move materially.

Currency Mismatches

Most larger companies do business in multiple countries and thus operate in multiple currency regimes. Business models vary, but the following are typical:

1. A company makes and sells products only in its own country—The perfectly foreign exchange (FX)–matched company buys its raw materials, and all expenses, and generates revenues in one currency. This is the case for some smaller businesses but few large companies.
2. A company makes products in its home country for sale primarily abroad—Many commodity producers, including Valle, the Brazilian iron ore company, fall into this category. Valle mines iron ore in Brazil for sale around the world. A depreciating local currency expands profits until higher inflation starts to close the arbitrage. Many of these companies borrow in other currencies that are better matched to their revenue streams.
3. A company makes products in foreign countries for sale primarily in its home market—The Gap manufactures primarily in low-cost countries, while its retail presence is in the United States. A weakening of the U.S. dollar increases costs and margins until it can reprice products higher in the United States.
4. A company manufactures and sells its products in multiple countries—The average S&P 500 company generates half its sales from other countries. This analysis is a bit more complex, with companies grouped into one of the following three buckets:

   - Manufacture in the United States and sell a portion of its production abroad—Boeing or Lockheed Martin produce mostly in the United States and purchase from a mix of U.S. and international suppliers.

- Manufacture in other countries because costs are lower, selling those goods to other customers around the world—Apple is a prime example. It manufactures much of its products in China for sale globally.
- Attempt to match manufacturing capacity with sales regionally or even by country—General Motors cars sold in the United States are mostly manufactured in the United States, whereas its sales into China are mostly manufactured there. This is the least risky approach because local demand and supply and FX exposures are matched.

Currency financing strategies—that is, how companies structure their debt profiles in these international settings—differ dramatically and tell us much about management and structural risks of businesses. Various strategies include the following:

1. Finance all debts in the home currency—Many companies situated in deeper less expensive capital markets such as the United States, United Kingdom, or Japan mostly borrow in their home currency.
2. Borrow when costs of financing are lower and available maturities have a longer duration—Many emerging markets companies based in Brazil, Argentina, Mexico, and Indonesia borrow in U.S. dollars regardless of their FX profile to lower interest expense and extend liability durations.
3. Match borrowings with local operations—UK real estate investment trusts with portfolios in mainland Europe will look to borrow in euros when purchasing properties outside of the United Kingdom.

Do Currency Mismatches Cause Major Pain in Unsteady Circumstances?

It is essential to ask whether currency mismatches could cause pain. Forecasting currencies is challenging, almost impossible, but stress-testing balance sheets for large movements in currencies is a prudent risk management exercise. Balance sheet mismatches occur quite often on the currency side, and the pain can be severe. It is typically less expensive to borrow in U.S. dollars, euro, or yen than to borrow in Turkish lira, Brazilian real, or the Thai baht. Companies domiciled in foreign countries with higher costs of debt often engage in this hidden currency arbitrage, borrowing in U.S. dollars to lower costs while generating revenues and income in other currencies. U.S. capital markets are deep, allowing an emerging markets company access to (1) lower interest rates, (2) longer duration borrowings, and (3) a greater proportion of fixed versus variable rates. This optically lowers financial risk because the debt maturity schedules and interest coverage appear to be stronger.

The consequences are hidden in a steady-state environment when FX rates remain relatively stable. When debts become due, they are repaid at the same exchange rate with earnings generated from their home country in the local FX. Imagine, however, a Brazilian utility with very long dated assets that borrows in U.S. dollars because the cost of debt is several hundred basis points lower and debt maturities are longer. The Brazilian real has fluctuated widely over time, from 1.0 BRL/USD while pegged to the U.S. dollars, collapsing to 1.8 BRL/USD in 1998, and bottoming out below 6.0 BRL/USD in 2020.

Maturing U.S. dollar debt will be more expensive to repay as the local currency devalues. Emerging market FX devaluation has been common in many markets, from most Asian economies in the 1997 Asian Crisis, to the Mexican Tequila Crisis in 1994, to the Russian Default in 1998, to the Argentine Default in 2001, to the 15 percent decline of the Chinese renminbi between 2017 and 2020 after the Trump tariffs were introduced. FX volatility is normal. Ensure that companies manage these risks prudently.

Table 11.3 illustrates this point. A base case manageable leverage for a Brazilian utility borrowing in U.S. dollars, at one and half times net debt to EBITDA, moves quickly to two times net debt to EBITDA with just a small

Table 11.3
Utopian Utility SA

	Base Case	FX Weaker
BRL to USD	3.00	4.00
EBITDA to BRL mm	2,000	2,000
Net Debt to BRL mm	3,000	4,000
Memo: Net Debt to USD mm	1,000	1,000
Net Debt to EBITDA	**1.50**	**2.00**

Note: BRL = Brazilian real; EBITDA = earnings before interest, taxes, depreciation, and amortization; FX = foreign exchange; mm = million; USD = U.S. dollar.

weakening of the Brazilian real. Imagine the havoc that larger moves can introduce.

U.S. Case Study: WeWork

WeWork (WE), the besieged provider of shared coworking space, has seen phenomenal growth since its 2010 founding. It became a unicorn not many years later, reaching the pinnacle of startups with a $1 billion private market valuation. A 2018 private market transaction gave WE a market value of $47 billion. It was slated for a third-quarter 2019 initial public offering (IPO), but the public market investors took issue with one primary issue: the asset liability duration mismatch. WE took out office space, much with twenty-year fixed rate leases with built-in inflation escalators. It rented that space out piecemeal to individuals and smaller companies by the month or year.

Liability duration = ten years
Asset duration = one year

The business model really boomed in 2009 following the GFC, during which time the appetite for coworking spaces flourished. The large unknown, how many tenants would remain through a challenging recession, was the outgoing tide. The public markets refused to ascribe a valuation for WE greater than $10 billion during the IPO process, even after the company had raised a total of $12.5 billion in cumulative funding. The 2019 IPO was pulled, and billions of debt financing conditional on the IPO being completed evaporated. Softbank, its primary private investor with $15 billion invested as of the end of 2019, took the company over at a 2020 valuation of $8 billion. This unfolded in a relatively benign environment that saw lots of credit extended to mediocre companies. A duration mismatch can be lethal. The saga continues: WeWork merged into a special-purchase acquisition company (SPAC) in October 2021, ascribing it a $7 billion valuation, which has since declined to $5 billion as of February 2022.

International Case Study: ING Direct

Sticking with the private theme, ING Direct was a direct-to-consumer bank utilizing virtual online branches to collect massive amounts of deposits in the mid-2000s. It was owned by ING, the publicly traded Dutch insurance company, and ING Direct had operations in multiple countries including the United States. It touted its risk mitigation techniques, including matching all deposit currencies with assets purchased in those same currencies to avoid any possibility of an FX mismatch.

Although this seemed prudent, its internet deposits received market or above-market rates of interest. Durations for collected deposits included a blend of demand deposits and short-duration certificates of deposits. Demand deposits could be withdrawn any time, whereas the majority of CDs had one- to two-year maturity schedules. Its deposits surged to $300 billion with twenty million customers by 2008. Banks are spread businesses, and deposits are invested into income earning assets at a positive spread. ING Direct originated a small amount of loans, but it mostly bought asset-backed and mortgage-backed securities (MBS). These assets had longer durations—three to five years on average. The bank seemed quite profitable because the upward-sloping yield curve generated asset yields 1 to 2 percent higher than their deposit rates. ING claimed to have modeled depositor behavior using sophisticated algorithms, but when MBS values plummeted in 2008, ING Direct saw billions of deposits withdrawing en masse, fleeing to safer institutions. It was forced to sell assets, crystallizing losses, to cover withdrawing depositors, and ended up with losses and an eventual sale to Capital One. Duration mismatch kills.

Reasons to Pass

Asset liability mismatches are an excellent way to judge management temperament. Intentional mismatches can boost short-term earnings but put longer-term results at risk. Companies are not the only culprits. Many investors have made a successful living off the carry trade. Borrow at LIBOR and invest in thirty-year treasuries, hoping for a stable yield curve. Borrow in Japanese yen at 0 percent and invest in euro-denominated Italian bonds, hoping for a stable exchange rate. Some Eastern European banks funded by local deposits have traditionally offered Swiss franc mortgages to their customers because interest rates were lower. Small rises in the Swiss franc resulted in large losses for mortgage borrowers who had to repay in Turkish lira. Many consumers borrow at variable rates, hoping that short-term rates remain low. Companies, investment funds, and individuals who utilize large mismatches may claim that they have the underlying balance sheet strength to withstand potential shocks, although in most cases, these are gamblers taking odds—speculators not investors.

Companies who aggressively use asset liability duration mismatches, or large FX mismatches, should be avoided. Also, pass on companies whose liability profile is heavily variable rate. These intentional management decisions signal either weakness in the underlying business or efforts by aggressive management teams to temporarily prop up earnings.

12

Deep Cyclical Companies
Near Cycle Peak

To state the obvious, the economic cycle fluctuates. Each country's economic history varies. There is no global "normal." The United States boomed after World War I, crashed in the 1930s, boomed again after World War II, crashed in the 1970s in an unprecedented era of stagflation (stagnation + inflation), the 1980s and beyond mostly boomed with two small downturns in the early 1990s and early 2000s, followed by the worst recession in a generation in 2008–2010. COVID gave us a taste of a worst-case economic crisis in which few companies remained unscathed and United States gross domestic product (GDP) collapsed 10 percent in the second quarter of 2020, equivalent to a 40 percent annualized drop. The post-vaccine boom in 2021 shaped up to be equally unprecedented. Many other countries experienced their own Great Depression in the 1930s, and the Great Financial Crisis (GFC) that began in 2008 was universally called the Global Financial Crisis. Banks around the globe struggled, and the interconnectivity of our global financial system was highlighted.

Although the United States, roughly 25 percent of global GDP, guides a large portion of global interconnectedness, many countries often diverge meaningfully from the U.S.-driven trend. Australia, for example, completed its eighteenth year of economic expansion in 2019. Japan, meanwhile, has been in recession for more than two decades beginning in the late 1990s.

Emerging markets (EM) also diverge from industrial countries but move in a more closely correlated fashion with each other. Many are over-exposed to commodities (e.g., iron ore and oil), and many depend on capital flows from the United States and other industrial markets. Concerns about one EM country often spill over into concerns for the asset class, further tightening correlations as capital withdraws from EM. Russia defaulted on its foreign debts in 1998 and Mexico remained in recovery mode after its 1994 Tequila Crisis.

Warrant Buffett has said that "market forecasters will fill your ear but will never fill your wallet" (Berkshire Hathaway annual letter, 2014). Macroeconomists spend their days predicting economic prospects, forecasting GDP, interest rates, and other variables they consider important. Equities correlate to some degree to the economic cycle because equity prices attempt to predict economic cycles. GDP declines, which hits companies' revenues and profits. Two relevant observations are as follows:

1. Predicting the economy is hard—really hard. Most economists do well at predicting the steady state yet fall flat when predicting inflection points. The most "successful" economists extrapolate the previous five years; the bravest forecast inflection points and are mostly wrong.
2. Even if one is to successfully predict the economy, the correlation with the equity markets is low. China grew at a blistering 8 percent per year between 2010 and 2019, yet its equity market peaked in 2012 and then faced a three-year equity market downturn that caught most pundits off-guard. The U.S. equity market, one of the strongest globally between 2010 and 2020, has done better than its mediocre economic performance would have predicted.

Given how hard economies are to forecast, and the tenuous connection with equity market performance, what really can be said about any consideration of where we sit in the economic cycle? Some investors utilize a pure bottom-up process, focusing only on one stock's investment merits, without considering the cycle. Hold a ten-year view, these investors postulate, and the question of where we are in the cycle does not matter so much. Rather, study what you can control, including barriers to entry, management quality, market share gains, and other relevant microeconomic variables. Other investors continue to rely on macroeconomic forecasts, knowing the odds of success are low but believing nevertheless that some forecast is better than nothing.

Charlie Munger raised this concern: "My fourth criticism is that there's too much emphasis on macroeconomics and not enough on microeconomics. I think this is wrong. It's like trying to master medicine without knowing anatomy and chemistry. Also, the discipline of microeconomics is a lot of fun. It helps you correctly understand macroeconomics. And it's a perfect circus to do. In contrast, I don't think macroeconomics people have all that much fun. For one thing they are often wrong because of extreme complexity in the system they wish to understand" ("Academic Economics: Strengths and Faults After Considering Interdisciplinary Needs," University of California–Santa Barbara speech, 2003).

I am sympathetic to the longer-term calls for notable investors to ignore the cycle. Just pick good stocks and don't overpay. This is rational and likely will generate above-average returns over the cycle. The problem is that certain stocks perform so poorly in downturns that exposing an investment portfolio to those risks at the peak of their cycle tilts odds toward failure.

A blended solution provides protection while allowing the bottom-up stock picking process to flourish. Keep it simple. Group the economic cycle into three categories. The first is a market trough, the second is a market peak, and any residual is considered midcycle or thereabouts—certainly close enough to be uncertain whether a peak or trough is in sight. This framework considers the world to be in midcycle most of the time, with only obvious extremes justifying modifications to investment behavior.

Defining a trough and peak can be challenging. Economists rarely get it right, so consider a practitioner's lens, someone in the field rather than a professor in the classroom. Many variables offer clues that point to the state of the current environment.

Variables Indicating a Market Trough

The following variables indicate a market trough:

1. Declines in real GDP over a one- to three-year period
2. Widening corporate debt credit spread, well above the long-term average
3. Increasing unemployment rate, often accompanied by large corporate layoffs

4. Loan growth in the banking system turns negative—no appetite to borrow more money or risk appetite amongst the banks to extend additional credit
5. Other banking metrics, including high nonperforming assets, reserves to loans at peak level, low or negative return on equity (ROE), and spiking cost-to-income ratio
6. Uptick in personal and corporate bankruptcies
7. Corporate profit margins below the long-term trend
8. Equity market valuations below long-term averages as measured by price over multiyear earnings
9. Investment banks laying off employees, bonus pools shrink, and trading desks closed
10. Companies scale back on capex, acquisitions, and large organic investments, preferring to pay down debt
11. Dividends decline, and dividend suspensions proliferate
12. Housing starts and new permits drop to well below the long-term average
13. Home prices decline, particularly in secondary and vacation markets
14. Auto sales fall well below midcycle
15. RV and boat sales collapse
16. Airfares collapse, and cruise lines offer high promotions to incent bookings
17. Share buybacks stall given uncertainty and corporate desire to preserve cash
18. Swelling federal deficit accompanied by new fiscal stimulus measures
19. Municipal government financial difficulties and state and local governmental layoffs

Variables Indicating a Market Peak

The following variables indicate a market peak:

1. Above long-term trend real GDP growth for several years
2. Tight corporate credit spreads, and high-yield debt issuances balloon
3. Debt underwriting standards loosen, with fewer covenants and longer durations

4. Short-term and long-term interest rates increase
5. A healthy banking system, with high ROE, low nonperforming assets, and strong loan growth
6. Unemployment near historical low levels
7. Corporate profit margins above the long-term trend
8. Equity market valuations above long-term averages as measured by price to multiyear earnings
9. Equity prices surge on narrow breadth, intense euphoria surrounds market leaders, and prices respond nonsensically to noneconomic factors, including stock splits
10. Near record margin debt, a sign of speculation
11. High consumer confidence—neighbors upgrade houses, cars, and vacations
12. Venture capital deals above trend, as are IPOs and corporate takeouts
13. IPOs in weak money-losing businesses surge, as do unconventional investment schemes—special-purpose acquisition company (SPACs) are one example
14. Share buybacks approach record levels, often funded by debt issuances
15. Investment banking hiring positive for extended period, bonus pools at record levels
16. Net debt to earnings before interest, taxes, depreciation, and amortization (EBITDA) at corporations steadily rises toward record levels
17. Cranes in the ground well above midcycle, and builders blame delays on a lack of skilled labor
18. Housing starts near record level
19. Housing prices rise above GDP for extended period to elevated level relative to median income, fueled by a systemwide loan to value increasing for residential real estate
20. Mega-development projects get underway—The Chrysler Building and the Empire State Building were built in the late 1920s, and Aria and Cosmopolitan were built in Las Vegas in the mid-2000s

Variables Indicating Midcycle Conditions

Everything in between a trough and a peak can be defined as too tough to call. Expect this to be the case 70 percent of the time or more. During this phase, the economic cycle likely expands by a sustainable amount, credit is generally available to decent borrowers, and market excesses are limited. Standard equity analysis applies, but you should pass on most names for reasons described elsewhere, while letting your fundamental work dictate portfolio composition.

Benjamin Graham warned: "As might be expected, the previous period of greatest enthusiasm about the economic prospects of the US coincided with the tumultuous bull market of the late 1920s. Then, as now, nearly everyone was convinced that we had entered a New Era of continued and dynamic prosperity which made all past markets experience worse than useless" ("Stock Market Warning, Danger Ahead!," University of California–Los Angeles speech, 1959).

Identify a Market Peak: Now What?

Peak market conditions exude optimism. Company projections are high, lending conditions are loose, expansionary plans may be commonplace, large project announcements are made, and consumer confidence is elevated, all of which drive large-scale discretionary spending. Equity valuations go along for the ride. Multiples of earnings increase on profit margins that are above midcycle. Corporate leverage increases as management teams and investors clamor for "optimal balance sheets," which is code for borrowing to buy back shares above intrinsic value.

This is a risky time to invest in deep cyclical companies, even for sophisticated investors. Your answers to a variety of questions will have few to no good answers—just guesses based on uncertain probabilities.

1. When will the economic cycle turn down?
2. How bad will the next downturn be?
3. How long will that downturn last?
4. What will governmental reaction be to any downturn?
5. How open will capital markets be to companies who need additional capital to withstand the downturn? Will lenders extend additional loans? Will equity investors provide more equity capital at reasonable prices?
6. Is the market fairly valuing deep cyclicals today to compensate investors for the real cyclical risks?

Does Valuation Protect?

If we found a good business tomorrow, we'd buy it. We've been
doing that all along. I'm not good at predicting macro things.
—CHARLIE MUNGER, WESCO ANNUAL MEETING, 2006

Although most investors are aware of the risks, many still advocate buying
deep cyclical shares near peak market environments if valuations become
sufficiently compelling. The equity market is not totally naïve. It attempts
to forecast upcoming conditions including a roll-over from a cyclical peak.
Buffett explained:

> The airline business, and I may be wrong and I hope I'm wrong, but
> I think it changed in a very major way, and it's obviously changed
> in the fact that they're four companies and each are going to bor-
> row perhaps an average of at least $10 to $12 billion each. You
> have to pay that back out of earnings over some period of time.
> I mean, you're 10 or 12 billion worse off if that happens. And of
> course in some cases they're having to sell stock or sell the right
> to sell stock at these prices. And that takes away from the upside
> down. And I don't know whether it's two or three years from now
> that as many people will fly as many passenger miles as they did
> last year. . . . And of course the airline business has the problem
> that if the business comes back 70 percent or 80 percent, the air-
> craft don't disappear. (Berkshire Hathaway annual meeting, 2020)

To some extent, Buffett took that view in 2016 when Berkshire Hathaway allocated $10 billion to the four large U.S. domiciled airlines. The
rationale was similar to their railroad bet in 2009. Airlines faced capacity limitations because the big four had the most desirable gate locations
locked up from competitors. This barrier to entry created the pricing
power that had been elusive over the industry's fifty-year history. Buffett
assumed their investment would generate $1 billion in average look through
earnings per year.

Airlines check virtually every box of the deep cyclical checklist. One
difference with Berkshire Hathaway's purchase of Burlington Northern,
Buffett's 2009 railroad purchase, was timing. The United States was just
beginning to emerge from a deep trough in 2009. By contrast, Buffett ended

up selling his entire airline stake at a 50 percent loss in April 2020, in the depth of the COVID downturn as airlines turned to government capital to plug negative cash flows.

Asking this question should protect capital while providing a reasonable rate of return: "Does the stock price adequately discount a company's financial performance in the next downturn?"

That question is unequivocally correct. Buy a stock below its intrinsic value, and it will (1) compound at the market rate of returns, (2) offer excess returns as its stock price eventually catches up with its intrinsic value, and (3) offer downside protection if your intrinsic value ends up being too high. Deep cyclicals are shunned by many investors, and stock prices are highly volatile, offering occasionally compelling buying opportunities for shrewd investors when margins of safety are large.

When evidence of a peak abounds, deep cyclicals become structurally riskier. The longer the peak, the greater the structural risk. Operating profitability and earnings are highly geared to the cycle, and an extended peak invites complacency on the part of both management and investors. Management often forgets how risky the earnings stream is and how unpredictable the cycle is, choosing to invest large free cash flows or raise additional debt to (1) increase the dividend, (2) buy back shares, (3) make large new capex investments to expand capacity, and (4) engage in mergers and acquisitions that take out a competitor or extend the footprint at high valuations. Investor complacency also creeps in, pushing management to "release excess capital" or accelerate growth plans. Deep cyclicals often trade at low multiples of peak earnings, and frustrated investors will demand some convergence with the overall market. Both constituencies act in unison to heighten risks at precisely the wrong time.

Deeply cyclical earnings quickly evaporate in a downturn, leaving the debt in place while cash balances and liquidity decline. This introduces stress and management action that can quickly degrade intrinsic values. Asset sales, equity raises, distressed debt issuances, and operating losses are all plausible outcomes. Bankruptcy by larger companies is often concentrated in the deep cyclical space because of its inherent earnings volatility—the longer the trough endures, the more distressed deep cyclicals become. Calling the shape of the cycle is inherently challenging, making the level of eventual distress impossible to forecast. Why play the forecasting game, particularly when deep cyclicals must navigate carefully to protect from permanent capital impairment? Buying near a peak economic environment coupled with deep cyclical names are hard to call. Intrinsic value becomes impossible to calculate, making it too hard.

Identifying Deep Cyclicals

Although the definition of a deep cyclical may seem obvious (you know it when you see it), a brief study is warranted to better understand what makes deep cyclicals so potentially risky heading into economic downturns. Better understanding will allow a refined view of how deeply cyclical a company may be, as this group comes in a sliding scale of riskiness. In other words, a deep cyclical is not simply an on-or-off decision. Check a company's performance in each of the following categories below through the lens of previous recessions. How did the company do between 2007 and 2010, a very deep recession, and how did it do between 1999 and 2002, a more shallow and isolated recession? Most recently, how did it navigate through COVID in the first half of 2020?

Following are the most important variables that define deep cyclicals:

1. Companies selling nice-to-have versus must-have products/services:
   a. No one will cancel their cell phone or Netflix accounts during a downturn. Nor will they defer replacement tires more than a few months. Utility bills will be paid. Most health care will continue.
   b. Consumer products/services postponed indefinitely: Cars, RVs, new homes, furniture, vacation homes, new clothes or jewelry, vacations, restaurants, children, new bank loans, elective health and dental care, and miles driven will decline.
   c. Commercial products/services deferred: Expansionary capex, new offices, many consulting services, business-class airfare and business travel, conventions, certain marketing expenses, new employees, high insurance coverage limits, discretionary borrowing, research and development (R&D), brand extensions, acquisitions, and geographic expansions stop.
2. Revenue declines: The deepest cyclicals may see revenue declines of 50 percent in deep declines. Check revenue declines in previous cycles for guideposts.

3. Gross and operating margin movements: Gross margins will decline but stay positive, whereas operating margins will turn negative for most deep cyclicals.
4. Free cash flow: Most deep cyclicals burn cash during downturns. Businesses with large working capital balances burn less because inventory liquidations will generate enough cash to partially offset operating losses.
5. Financial debt increases: As losses mount and free cash flow turns negative, companies' cash reserves shrink and they are forced to borrow to offset cash burn.
6. High fixed costs: Most deep cyclicals have high fixed costs.
   a. Auto companies, auto parts, airlines, steel companies, and other manufacturers operate large and heavily capital-intensive plants.
   b. Retailers and logistics centers have large real estate footprints that cost the same even if utilization and throughput decline.
   c. Not all deep cyclicals have high–fixed cost structures, as some are more variable-cost business models. Real estate brokers, for example, mostly pay commissions for transactions, so labor costs make up a large part of their cost base.
   d. High-advertising or R&D-intensive businesses appear to be high–fixed cost businesses, although these costs are relatively quickly rebalanced and thus are less burdensome on the fixed cost structure.

A Starting Point for Identifying Deep Cyclicals

Companies globally are grouped into sectors. MSCI labels its sectors Global Industry Classification Standard (GICS). These frequently are used by institutional investors to group companies of similar characteristics together. Certain sectors are more cyclical, and each sector contains multiple subsectors, which will vary in their exposure to the economic cycle. In general, think of sectors along the following lines:

Deep Cyclical GICS: Energy, materials, financials, some industrials, and some consumer discretionary

Moderately Cyclical GICS: Real estate, some consumer discretionary, some industrials, and some IT

Less Economically Sensitive GICS: Some IT, communication services, utilities, consumer staples

Case Study: Winnebago

Winnebago is the iconic U.S. manufacturer of an assortment of recreational vehicles. Few industries are as far out on the tail of the consumption curve. RV sales take place after most other needs and wants have been satisfied. Figure 12.1 shows the U.S. RV industry volumes since the 2007 peak. WGO sales correlate highly with industry unit sales, dropping 50 percent between 1989 and 1991, dropping 10 percent between 2000 and 2001, and dropping 81 percent between the 2004 peak and 2009. Sales then fell 40 percent between first quarter 2020 and second quarter 2020, but rebounded dramatically throughout 2021 to what can only be described as a current mega peak. The stock price traded to $75 at year-end 2021, placing it at thirty-five times 2020 earnings and eight times 2021 earnings, a level likely around peak earnings. Most deep cyclicals trade below ten times peak earnings. Its franchise quality is high, making it a likely survivor, yet downturns are brutal for fundamentals and likely the stock price. Winnebago has survived because (1) its cost structure is variable (it assembles rather than

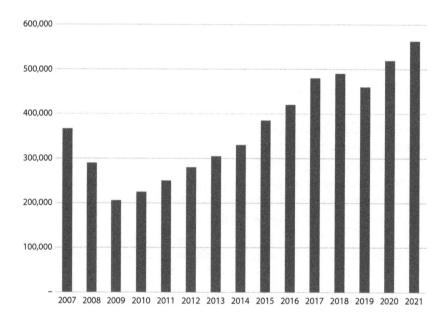

Figure 12.1
North American RV industry—retail unit sales, 2007–2021 (Statistical Surveys Inc.)

manufactures RVs), (2) it has a strong brand that consumers gravitate to, and (3) it has maintained a conservative balance sheet.

This data, sourced from Winnebago's February 2, 2022, investor presentation, offers a glimpse into the industry's volatility (figure 12.1).

Case Study: Micron Technology

Micron Technology is best known for its flash memory and DRAM, which are critical components of PCs and servers. The DRAM industry has been quite volatile because of large fluctuations in supply over time. PC and server sales exhibit some cyclicality, with suppliers like Micron toward the cyclical tail of the distribution. Since its initial public offering (IPO) in 1984, its revenues declined 25 percent from 1989 to 1990, 60 percent from the enormous 2000 tech peak to 2002, and 15 percent from the 2008 peak to 2009. The 2000 mega-peak revenues were not exceeded until 2010, which was surprising given a host of interim acquisitions and a structural tailwind toward digitization.

Operating losses summed to $3 billion in the early 2000s and again similarly through the 2008 GFC. The environment has been very strong since 2009 with record high margins in 2017–2019. Results into 2021 were even stronger as PC demand spiked during the COVID shutdowns. Recency bias skews investors to overweight these results, forgetting the pain of previous cycles. A cyclical downturn will likely be severe, plausibly causing material intrinsic value dilution.

Management is sensitive to this operating volatility, and its messaging both confirms the historical volatility while also expressing confidence that DRAM share gains should improve margins over time. Figure 12.2, with data pulled from Micron's annual reports, offers clues that (1) margins remain volatile, and (2) that margins in 2021 are nearer to peak than trough conditions. The third and fourth quarter 2021 margins demonstrate peak conditions. Investors should be wary.

Case Study: Voestalpine AG

Few industries suffer more from deep cyclicality than steel companies. Voestalpine AG is a high-quality Austrian steel manufacturer listing BMW among its clientele. Its stock price peaked at euro (EUR) 55 at the beginning of 2018, dropping to a low of EUR 13 in March 2020. Fundamentally, its revenues in

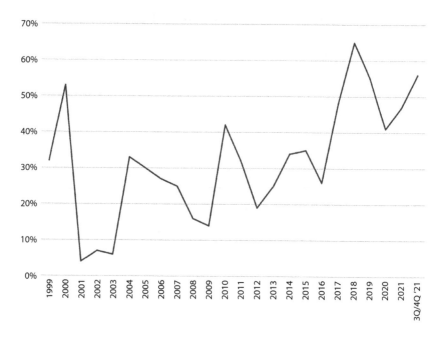

Figure 12.2
Micron—EBITDA margin over time, 1999–2021 (Micron Annual Reports)

the 2008 GFC dropped 25 percent, a challenge for any business, although it outperformed many of its industry peers. U.S. Steel, its dominant U.S. counterpart, saw revenues decline 51 percent during that time, generating enormous losses in the process. Steel demand has been strong in recent years, and the post-COVID boom has created a windfall of cash flows that will soon result in most steel companies becoming net cash by the end of 2022: boom and then bust. It is impossible to predict the shape of the cycle, and the enthusiasm seen at the end of 2021 (figure 12.3) calls for renewed caution, as U.S. Steel's EBITDA historical margins, sourced from their annual reports, warily attest.

Reasons to Pass

Less cyclical businesses may be bought near peak macroeconomic conditions if valuation allows, balance sheet flexibility exists, and other factors justify a purchase. Deep cyclical companies, even those trading at low valuation

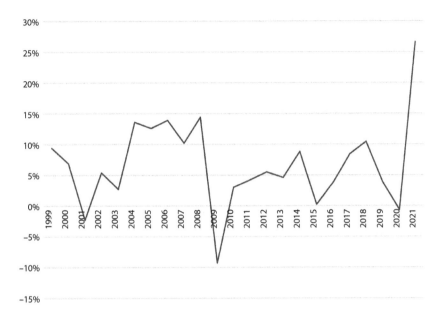

Figure 12.3
U.S. Steel—EBITDA margin over time, 1999–2021 (U.S. Steel Annual Reports)

levels, create a too-tough-to-call environment when peak macro conditions trigger alarm bells. Buying deep cyclicals near peaks is a bit like trying to squeeze a few basis points out of a higher yielding money market fund. You might end up with a little more income or a distressed fund that breaks the buck with "unexpected" investment impairments. It is not worth the risk.

The primary problem is one of prediction. Predicting the cycle is really, really, hard—the fool's gold of investing. Everyone tries to predict the cycle and invest accordingly, tries to invest around inflection points, and tries to time the bottom. Good luck. The shape of the cycle is unknowable, and deep cyclicals near peak conditions respond painfully to the next downturns. It's too hard. Just pass.

13

High-Cost Commodity Businesses

One of the ironies of capitalism is that most managers in commodity industries abhor shortage conditions—even though those are the only circumstances permitting them good returns. Whenever shortages appear, the typical manager simply can't wait to expand capacity.
—WARREN BUFFETT, BERKSHIRE HATHAWAY
ANNUAL LETTER, 1987

Any industry lacking in differentiation is essentially commoditized, and ubiquitous products seamlessly substituted for each other are commodities. Every commodity has its own cost curve. The obvious industries (i.e., copper, steel, oil, forestry, pulp, petrochemicals) present publicly available cost curves. Other industries' cost curves, in which products are near-perfect substitutes, are more subtle. Companies in high-cost positions make less money at cycle peaks and lose more money in cycle troughs. These companies should be, but are not always, less financially leveraged to account for this riskier profile. Cash burn for high-cost competitors in the troughs can be severe, and the balance sheets must be prepared for this circumstance. Low-cost business models offer obvious investment advantages.

Retail: Low-Cost Examples

Following are retail companies in low-cost positions:

1. Walmart: Walmart combines enormous purchasing power with large well-situated stores that raise sales per square foot while

keeping labor costs at reasonable levels. Its 2020 sales of $520 billion compares favorably to even Amazon's $380 billion.

2. Amazon: Amazon eliminates the storefront, which lowers costs, although that is partially replaced with direct to home shipping costs. Other online retailers have problems competing with AMZN because (1) they don't have the same brand awareness, which must be earned; (2) they suffer from distribution disadvantages that prohibit them from two-day/one-day/same-day delivery options; and (3) they suffer from other scale disadvantages that become increasingly challenging to overcome.

3. Dollar General: The behemoth of the dollar discount stores, it has a 50 percent market share in the United States. It combines purchasing scale with secondary locations at lower rents, low-cost labor, and unique product sizes that make comparison shopping challenging.

4. Aldi: The German discount retailer has branched out to Switzerland, the United Kingdom, and increasingly the United States. It carries roughly 2,000 SKU's per store, about one-tenth of the number seen in traditional grocery retailers. This lowers logistics costs and raises purchasing power. It also carries a larger percent of house brands versus other grocery retailers, helping to lower costs further. Finally, it selects secondary locations near population centers but outside of Class A locations to lower rent expense.

Basic Materials Examples

Following are examples of basic materials companies with structural cost advantages:

1. Nucor: The largest of the U.S. mini-mills, its plant configurations and scale advantages allow for higher margins in an industry in which competitors are price takers.

2. Valle: The world's largest iron ore producer, its Brazilian deposits are so concentrated that secondary processing is not required for a large portion of its iron-ore output.

3. Posco: The Korean steel giant has two well-engineered plants in excellent waterfront locations that offer both scale and logistical advantages. Its structural low-cost advantage allows it to generate profits and positive cash flow in any steel price environment.

4. Antafagasta: The Chilean copper producer sits on high-quality deposits that offer it a durable competitive advantage. Its cost structure may be slightly above average, although its substantial brownfield expansion possibilities offer high returns on investment.

5. Baosteel: Situated in China, its facilities are world class both in size and technology, and its logistics offer it a low-cost advantage that U.S. and European legacy steelmakers cannot replicate.

6. Fibria: This Brazilian pulp manufacturer owns some of the lowest cost pulp production globally. Its eucalyptus trees grow to maturity every seven years versus twenty years plus in most markets, including the United States.

Other Low-Cost Examples

Many industries offer examples of high and low-cost business models:

1. Ethanol production: Ethanol production in Brazil is substantially lower cost than ethanol production in the United States. Highly productive sugar fields offer greater energy per hectare output relative to U.S. corn production. Ethanol economics in the United States work only because of governmental subsidies. Eliminate the subsidies, and the market will rightsize U.S. ethanol production to its rightful market share—zero.

2. Tech assembly: Electronics manufacturing services (EMS) companies exist primarily in China and other low-cost centers. These facilities are variable cost with labor the largest input, and labor costs are a fraction of those seen in developed Europe and the United States. Although Chinese labor costs have risen steadily, productivity per unit of labor has expanded alongside this growth, protecting the Chinese low-cost advantage. Other low-cost centers (e.g., Vietnam) have risen as viable alternatives. One certainty, the United States is unlikely to regain its strength in labor-intensive assembly regardless of government rhetoric.

3. Online insurance: GEICO and Progressive in the United States have been gaining share against incumbents dealing with high-cost legacy distribution channels, including a captive salesforce and third-party agents. GEICO has steadily gained market share, from 2 percent in 1994, to 5 percent in 2000, to 14 percent in 2020,

taking the second position in the United States behind State Farm (17 percent). Its expense ratio, consistently in the mid-teens, is best in class over any time period and consistently compares favorably to State Farm's 35 percent. It has retained its expense advantage since its inception in the 1930s, only once temporarily falling off the top when it tried to diversify into other less advantaged areas. That misstep led to Berkshire Hathaway attaining its first 40 percent ownership.

Buffett wrote, "When I was first introduced to GEICO in January 1951, I was blown away by the huge cost advantage the company enjoyed compared to the expenses borne by the giants of the industry. It was clear to me that GEICO would succeed because it deserved to succeed" (Berkshire Hathaway annual letter, 2015).

Its substantial advertising budget has created strong brand awareness, and its well run and efficient back office receives high reviews from customers. It is large enough that its substantial advertising dollars are well covered by existing and net new policy counts. Scale, disciplined operations, and high recognition are moats around this business. Berkshire Hathaway paid less than $3 billion for the entirety of GEICO, with an estimated value today of more than $100 billion.

4. Low-cost airlines: Ryan Air and easyJet compete in Europe, Southwest and Spirit in the United States, Westjet in Canada, and Azul and TAM in Brazil. Many larger countries have one or more discount airlines. Low-cost airlines utilize a combination of direct booking, secondary airports, limited plane varieties, labor advantages including less union representation, and no-frills approaches to reduce costs per mile. They are newer airlines so are unencumbered with legacy pension costs, which are a material burden on incumbents. In down cycles, seen frequently in the industry, legacy carriers go under while low-cost airlines gain market share.

Discount business models the world over generally have gained share against higher cost incumbents, particularly in areas in which incumbents ceased to innovate or rested on their laurels. Customers gravitate to value. Incumbents bring with them structural barriers to innovation because change threatens their existing products. Also, legacy processes are difficult to reconfigure without disrupting current output, and major changes to labor utilization take time, require capital, and risk resentment within the remaining workforce. The decision to retain the status quo is easier and perhaps logical in the short run. As a result, many high-cost incumbents struggle with declining units, becoming less profitable cycle after cycle.

Certain businesses, however, are most at risk from low-cost competition and justify an immediate pass irrespective of valuation:

1. Structurally high-cost competitors that offer no differentiation. Basic materials companies are particularly at risk because of the lack of product differentiation. A barrel of oil has a global market clearing price. The same can be said for platinum, gold, copper, most paper grades, and steel. Each unit produced will find a buyer at the quoted global price. Management must focus its expertise into relentlessly managing costs. Predicting commodity prices is a fool's game, and unexpected declines in prices can quickly lead to distress if assets are structurally high cost. Commodity producers have few levers to pull that can materially lower costs.

2. High-cost producers that face structural impediments to change over the long run. The legacy airline carriers have worked hard to close their cost disadvantages against Southwest with little success, even in the face of Southwest's own increasing cost structure. Its business model is simple: incumbents should have had little trouble replicating its success. Yet many have gone into and through the bankruptcy process, slimming down but still not eliminating their competitive disadvantage.

3. High-cost producers with large debt loads should be especially avoided. Commodity producers at the top of the cost curve with large debt loads are among the most likely companies to be forced into bankruptcy eventually or to sell themselves at large discounts to their asset values. Capital markets will ruthlessly withhold further credit once operating losses emerge. Intrinsic value will then swing wildly and unpredictably, making any investment speculation, not investing.

To state the obvious, the economic cycle affects commodity prices. Commodity companies often have relatively fixed levels of production, and altering units produced in the short run is challenging. During market peaks, economic activity is high, bidding up the unit prices for many commodities. The reverse holds true in a downturn—the deeper the downturn, the greater the collapse in commodity prices. Once prices extend below marginal costs of production for a portion of global capacity, prices start to stabilize, and then eventually to recover. High-cost producers will be quick to post operating losses as they shut their highest cost production, their capacity that burns the most cash.

Charlie Munger explained:

> For example, when we were in the textile business, which is a terrible commodity business, we were making low-end textiles—which are a real commodity product. And one day, the people came to Warren and said, "They've invented a new loom that we think will do twice as much work as our old ones." And Warren said, "Gee, I hope this doesn't work because if it does, I'm going to close the mill." And he meant it. What was he thinking? He was thinking, "It's a lousy business. We're earning substandard returns and keeping it open just to be nice to the elderly workers. But we're not going to put huge amounts of new capital into a lousy business." And he knew that the huge productivity increases that would come from a better machine introduced into the production of a commodity product would all go to the benefit of the buyers of the textiles. Nothing was going to stick to our ribs as owners. ("A Lesson on Elementary, Worldly Wisdom as It Relates to Investment Management and Business," University of Southern California speech, 1994)

High-cost commodity businesses should logically be placed into runoff and then should be run to maximize cash flow with minimal investment in capex. This strategy squeezes value out of dying assets. Management most often sees things differently, looking to elongate the runoff period through continued reinvestment, hoping to outlast the other weakest competitors. They continue to get paid and hope secretly that a super-cycle boom bails them out from their otherwise lackluster existence. Eventually, the capacity closes with little cumulative free cash flow distributed to investors.

Case Study: Southern Copper Corporation

Southern Copper Corporation, ticker SCCO, has the number-two copper reserves globally and one of the longest reserve lives seen anywhere: seventy years. It doubled copper production over the past ten years and has lots of growth options available to it in the future. Finally, it boasts low costs, $0.87 per pound for 2018, placing it at the low end of the global cost curve. Its forecast calls for continued declining cash costs. Operating costs came in at $1.54 per pound in 2018, covering even the lowest copper prices seen in the past fifteen years. Costs tend to be inflationary, rising over time. In 2018, $1.54 likely was equivalent to a much lower cost in the year 2000.

The 1998–2001 period was the worst global trough experienced in the commodity area over the past forty years. Commodity prices were low, too much supply versus demand, and companies eliminated all nonessential capex and exploration to preserve cash to weather the downturn. SCCO was still profitable during this trough, averaging a 4 percent return on invested capital. Many competitors shut large amounts of capacity, raised new equity, sold assets at distressed prices, and went bankrupt.

The copper price, consistent with other commodities, has a volatile yet generally rising price. This volatility creates lumpy earnings for SCCO, and large losses for high-cost producers during cycle troughs (see figure 13.1). Downturns are unpredictable, and a structural low-cost position offers companies a position of strength from which to navigate cycles. Stock prices are

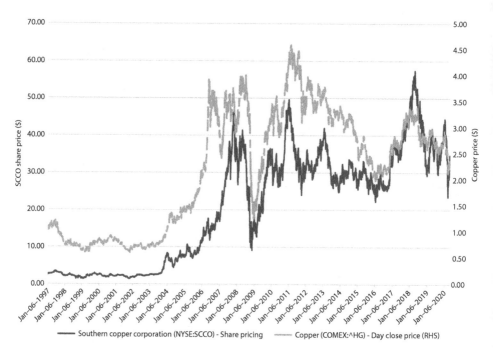

Figure 13.1
SCCO stock price versus global copper spot price, 1997 to calendar year-end 2021

correlated to commodity prices, giving investors occasional opportunities for value accretive investments.

A Structural, Low-Cost Position Offers Investors an Operational Margin of Safety

Global cost curves are available in many industries, including the copper mining industry, and can be generously found online and in many exposed companies' investor decks. Brook Hunt provides a standardized definition abided to by most copper companies, C1 costs per pound, standardized in U.S. dollars, and includes all direct costs, local general and administration (G&A), transportation, and selling expenses. Other firms, most notably Wood Mackenzie, base their global cost curves off this standardized framework.

Wood Mackenzie in 2021 reported that the average copper company globally incurred costs of roughly $1.40 per pound. Per their methodology, SCCO sat near the low end at $1.00 per pound, whereas other large producers, including Glencore, Antafagasta, BHP, and Freeport McMoran, all large competitors, sat above the average. More than 20 percent of global capacity sits with a cost base above $1.75 per pound, placing that capacity most at risk of shutdowns in an extended cyclical downturn. SCCO, in contrast, is likely to remain open and cash flow positive in most any cyclical environment. Risks exist when one invests in the high-cost tail of the cost curve, while a margin of safety exists when investing to the left where costs are below average. These cost advantages, and SCCO is no exception, protect their earnings, cash flow, and balance sheet even when commodity prices plummet while still providing an excellent upside during a cyclical boom.

Reasons to Pass

Good jockeys will do well on good horses, but not on broken-down nags.
—WARREN BUFFETT, BERKSHIRE HATHAWAY ANNUAL LETTER, 1989

When offering career advice to university students, be sure to include the suggestion that they seek out good businesses with good prospects. Having such a firm on their resumes can enhance reputation. High-cost commodity businesses, however, are unworthy candidates for employment when using this screen. These businesses are notoriously difficult to manage and almost impossible to fix.

Investment gains in high-cost businesses are possible with a short time horizon and opportunistic pricing, although much can go wrong. Simply mis-timing the cycle, a major risk with these cigar butts, can eliminate any perceived margin of safety, or worse.

With a lengthy enough time horizon, investors eventually will lose all capital invested in companies facing a high-structural-cost disadvantage. Low-cost competitors will gain share, the high-cost companies will down-size, margins will contract cycle over cycle, and free cash flows will shrink and eventually turn negative. Just pass.

14

Cash Flow and Earnings Disconnect

Why focus on cash flows? Because a share of stock is a share of a company's future cash flows, and, as a result, cash flows more than any other single variable seem to do the best job of explaining a company's stock price over the long term. If you could know for certain just two things—a company's future cash flows and its future number of shares outstanding—you would have an excellent idea of the fair value of a share of that company's stock today. (You'd also need to know appropriate discount rates, but if you knew the future cash flows for certain, it would also be reasonably easy to know which discount rates to use.) It's not easy, but you can make an informed forecast of future cash flows by examining a company's performance in the past and by looking at factors such as the leverage points and scalability in that company's model. Estimating the number of shares outstanding in the future requires you to forecast items such as option grants to employees or other potential capital transactions. Ultimately, your determination of cash flow per share will be a strong indicator of the price you might be willing to pay for a share of ownership in any company.

—JEFF BEZOS, AMAZON ANNUAL LETTER, 2001

Wall Street analysts love to focus on earnings. Are earnings increasing? What is a company's earnings per share (EPS), and what multiple should I apply to that EPS? Many investors only buy shares in companies with high returns on equity. Equity strategists and economists talk about earnings recessions and peak earnings, and the Fed discusses corporate earnings to justify its actions. CNBC reports that a company has missed its earnings by 10 percent, and the stock plunges at the next day's open.

The irony is that one cannot spend a company's earnings. They are "best estimates" of profits as defined by governmental accounting standards. Earnings are absolutely relevant and should be carefully scrutinized. Various reasons exist, however, why earnings may not tell the full story of a company's economic results:

1. Many assumptions go into an earnings report. Investments into long lived assets are capitalized, with depreciation expense an estimate of wear and tear for the year.

2. Intangible assets are capitalized on the balance sheet. Goodwill is perpetual, whereas most other intangible accounts are assumed to wear out so are amortized as expenses over their "useful lives." Investors frequently see large, extraordinary intangible write-downs because their useful lives were inconsistent with financial performance. Some intangible amortization is economic, and some is no more than accounting convention.

3. Some subsidiaries are partially owned and thus are equity accounted. Their operating profits are proportionately included in a company's earnings and are subject to the same issues that the consolidated income statement faces. One difference, equity interests provide much less disclosure to determine risks and underlying economics. Companies sometimes use equity interests to hide unflattering businesses. Most often, no cash flows come from equity affiliates.

4. Revenues are not cash receipts. Such revenues are often promises customers make to pay at a later date, and as a result, accounts receivable is debited on the balance sheet rather than cash. Collectability can be uncertain. Unethical management can pull sales forward by building up large accounts receivable balances that later end up being written off.

5. Working capital (WC) movements can either help or hinder cash flow and are entirely excluded from earnings. WC increases lowers cash flows relative to earnings. Companies that are too aggressive in how they manage WC, often with the intent to make cash flows

look stronger than they are, may require years of WC rebuild in the future. A post-COVID world likely will see a major rethink on how companies approach just-in-time inventory management, pushing WC higher to protect against external shocks. This will lead to many companies underreporting cash flows relative to earnings in 2022 and 2023.

6. Other assumptions embed themselves into earnings. Pension and postretirement costs are calculated using expected investment performance achieved over the long run, and discount rates present value back outflows. Companies have some discretion on what assumptions to use. Higher expected asset returns equal smaller earnings hit. A separate line item reports cash paid into the pension fund, but the disconnect between cash payments and accounting costs can be massive. Many derivatives are "level 3," marked to model on the income statement because no liquid market for them exists. Lots of assumptions equal opportunity for aggressive managements to manipulate earnings.

7. Many extraordinary charges sit within earnings: gains and losses on investments, restructuring costs related to layoffs or other charges, adjustments to amortization rates when previous assumptions were incorrect, asset write-downs, and intangibles impairments. Some of these extraordinaries are noncash, which distort earnings relative to cash flow.

8. Tax expense on the income statement often is different from cash taxes paid. Quite often the cash tax paid disclosure, seen on the cash flow statement, is much lower because of shrewd tax planning, offshore entities, and so forth.

9. In certain countries, preferred dividends are deducted from net income, whereas in others, they are assumed to be below the net income line. Because they are a financing expense they should be deducted from earnings and cash flows.

Over the long run, free cash flow (FCF) to equity holders should approximately equal net income. Disconnects require investigation, adjustments to your valuation and desired purchase price, or possibly an immediate pass if material and concerning enough. Some investors disregard reported earnings, focusing almost exclusively on cash flows. In their eyes, cash is king.

Financial Statement Analysis

A brief discussion of financial statement analysis, and the major issues found herein, is warranted.

Earnings: The Income Statement

Review earnings in detail whenever digging into annual reports. Earnings is defined as net income available to common shareholders. Relying primarily on annual earnings rather than quarterly will smooth out some of the earnings volatility, whereas average earnings over a peak-to-trough cycle should be reflective of true earnings power. Earnings is filled with accrual estimates that should provide a "best guess" as to the actual earnings power of a business, but it is not cash—not by a long shot.

Cash Flow: The Cash Flow Statement

Ignore cash flow at your peril. It begins with earnings, converting accrual accounting into cash flow ins and outs. It reverses accrual adjustments built into earnings to describe where money is being spent and how it is generated. Most companies globally present cash flows similarly using the indirect method, grouping cash flows into three sections.

SECTION 1—CASH FLOWS FROM OPERATIONS

Accountants use cash flows from operations (CFOs) to define cash generated from the operations. It includes both cash flows from the underlying operations and changes in WC, a critical source or use of cash to fund operations. CFO begins with the accrual-based net income and adjusts for noncash estimates. Depreciation expense, often the most material adjustment, is added back to net income because it is a noncash estimate of plant, property, and equipment (PP&E) wear and tear. Amortization expense is an accrual estimate of the value reduction in intangibles previously booked on the balance sheet and is added back. Interest expense, a cash payment, is already deducted, making the CFO representative of operating cash flows to equity holders. Options expense accruals are adjusted, as are asset write-downs and other noncash items. Pension accounting accruals are reversed.

CFO excluding movements in WC is a decent proxy for how much cash the underlying operations were able to release. Analysts should average out the CFO ex-WC over a full economic cycle. Most businesses should generate positive CFO ex-WC over a cycle except those in the earliest stage of their life cycle or those in deepest distress. Neither category is likely of interest to *Reasons to Pass* investors. *When seeing companies with full cycle CFO ex-WC near or below zero, just pass.*

WC movements can materially swing CFO. WC analysis begins with the other financial statements. Study accounts receivable, inventory, accounts payable, short-term accruals, and other material current assets and liabilities relative to sales over time to get a sense of where each business sits with its WC usage. Companies operating with a high level of WC may have room in the next few years to release cash, whereas others managed too lean may need to consume cash to rebuild overly aggressive management of WC.

Beyond cyclical considerations, companies have been running with less and less inventory, a product of just-in-time (JIT) manufacturing and generally greater emphasis on capital efficiency. Tying up lots of capital on inventory without increased pricing power reduces return on invested capital (ROIC). The global supply chain has faced unprecedented strains during 2020 and 2021 because of COVID restrictions and strong demand. Companies have begun to ask whether vulnerability of JIT manufacturing is worth a 1–2 percent increase in ROIC. Expect companies to at least temporarily raise inventories to protect their businesses, with companies most reliant on inventories seeing larger cash flow strains.

Case Study: Glenair Inc.

Glenair Inc. is a privately held manufacturer of electrical components based in Los Angeles, CA. It is run by Peter Kaufman, who is well known for his multidisciplinary and highly independent views of the world, and for his deep friendship with Charlie Munger. Glenair began operations in 1956, growing into a premier supplier of mostly commoditized, smaller value but mission critical items for aerospace, manufacturing, and government applications. They house more than 100,000 SKUs and pride themselves on excellent service, including same-day delivery. Given Kaufman's proclivity for independent thinking, they manage inventories differently than their many peers. They keep too many items of each SKU in inventory, ensuring that any order can be quickly met. Their turnaround time averages two days versus two weeks or longer for competitors. No company wants to see a line down for two weeks because of a low-price electrical connector, and they are happy to pay substantial premiums for rapid delivery. This more than compensates for greater capital deployed, giving Glenair an industry-leading ROIC.

SECTION 2—INVESTING CASH FLOWS

This section contains important information on how operating cash flows are deployed into capex (i.e., PP&E) and acquisitions.

Capex includes investments in factories, machinery, distribution equipment, and facilities with useful lives beyond one year. Capex typically will be larger than depreciation expense because of inflation and the fact that most businesses grow over time so require slightly larger facilities. Companies investing less than depreciation expense in capex are in harvest mode, most likely either financially distressed or in structural decline. *Both are easy passes for long-term-oriented investors in most cases.* Increasingly, companies are becoming less capital intensive. Software companies may carry little PP&E on their balance sheet, making analysis around capex less material.

Net acquisition activity is lumpy and varies widely by company. Some acquisitions are truly expansions of footprints that will improve earnings in the future. Some acquisitions are vital purchases of research and development (R&D) that compensate for R&D misses internally. These acquisitions may not raise future earnings as much as retain earnings power that otherwise would be lost. This distinction is important. Most acquisitions are value destructive for acquirors for reasons discussed elsewhere, yet investments that boost future earnings may be acceptable to incumbent shareholders if bought at a reasonable multiple. Beware of companies making material acquisitions without long-lasting increases in revenues and earnings. Finally, beware of companies making large acquisitions near cycle peaks, or divestments near cycle lows. True owners will strongly oppose such actions. *Absent the necessary depth of knowledge to fully understand large acquisitions that do not translate into revenue and earnings contributions, pass.*

SECTION 3—FINANCING CASH FLOWS

Although not directly relevant to the analysis of cash earnings versus accrual earnings, financing cash flows speaks volumes and should be scrutinized. How is FCF allocated, to dividends, share buyback, to net debt repayment? When FCF is insufficient, is the company issuing new stock, or new net debt?

Free Cash Flow

Investments may or may not generate FCF today, but investors expect FCF to trend higher in the long run. Amazon heavily invests into its operations, so FCF is minimal versus valuation, but survey any investor, and they will assume that at some point in the future FCF will ramp up dramatically to justify its $2 trillion valuation at mid-2021.

*Free Cash Flow to Shareholders = Cash Flow from Operations –
Capex – Acquisitions made to keep business
earnings power stable*

Over time, you should expect convergence between earnings and FCF. The slower the growth rate, the less reinvestment should be required beyond what is necessary for maintenance capex so the more closely FCF should correlate with earnings. The number of years you need to average results to get a statistically significant perspective varies based on where the company sits in its life cycle, but typically a full market cycle is required for mature, slow-growth companies, whereas 10 years or longer are required for early stage, higher-growth companies.

In a perfect world, FCFs will correlate to net income as follows:

1. FCF will equal earnings over a cycle for no growth companies.
2. FCF will exceed earnings over a cycle for shrinking companies.
3. FCF will fall below earnings over a market cycle for growth companies. The greater the growth rate the lower the FCF.

- High-growth companies may be FCF negative for many years until growth slows; Amazon was FCF negative from its inception in 1994 until 2002, at which point FCF grew each year.
- Moderate-growth companies with growth above the market should generate some FCF over a cycle, 40 percent to 80 percent of earnings, depending on their level of growth.
- Slow-growth companies with growth rates below the market should generate FCFs at 70–90 percent of earnings.

Case Study: Netflix

Netflix operates with a wide divergence between cash flow and earnings. Looking through the lens of year-end 2018, it was a quickly growing business, with revenues up 32 percent and 35 percent in 2017 and 2018. This blistering growth rate should be expected to result in investment needs that are far in excess of those implied by earnings. Negative FCF from its inception was no surprise. Of some concern, however, was (1) the magnitude of the divide between FCF and earnings; (2) the operating profits trend; and, most important (3) the specific line item that consumed all the cash. Our conclusion is that this situation in 2018 is unanalyzable and so it is an obvious pass despite its global presence and seemingly strong market position. It's too hard!

First, see the Netflix 2018 income statement in table 14.1.

Earnings improvement has been remarkable. The company claims that this is the result of their highly scalable platform, which is experiencing improving economics as subscription numbers grow. Looking more closely, the largest expense by far is their cost of revenues. This is the cost of content, most of which is amortized over Netflix's estimate of the content's useful life. A company's largest expense is typically input costs in the manufacturing process, or compensation expense, but it is rarely a line item that is so reliant on management estimates. This amortization charge is roughly 60 percent of revenues over the previous three years. Amortization on Netflix's owned content is particularly subject to management discretion.

Table 14.1
Netflix Income Statement, 2018

	Year-Ended December 31		
	2018	2017	2016
Revenues	$ 15,794,341	$ 11,692,713	$ 8,830,669
Cost of revenues	9,967,538	8,033,000	6,257,462
Marketing	2,369,469	1,436,281	1,097,519
Technology and development	1,221,814	953,710	780,232
General and administrative	630,294	431,043	315,663
Operating income	1,605,226	838,679	379,793
Other income (expense):			
Interest expense	(420,493)	(238,204)	(150,114)
Interest and other income (expense)	41,725	(115,154)	30,828
Income before income taxes	1,226,458	485,321	260,507
Provision for (benefit from) income taxes	15,216	(73,608)	73,829
Net income	$ 1,211,242	$ 558,929	$ 186,678

Second, see the Netflix 2018 CFO in table 14.2.

Netflix spent $13 billion on new content in 2018, a significant cash drain. This was almost twice its $7.5 billion amortization expense. If the platform was already fully scaled up, we might expect content costs in 2018 to approximate those of 2017. Coupled with rising membership, FCFs would start to improve dramatically. The opposite, however, is true. Membership is rising, but content costs are rising more quickly, a serious concern at year-end 2018.

The divide between earnings and cash flows is too extreme, and the nature of the account producing this large divide is subject to an enormous amount of management discretion. Fast-forwarding to 2020, the analytical challenges remain, with amortization of its library still amounting to roughly 60 percent of revenues. Scale benefits for Netflix likely will result in

Table 14.2
Netflix Cash Flows from Operations, 2018

	Year-Ended December 31		
	2018	2017	2016
Cash flows from operating activities:			
Net income	$ 1,211,242	$ 558,929	$ 186,678
Adjustments to reconcile net income to net cash used in operating activities:			
Additions to streaming content assets	(13,043,437)	(9,805,763)	(8,653,286)
Change in streaming content liabilities	999,880	900,006	1,772,650
Amortization of streaming content assets	7,532,088	6,197,817	4,788,498
Amortization of DVD content assets	41,212	60,657	78,952
Depreciation and amortization of property, equipment, and intangibles	83,157	71,911	57,528
Stock-based compensation expense	320,657	182,209	173,675
Excess tax benefits from stock-based compensation	—	—	(65,121)
Other noncash items	40,428	57,207	40,909
Foreign currency remeasurement loss (gain) on long-term debt	(73,953)	140,790	—
Deferred taxes	(85,520)	(208,688)	(46,847)
Changes in operating assets and liabilities:			
Other current assets	(200,192)	(234,090)	46,970
Accounts payable	199,198	74,559	32,247
Accrued expenses	150,422	114,337	68,706
Deferred revenue	142,277	177,974	96,751
Other noncurrent assets and liabilities	2,062	(73,803)	(52,294)
Net cash used in operating activities	(2,680,479)	(1,785,948)	(1,473,984)

an eventual decline in this ratio. One improvement already noted is that the size of its capitalized asset has flatlined. This could signal greater conservatism, or it could signal greater purchased content with shorter contract lives. The situation is becoming more analyzable, but for the time being, the appropriate conclusion is still pass!

When a puzzle is hard, bright people press on, determined to conquer that Everest and solve the puzzle, almost at any cost. It's a game. Solve the puzzle and prove your intellect. The cagiest companies are most likely to force you into your puzzle pose. Invested effort into these puzzles is likely to (1) disappoint because companies will not prove investible, or (2) draw even intelligent investors into an investment because the simple act of expending resources on an idea weighs as a favorable variable justifying that investment. The hidden cost is where you otherwise could be allocating your time, finding the few easy-to-understand compelling investments with fewer unknowns or complexities. Invest time where you are most likely to gain an edge. Return on invested time matters.

Reasons to Pass

What counts, however, is intrinsic value—the figure indicating what all of our constituent businesses are rationally worth. With perfect foresight, this number can be calculated by taking all future cash flows of a business—in and out—and discounting them at prevailing interest rates. So valued, all businesses, from manufacturers of buggy whips to operators of cellular phones, become economic equals.

—WARREN BUFFETT, BERKSHIRE HATHAWAY ANNUAL LETTER, 1989

Some businesses never generate great FCF. Beware of wide and chronic divides between net income and FCF that are not readily explainable. Perhaps assumptions underlying earnings are too aggressive. Perhaps unit economics don't pencil out because of high reinvestment needs. High investment in "growth" opportunities often are management justification for low FCFs, yet revenue or profit growth after investments are lackluster. Management explanations can be difficult to refute or may require intensive investigation to substantiate. Rather than allocate precious time to situations in which odds tilt against, just pass and move on. Identify other investment opportunities in which FCFs connect better with earnings. Tilt the odds in your favor.

15

Structurally Declining Businesses

If you buy a stock at a sufficiently low price, there will usually be some hiccup in the fortunes of the business that gives you a chance to unload at a decent profit, even though the long-term performance of the business may be terrible. I call this the "cigar butt" approach to investing. A cigar butt found on the street that has only one puff left in it may not offer much of a smoke, but the "bargain purchase" will make that puff all profit.

—WARREN BUFFETT, BERKSHIRE HATHAWAY
ANNUAL LETTER, 1989

The natural trajectory of corporate earnings is up over time. The rate varies, but factors driving earnings higher over time are as follows:

1. Employment—The long-run employment level in the United States increases by 0.5 percent per year because of net positive immigration coupled with two children per family. Some countries, including China, Japan, and Germany, have lower birth rates and lower level of net immigration, leading to lower structural upward growth in corporate profits or even structural declines. Negative 1 percent per year in overall employment level for Japan and China is a reasonable guess.

2. Productivity—Increases of 1 percent per year have been seen over the long run and continued future improvements should be expected. Managements are highly incentivized in many countries to grow earnings, with incentive plans that are partially linked to earnings per share (EPS) or net income growth. They will cut

employment, reengineer processes, and increasingly automate to a lower marginal cost of production. Technology shifts facilitate efficiency improvements. Consider your personal efficiency gains made from technology over your careers. Are you 20 percent more efficient than you were twenty years ago because of automation, video conferencing, and process improvements? Many support professionals have become obsolete (e.g., administrative assistants and travel agents).

Although productivity growth has stalled somewhat in the United States of late, growth spurts tend to ebb and flow. The advent of the PC around 1980 did little to boost productivity (AI) in the short run, taking a decade or longer to materialize. Artificial intelligence may be all the rage today, but productivity improvements may again take years or decades to fully materialize. It will make us all smarter and allocate resources more efficiently while hastening critical decision-making. Expect productivity growth to again resume toward trend as the benefits of AI become incorporated into our processes.

Government policies can influence productivity growth. Higher regulations, all equal, create impediments to productivity growth. The requirement to buy local may drive up costs. Tougher labor regulations reduce operational flexibility. Time will tell whether shifting political winds will affect forward-looking productivity growth.

3. Inflation—The long-run historical inflation rate has averaged just over 2 percent per year in the United States. Expect costs and revenues to increase similarly for the average business, leading to nominal EPS growth of 2 percent in this circumstance. Japan's inflation rate has averaged 0 percent over the past twenty years. Corporate earnings everywhere is a nominal output, and no factor may influence forward-looking nominal EPS growth more than the rate of inflation.

4. Share Repurchases—The average large-cap business will invest a portion of its retained earnings into buying back its own shares. This lowers the share count outstanding and thus increases EPS even if earnings are flat.

5. Other Factors—China consumers are savers, with strong balance sheets and a historically high savings rate. This is now changing. Increased consumption over time is accelerating consumer exposed companies' EPS growth. Watch the rate of change in

national savings rates for clues. U.S. consumers housed excess liquidity from large COVID stimulus packages and did not spend this capital during the lockdowns of 2020. This will provide EPS growth a temporary boost as personal balance sheets normalize.

Another way to think about earnings growth is the retained earnings method. As an example, assume a company trades at two times book value and earns a 15 percent return on equity (ROE). The stock price is $100, book value is $50, and earnings per share is $7.50. A 50 percent payout ratio implies retained earnings of $3.75. Reinvest this retained earnings at the same ROE, and then next year's earnings will be $8.06, implying a 7.5 percent growth rate. A lower 10 percent ROE on incremental capital deployed implies a 5 percent growth rate.

Investors in the typical U.S. public company have experienced long-run historical EPS growth of 5 percent per year. Emerging markets historical EPS has been somewhat higher, whereas developed Europe and Japan have seen lower EPS growth, in the neighborhood of 2–3 percent per year. Small cap stocks average slightly higher EPS growth.

A discounted cash flow (DCF), the theoretically correct determinant of intrinsic value, embeds two distinct phases. The first forecasts individual years based on near-term annual projections. This period may include a cyclical correction or company-specific factors, including restructuring efforts or competitive shifts. A DCF valuation does not typically move dramatically as a result of changes to short-term growth projections. The most significant valuation impact comes from changes to the terminal growth assumption. This represents a midcycle forward projection—that is, how the company should fare in an average year into perpetuity. A terminal growth rate of 3 percent, 4 percent, or 5 percent has a material impact on a DCF value. In this scenario, a valuation synthesizes the long-term structural growth into one number that, to a large degree, determines the intrinsic value of any company.

Determining which companies have a 3 percent or a 5 percent terminal growth rate is a hard ask. Larger cyclically exposed companies with global footprints and operations spread around the world are challenging to differentiate. Analysts have to determine around a relatively tight band what a long-term structural growth trajectory should be for each competitor. Who among ABB, Siemens, Hitachi, United Technologies, and Honeywell have the highest and lowest structural long-term earnings growth prospects? Remember, you are making a call out twenty years into the future! Based on history, Hitachi would be an obvious contender for low expectations, but that is a tougher call to make over the next twenty years. Or consider Bank of America compared with HSBC, RBS, UBS, and BNP. Odds are high that analysts will embed similar terminal growth estimates into each of these competitors because they will not see the future well enough to differentiate. More likely, analysts will extrapolate those with higher historical growth into their terminal forecasts. This is dubious analysis at best.

Some situations are easier to differentiate. Dell and HP Inc. may have similar growth rates, but HP Inc., in particular, will likely show a lower terminal growth rate given its highly mature consumer PC and printer businesses. It will grow more slowly than the average large-cap cyclical name, and the valuation should reflect that through a lower terminal growth rate, which suppresses the multiples of earnings and free cash ascribed to their business. Nestle versus Unilever is tough to call, as both are overexposed to strong franchises in underrepresented and more quickly growing emerging markets. Nestle, however, should be expected to grow more quickly than P&G given its larger high-growth footprint.

Warren Buffett explained: "Not all of our businesses are destined to increase profits. When an industry's underlying economics are crumbling, talented management may slow the rate of decline. Eventually, though, eroding fundamentals will overwhelm managerial brilliance. (As a wise friend told me long ago, 'If you want to get a reputation as a good businessman, be sure to get into a good business.')" (Berkshire Hathaway annual letter, 2006).

International Paper (IP), by contrast, likely will generate a below-average earnings growth over time. True, they generate retained earnings that are reinvested in their business. Management teams mostly invest in what they know, and IP executives know forestry and paper manufacturing and distribution. Paper usage will decline slowly over the next twenty years, so IP will invest in efficiency gains to protect their competitive position. This may increase the longevity of their survival and be a necessary cost of doing business. Management will argue that these investments generate a positive return on investment, and they are correct in one sense. Devoid of these investments, earnings will shrink faster because competitors will make those investments. Segmental profits have been increasingly allocated away from printing papers, which now accounts for only 20 percent of profits. This segment, in particular, is slated to decline in future years.

No industry competitor wants to be the first to exit unless their structural cost position is at the wrong end of the industry cost curve. These companies inevitably will fail or be taken under at low prices and their assets will be heavily restructured or closed. The remaining competitors will fight for market share in a declining market. Assuming that companies' starting cost positions are viable, they will invest as much as necessary to retain their market positions. Some will overinvest in an effort to irrationally gain share. The industry collectively will earn low incremental returns on capital as this prisoner's dilemma evolves into chaos. In the end, commodity prices will stay stable, volumes will decline, and most retained earnings will have been reinvested to keep profits from plummeting. Consumers, of course, benefit through lower prices.

One potential alternative strategy for companies facing declining business prospects is to accept the futility of additional investments in their core business and then to run it to maximize cash generation. Assets will slowly decay, and the business will face a moment of eventual reckoning at which point a complete shutdown makes sense. Interim cash flows can be distributed to shareholders to maximize returns.

Sometimes, management teams will take the first part of this strategy to heart but decide to invest in noncore businesses rather than distributing free cash flow back to shareholders. These managements will not have any particular expertise or competitive advantage in this new area, which presents an entirely different set of capital allocation risks. Imagine buying a stock in which you have no familiarity, or a nonprofit donating to a cause without thoroughly understanding the needs of the beneficiaries. Would you buy a car without learning about the alternatives, or a house in a city you never visited? Finally, would you prefer that free cash flow available be distributed to you, or should it be reallocated by a management team into an unfamiliar area?

Another issue with structurally declining businesses is gauging profitability. Businesses have fixed costs, semivariable costs, and truly variable costs. Volume declines lead to lower revenues, and fixed and semivariable costs need to be allocated across fewer units. This drives down gross margins and, most painfully, operating margins. Estimating the rate of decline of revenues is hard. Estimating its impact on the operating profits is really hard. *If profit evolution is too hard to call, just pass.*

What multiple of current earnings should an investor ascribe to structurally declining businesses? The U.S. equity market has traded at sixteen times earnings on average over the past forty years. This embeds an average 5 percent EPS growth. Other markets mostly trade lower because of lower historical growth rates or higher implied discount rates. Declining businesses should trade at lower multiples—ten times or lower based on their current earnings. The appropriate multiple, however, proves to be elusive because of uncertainty surrounding (1) the fade rate of revenues, (2) the resulting impact on margins, (3) management's capital allocation decisions once declines are evident, and (4) the uncertain competitive response. *Growth drives intrinsic value compounding.*

Case Study: Deluxe Corporation

Deluxe Corporation is best known for bringing checks to the banking system in the early 1900s. They are still the dominant checks printer in the United States, a structurally declining business with an uncertain fade rate. Sweden eliminated checks from their banking system in 1999, and most other countries have followed. Inevitably, so will the United States. Management saw the risks to their core business in the early 2000s and decided to focus on a targeted acquisition strategy. Their largest purchase was New England Business Service in 2004. This effectively doubled down on checks but also expanded their product offerings to other printed services offered specifically for small and midsize enterprises. Other acquisitions in the 2000s focused on web hosting, logo design, digital marketing, and marketing intelligence. In 2008, it declared its rebirth, calling itself a small business services company rather than a check printer. Revenues, indeed, have increased again after years of declines, as did earnings before interest, taxes, depreciation, and amortization (EBITDA). Free cash flow looks fine if considering only cash flows from operations less capex, as capex has been minimal. Free cash flow has averaged $140 million per year over the 2016–2020 period. Revenues and EBITDA, however, have been driven higher by its continuing acquisition strategy, but it is unclear from the numbers whether their platform extension will prove successful. Management must have high confidence in its prospects as it levered itself to three times net debt to EBITDA at year-end 2019. *Because this is too hard, pass.*

Case Study: China Coal Energy Company Ltd.

China Coal Energy Company Ltd. is one of the dominant coal producers in mainland China. China has materially expanded its footprint of coal-fired power plants over the past two decades, from 400 MW power plant equivalents to 1,500 today. China burns four billion tons of coal per year

STRUCTURALLY DECLINING BUSINESSES 203

as of 2020, more than four times as much as the United States and six times as much as the European Union. Although some new capacity is still under construction, it seems likely that coal-fired energy production will peak and then slowly decline in upcoming decades. The rate of decline is unknown, and a gradual decline seems likely based on history. Usage in the United States, however, declined much more quickly once climate change urgency intensified and alternative energy options emerged.

China Coal's revenues have increased 20 percent per year over the past five years, EBITDA has grown similarly. It produced more than two hundred million tons of coal in 2019 and profits hit a record high. According to their year-end 2000 press release, "coal will maintain its dominant role during a comparatively long period in China's energy structure. The Company is not afraid of the dark clouds blocking its view and is looking ahead with a positive mind." *This may be the case, but the dark clouds of uncertainty make this too tough to call. Pass.* Note that this pass is irrespective of balance sheet risk, which, in this case, is significant with three times net debt to EBITDA, which is far too high for businesses facing potentially severe decline rates. As is often the case, valuation in structurally at-risk businesses appear optically tempting, trading at a mere four times forward earnings at year-end 2021. The siren's allure may be strong, but resist the urge.

Reasons to Pass

In all cases, the people who sell the machinery—and, by and large, even the internal bureaucrats urging you to buy the equipment— show you projections with the amount you'll save at current prices with the new technology. However, they don't do the second step of the analysis which is to determine how much is going to stay home and how much is just going to flow through to the customer. I've never seen a single projection incorporating that second step in my life. And I see them all the time. Rather, they always read: "This capital outlay will save you so much money that it will pay for itself in three years." So you keep buying things that will pay for themselves in three years. And after 20 years of doing it, somehow you've earned a return of only about 4 percent per annum. That's the textile business.

—CHARLIE MUNGER, "A LESSON ON ELEMENTARY, WORLDLY
WISDOM AS IT RELATES TO INVESTMENT MANAGEMENT,"
UNIVERSITY OF SOUTHERN CALIFORNIA SPEECH, 1994

The spectrum of structural decline rates is wide. One can argue that beer sales are peaking as seltzers or spirits gain share, or that the mega brewers will face increasing competition from craft beers. The theory of peak oil has been postulated for decades, although finally the inflection point seems to be nearing. PC demand declined substantially as tablets and mobile devices began to replace traditional computing solutions. PC demand appears to have stabilized and then to have grown again through the COVID crisis. It is not yet known whether that trend has perpetually reversed. Newspapers declined for many years but seem to now be finding their way as content providers with monetizable digital content.

Some cigar butts are worth a drag, but few can be held as perpetual investments. The lens of a ten-year investor is different from the lens of a reversion to the mean investor or to the one looking for a temporarily deeply discounted equity. *Holding twenty to forty names over one or more market cycles means targeting certain characteristics, including the ability to compound some level of intrinsic value growth over time. Declining businesses are unlikely to fit into this portfolio.*

16

Obsolescence Risk

Our criterion of "enduring" causes us to rule out companies in industries prone to rapid and continuous change. Though capitalism's "creative destruction" is highly beneficial for society, it precludes investment certainty. A moat that must be continuously rebuilt will eventually be no moat at all.

—WARREN BUFFETT, BERKSHIRE HATHAWAY
ANNUAL LETTER, 2007

Eastman Kodak was formed in the late 1800s, cementing its position as the U.S. market leader throughout most of the twentieth century with a dominant 85 percent market share in camera equipment by the mid-1970s. Its engineers invented digital images around that time but refused to invest in the digital market, a combination of skepticism of market potential and fear of cannibalization of its analog products. Facing the prospect of obsolescence, it finally devoted resources to digitization in the late 1990s. This move was too little too late, as it turns out, and the company declared bankruptcy in 2012.

Incumbent management teams and owners who built up a company's historical success are unlikely to be the disrupters that steer that company into the future. Generational shifts in technology, fashion, or other product characteristics often catch the incumbents by surprise. Step change risks are challenging for any industry, although certain industries and companies are most at risk. It is difficult to predict in both timing and intensity, and the only certainty is that incumbents have low odds of dominating both the last step and the next step on the innovation staircase. Lightning rarely strikes twice.

Single-product companies exposed to markets vulnerable to step changes face the greatest risk. Smaller semiconductor equipment companies may dominate a niche, but next-generation fabs may require, or competition produces, different configurations or other advances that lead to step-change innovation. Figuring out whether incumbents have the edge in next-generation technologies is hard or impossible. *If it's too hard, just pass.*

Single-product biotech investments sit at the opposite end of the innovation spectrum but suffer from the same decision-making challenges. Small biotechs rarely generate revenues. Their research and development (R&D) portfolio consists of one, or a handful, of potential big winners in various phases of U.S. Food and Drug Administration (FDA) clinical trials. They are the disruptors making other companies' products obsolete. Odds of success are uncertain, and quite possibly are unknowable. Investors dissect FDA filings, management backgrounds, and lead investor credentials; hire scientific experts; and look for other indicators to stack the odds in their favor. A basket of diversified investments at reasonable prices may do well. Yet the logical home for this position is not in concentrated portfolios but rather in specialist funds. *When expertise is lacking, or the range of outcomes is too wide, they are too hard to quantify. Just pass.*

Charlie Munger shared this insight: "Then there's another model from microeconomics which I find very interesting. When technology moves as fast as it does in a civilization like ours, you get a phenomenon which I call competitive destruction. You know, you have the finest buggy whip factory and all of a sudden in comes this little horseless carriage. And before too many years go by, your buggy whip business is dead. You either get into a different business or you're dead—you're destroyed. It happens again and again and again" ("A Lesson on Elementary, Worldly Wisdom as It Relates to Investment Management," University of Southern California speech, 1994).

Obsolescence comes in many forms and spans industries and countries. Historical examples demonstrate some of the fragility that is rarely built into stock prices until the threat of disruption imminently looms over the horizon. Consider the following examples:

1. Retail—The shift away from storefronts began in the late 1990s. Cap rates for mall operators should have increased years ago to account for obsolescence risk. Yet publicly listed malls and strip centers only recently began diverging materially from other real estate asset classes. Simply passing on retail real estate made sense as far back as the 2005–2006 peak.

2. Discount airlines—Legacy airlines carry high-cost structures, including higher labor costs, large unfunded pension and health-care obligations and other structural rigidities. Discount airlines emerged post deregulation in the late 1970s. Investors selling the incumbents needed only to make the prediction that structural advantages of discounters were long-lasting. Forty years later, the cost divide continues to exist.

3. Coal—The upcoming shift away from coal was unforeseen in the early 2000s by most investors. Coal's cost advantage seemed too great in the United States and China, and the climate implications were discounted. Step changes do not need to occur overnight. The history of adoption curves varies between new technologies. Solar and wind have required twenty years of innovation to get cost structures down toward fossil fuels, and the call to climate change action intensified over that timeframe. Coal captured 50 percent of U.S. energy production between 1950 and 2005, at which point demand began to decline at roughly 2 percent annually. Today less than 30 percent of energy production comes from coal, and continued declines from here are likely. The demand decline has been enough to bankrupt most coal producers. A shrinking market with desperate competitors vying for survival is a challenging market in which to pick the winners, and even the winners may do poorly relative to other investment opportunities.

4. Wireline to wireless—This step-change revolution would have hit telecoms incredibly hard except they also controlled the wireless spectrum. In 2000, more than 90 percent of households in the United States still had a landline. It sat below 50 percent as of 2021. The advent of 3G networks in 2001 provided the foundation for smartphone adoption, and cell phones have been getting faster and smarter ever since. Search engines went mobile, and social networks rose. Wireless barriers to entry increase each time data speeds are upgraded.

5. Dial-up to DSL to cable modems—The shift to high-speed home internet access allowed the internet to proliferate. Online retail was a painful affair in the 1990s. It took several minutes to dial into your AOL network, to be faced with long load times and frequent connection glitches. Jeff Bezos saw the trend perfectly, convinced that the online retail experience would improve as bandwidth problems were solved. High bandwidth speeds offered by cable companies

took a source of revenue away from telecoms until, perhaps, the advent of 5G in 2021 and 2022.

6. Global Positioning System (GPS)—Garmin manufactured navigation systems that became mostly obsolete when smart phones linked efficiently to the GPS network. It has astutely remade itself with niches linked to their GPS technology. Its GPS watches, for example, command high prices and strong market shares.

7. Channel Tunnel—Eurotunnel, the entity which privately financed this record-setting construction project, gave life to this project in 1985. It was accorded a sixty-five-year operating concession. Ferry companies protested the project, fearing they would become obsolete. Ironically, it was Eurotunnel that became obsolete as European discount airlines Ryanair and Easy Jet emerged to underprice London to Paris train tickets by a wide margin. The company declared bankruptcy in 2006.

8. Gaming—Arcades were common in the 1980s, places for teens to gather after school. Arcade games were replaced by consoles, which eventually became a duopoly. The current shift toward PC gaming brought on by greater processing speeds and high bandwidth has created the risk that gaming consoles will become obsolete. Content providers should continue to thrive, whereas Sony and Microsoft may struggle to compete.

9. Children's toys—Mattel was the world leader in toy manufacturing. Its Barbie franchise peaked at $1.7 billion annual revenue in 1997 dropping to below $1 billion in recent years. iPads and phones increasingly stole share from physical toy markets. Major toy retailers have gone under, including the venerable New York City–based FAO Schwartz, Toys R Us, and K-B Toys. Jakks Pacific stock price bottomed at $3 before its COVID-induced recovery. Mattel has invested in various digital projects, but its skill set has been lacking.

10. Hearing aids—Hearing aids used to be the domain of audiologists, charging $5,000 for high-end devices. Startups are in the process of selling comparable units, some using slick next-generation technology, which better filters out background noise and are less visible to others. Price points are up to 90 percent lower.

11. Globalization—Globalization killed the U.S. textile industry and severely injured many other industries. The principle of comparative advantages justified low-cost assembly in China, IT outsourcing

to India, and Philippine call centers. Adaptable U.S. companies benefited, and many single-product companies failed. Chinese electronics manufacturing services, or EMS companies, benefited. Hon Hai, the public owner of Foxconn, calls Apple its primary customer. It has benefited immensely from globalization.

A Particularly Dangerous Risk: Single-Product Obsolescence

So many companies have faced, or are facing, some form of obsolescence risk. Nautilus generated most of its revenues from its Bowflex exercise equipment, making it overly dependent on one product with limited success in product diversification. Its revenues peaked in 2006 at $681 million declining to $168 million in 2010. New product launches since then brought sales back to $400 million in 2016 though declining 25 percent through 2019. Product dependence often leads to high revenue and earnings volatility. Sharper Image by 2006 had a similar reliance on Ionic Breeze purifiers and massage chairs. It declared bankruptcy in 2008. Brooks Brothers has struggled with a structural shift away from business attire, its primary fashion category. Founded in 1818, it has dressed forty U.S. presidents, yet just in 2021, it declared bankruptcy. Fitbit, the early innovator of fitness watches, has lost substantial market share to better engineered competitors, and it sold in 2019 at a deep discount to Google. Its stock price peaked at $52 in 2015 compared with its agreed-to takeout price of $7.35. Plantronics designs high-end headsets for the corporate market. Its premium-priced products are under increasing threat from lower-priced entrants who are closing the gap on sound quality. Its stock price peaked at $75 in 2018, collapsing to $10 in 2020. Housing construction has increasingly relied on engineered wood, such as oriental strand board (OSB). This has led to structurally declining shares for natural wood products, hurting traditional lumber companies and benefiting OSB producers, including Louisiana Pacific in the United States and Norbord in Canada. Munger discussed this risk in an interview:

> Over the long term the companies of America behave more like biology than they do anything else. In biology all the individuals die—so do all the species—it's just a question of time. And that's pretty well what happens in the economy too. All the things that were really great when I was young have receded enormously. And new things have come up and some of them have started to die.

That is what the long term investment climate is, and it does make it really interesting. Look at all what's died, all the department stores, all the newspapers, US Steel, John D Rockefeller's Standard Oil is a pale shadow of its former self. It's just like biology, they have their little time then they get clobbered. (CalTech interview, 2020)

So many challenges exist when considering an investment in companies subject to obsolescence risk. At inception, predicting which innovations will become a hit is difficult. Even when successfully identified, more than one company often competes with similar products, forcing the correct company call. Success in company selection then requires calling the growth ramp correctly, because continued investment once sales flatline or decline can be costly. Finally, will management do the prudent thing at each stage of growth, deploying capital judiciously? Establishing any intrinsic value is too challenging in most situations. *It's too hard, so just pass.*

Future obsolescence case studies are an inevitable part of the investing landscape. Investment stories will be compelling, and some of your peers will successfully navigate the cycle, buying an emerging one-hit wonder on its way to temporary stardom. Peloton anyone, or perhaps Lululemon Athletica? The temptation to participate in next-generation successes is enticing. Resist the siren's call. The cost of miscalculations is severe. Investing in companies subject to obsolescence risk in most cases is just gambling.

For entertainment purposes, let us evaluate a handful of possible future waves of obsolescence risk:

1. Office real estate investment trust (REIT) cap rates will increase, and rental prospects will decrease, as a greater portion of the workforce chooses to work remotely. Higher job satisfaction and greater productivity will support the decision. Office REITs will dramatically underperform the broader market for an extended period, ten to twenty years, similar to recent underperformance of retail REITs.

2. 5G bandwidth speeds will place pressure on cable companies. If true to its promise of more than 1 GB download speeds, cable modem demand will decrease, and price competition will ensue. Cable companies already facing cord cutters and laden with large debt burdens will face uncertain financial futures.

3. Canada Goose, the purveyor of $1,000 high-end coats, and Lululemon, the fitness fashion company, both with large operating margins

and tantalizing historical share gains, will be supplanted by next-generation fashion. Lulu forecasts continued 10 percent annual revenue gains through 2025, with 20 percent operating margins. The stock trades at fifty times 2021 earnings, a rich valuation. Investors are discounting no risk to its franchise over the forecast period. Quite often, fashion trendsetters receive premium valuations without regard for obsolescence risk.

4. Relocalization of the supply chain will begin in earnest in 2022. Companies will diversify sourcing, some closer to home, and build inventories in nearby warehouses. Inventory days will increase, creating a one-time spike in demand until "new normal" inventory levels are built. Logistics assets will see greater demand, which will be filled eventually by greater supply.

5. Three-dimensional (3D) printing solutions will become ubiquitous, allowing small-batch local manufacturing to better customize customers' needs. Localization will accelerate this trend. Customers will benefit through the emergence of greater choice as mass assembly lines are partially replaced, placing additional pressure on industrial companies servicing those markets. Industrial 3D printing technology will increasingly make its way to consumers, and new companies will streamline software interfaces and engineer printers for a larger number of materials. Trips to Home Depot, and Amazon clicks, may decline.

6. Artificial intelligence (AI) will bring proper science and decision-making to medical treatments. AI superiority in radiology diagnosis is clear, an early indicator of its potential. This advancement will drive down consumer costs and improve outcomes. It also will reduce revenue for the health-care system globally, affecting service providers on the wrong end of this more scientific decision-making ability. Margins in health care are high, and standards of care are too low.

The only thing we can attest to is that these predictions are either (1) too obvious and thus already are properly reflected in valuations, or (2) too hard to call and thus unlikely to lead to serious excess return opportunities.

Warren Buffett explained: "Tech or not, we base our decisions on the durability of competitive advantage and if we think we are better at assessing the probability of improving that durability. Amazon doing what it did

I thought would be something close to a miracle, and I tend not to bet when I think something takes a miracle. I would've been far better if I had insights. Bill told me early on to switch from Altavista to Google, but I wondered who would then skip past Google" (Berkshire Hathaway annual meeting, 2018).

Case Study: Peloton Interactive Inc.

Peloton Interactive Inc. manufactures fitness bikes and offers monthly fitness subscriptions, linking its fitness devices to group classes. Its revenues, $220 million in 2017, have increased to $4 billion for its fiscal year-end 2021. Its subscription services, the high-value portion of revenues, has risen from $30 million to $870 million over that period. Wall Street forecasts call for continued 10 percent to 15 percent per year increases over the next three years. This recent decline in growth expectations has hit its stock price hard, dropping from $150 to $50 during mid-2021. Peloton has continued to invest in both its platform and new products, introducing a $4,000 treadmill to a lukewarm audience. Meanwhile, an increasing number of competitors, including NordicTrac, Nautilus, and Echelon, and a large group slated to present this year at the Consumer Electronics Show have created copycat products. The social network subscription element is the barrier to entry, and it remains to be seen how durable that moat will be. Its $15 billion market cap at year end 2021 implies a high level of continued success, including an eventual transition to positive operating margins and free cash flow. *Technological obsolescence risk is too high, and odds are too hard to call. Just pass.*

Reasons to Pass

Splashy businesses with successful products are sexy businesses and may be appealing at first glance. High revenue growth, increasing margins, lots of free cash flow, and high brand recognition create the euphoria that elevates valuation multiples. Avoid the siren call because forecasting the staying power, future growth prospects, and competitive responses are too hard. Results bracket widely and capital protections are limited. Although precision indicators to identify which companies are the most at risk of obsolescence are less quantifiable, certain variables can offer clues. The following types of companies that break more than a few of these indicators should be included in the pass category:

1. New product or product category falling within the technology or consumer segments
2. A successful multiple year revenue ramp-up, and companies now hitting high-growth screens
3. Undiversified product mix, with most or all revenues coming from one successful product
4. High margins for multiple years once sales spike—high price points with limited competition
5. The eventual emergence of copycat competitors, many of them at lower price points, and some with innovative features
6. High and increasing advertising costs indicating a heavy push to further expand sales
7. High and increasing R&D costs indicating heavy investment in next-generation products
8. The introduction of new products that receive lackluster marketplace traction

17

Valuation

A Critical Protector of Capital and Returns

Well, Berkshire's whole record has been achieved without paying one ounce of attention to the efficient market theory in its hard form. And not one ounce of attention to the descendants of that idea, which came out of academic economics and went into corporate finance and morphed into such obscenities as the capital asset pricing model, which we also paid no attention to. I think you'd have to believe in the tooth fairy to believe that you could easily outperform the market by seven-percentage points per annum just by investing in high volatility stocks.

—CHARLIE MUNGER, "ACADEMIC ECONOMICS: STRENGTHS
AND FAULTS AFTER CONSIDERING INTERDISCIPLINARY
NEEDS," UNIVERSITY OF CALIFORNIA–SANTA
BARBARA SPEECH, 2003

How does an analyst value a lemonade stand down the street, or the flower stand one corner removed that pays rent for the semipermanent dwelling it occupies? How does the financial adviser value her book of business that she looks to divest at the end of her career? Buying rental property? How will you know if you are paying a fair price? What about the family business put up for sale after the founder's passing? Finally, what about one share in Alphabet?

It is an obvious truism that valuation matters. Pay too much and your return declines. Buy a stock at thirty times earnings when only fifteen times is justified, and your theoretical loss on day one is 50 percent. Hold to perpetuity, and your internal rate of return (IRR) is slightly lower. Paying too much for an asset leaves less capital remaining for other income-earning assets or leaves less for consumption. The opportunity cost is rarely considered but is the most relevant.

The Trouble with Valuation

It's my view that economics could avoid a lot of this trouble that comes from physics envy. I want economics to pick up the basic ethos of hard science, the full attribution habit, but not the craving for an unattainable precision that comes from physics envy."
—CHARLIE MUNGER, "ACADEMIC ECONOMICS: STRENGTHS AND FAULTS AFTER CONSIDERING INTERDISCIPLINARY NEEDS," UNIVERSITY OF CALIFORNIA–SANTA BARBARA SPEECH, 2003

Certain mathematical formulas are absolute. The Pythagorean theorem $(a^2 + b^2 = c^2)$ calculates the length of the hypotenuse, Newton's second law, $\vec{F} = m\vec{a}$ (force = mass × acceleration), and of course, Einstein's E = mc^2 (energy = mass × the speed of light squared) are equally definitive.

Finance has its own formulas. Compound interest is universally calculated as $A = P\left(1 + \dfrac{r}{n}\right)^{nt}$. A discounted cash flow analysis (DCF) is the theoretically correct way to value any asset. Capital invested is compared with FCF from now to perpetuity and then is discounted back to present day. What could be easier? At a CFA Institute seminar, Benjamin Graham offered this answer:

So far I have been talking about the virtues of the value approach as if I had never heard of such newer discoveries as "the random walk," "the efficient portfolios," the Beta coefficient, and others such. I have heard about them, and I want to talk first for a moment about Beta. This is a more or less useful measure of past price fluctuations of common stocks. What bothers me is that authorities now equate the Beta idea with the concept of "risk." Price variability yes, risk no. Real investment risk is measured not by the percent that a stock may decline in price in relation to the general market in a given period, but by the danger of a loss of quality and earning power through economic changes or deterioration in management. ("Renaissance of Value," 1974)

A DCF hinges, to a large degree, on the capital asset pricing model (CAPM), written as $ERi = Rf + \beta i(ERm - Rf)$, where the equity risk premium is equal to beta × (expected market return – risk free rate). This formula may be universal and central to valuation, yet it is here that we begin to see cracks in the precision sought by investment professionals. Inputs in physics are absolute: mass is mass. In finance, beta is squishy. Most academics define it as historical price volatility of an asset, but over what time period? And why would long-term-oriented investors care about short-term price movements? True investors concern themselves with variables affecting their long-run investment thesis—in particular, the structural risk of future declines in earnings. Although this may be measured, imprecisely, by a fundamental beta, one that measures the risk of structural decline compared with the market, traditional beta measuring volatility is easy for academics to calculate but is irrelevant to true investors like Warren Buffett and Charlie Munger.

Buffett explained: "Forecasting interest rates has never been our game, and Charlie and I have no idea what rates will average over the next year, or ten or thirty years. Our perhaps jaundiced view is that the pundits who opine on these subjects reveal, by that very behavior, far more about themselves than they reveal about the future" (Berkshire Hathaway annual letter, 2019).

The risk-free rate used to discount future flows in a DCF is equally ambiguous. Should investors use the thirty-year treasury, the ten-year treasury, today's interest rate, a historical average, or some reversion to the mean estimate? Should they use the U.S. yield curve, some other country, or a blended country rate? Most investors take some form of the current yield curve as their input because it's easily accessible and readily identifiable. When long-term risk-free rates drop to zero, say from 2 percent, does it make sense that a DCF will automatically use a 2 percent lower cost of capital? Long-term interest rates vacillate, sometimes materially. Equity valuations should be more stable.

Munger offered this suggestion: "If you take the best text in economics by Mankiw, he says intelligent people make decisions based on opportunity costs—in other words, it's your alternatives that matter. That's how we make all of our decisions. The rest of the world has gone off on some kick—there's even a cost of equity capital. A perfectly amazing mental malfunction" (*Poor Charlie's Almanack*, 2005).

Opportunity cost is an essential yet difficult-to-measure indicator. If your entire investment portfolio is expensive, and known investment options are unappealing, the logical escape hatch is cash. If a new investment alternative comes to the forefront that is still less compelling than a current investment, continue to sit in cash or increase your existing position further. The academically rigid exercise of allocating to investments whose returns exceed your cost of capital is fatally flawed. There is no magical cost of capital. There are only opportunities that present themselves that must be measured against other available and known opportunities. Cash is the baseline against which everything else is measured. Do the best with what you have.

Buffett explained: "Obviously, we can never precisely predict the timing of cash flows in and out of a business or their exact amount. We try, therefore, to keep our estimates conservative and to focus on industries where business surprises are unlikely to wreak havoc on owners. Even so, we make many mistakes: I'm the fellow, remember, who thought he understood the future economics of trading stamps, textiles, shoes and second-tier department stores" (Berkshire Hathaway annual letter, 2000).

The core of a DCF lies in predictions of future free cash flows. This embeds estimates of revenues, margins, and capex, which are rooted in understanding the broad economy, competitive dynamics (including barriers to entry), substitution effects, and so forth. Management action shifts over time, as does competitive reaction. Single-factor models do not do the complex landscape justice, and multifactor models, linear or nonlinear, are impossible to construct so that they approximate reality. Artificial intelligence (AI) won't help, nor will extra due diligence.

What about price to earnings (P/E)? The market has averaged sixteen times earnings over the very long run. Good growth companies and high-quality franchises trade higher, whereas weaker franchises or those earning near cycle peak returns trade lower. P/E has been moderately predictive of future returns when looking at asset class returns. Leuthold Group, an outstanding research boutique in Minneapolis far from Wall Street, has studied both individual P/E and price-to-average earnings over time looking for return relationships. They concluded that the index price over their version of normalized earnings, the average of fifty-four months back to six months forward, correlated inversely with future five-year returns. The higher their normalized P/E is, the lower forward returns. Price-to-normalized earnings does not work well for timing, and it does not work well for extended cycles nor for individual stocks. Overall, on its own, P/E is not a reliable indicator of valuation. It must be combined with other factors. Munger wrote:

> It's such a huge advantage to be by far the best-known gum company in the world. Just think of how hard it would be to replace that image. . . . The trouble with the Wrigley Gum-type investments is that everybody can see that they're wonderful businesses. So you look at it and you think, "My God! The thing's at eight times book value or something. And everything else is at three times book value." The ability to answer such questions explains why some people are successful investors and others are not. On the other hand, if it weren't a little difficult, everybody would be rich. (Quoted in *Damn Right, Behind the Scenes with Berkshire Hathaway Billionaire*, 2000)

What is price to book (P/B)? CPAs are attracted to book value. If you can raise $1 million in an equity offering, the book value is just that. Use half to buy property, plant, and equipment (PP&E), the book value remains $1 million. Earn $100,000 the next year with no dividend, and the book value increases to $1.1 million. Depreciate the PP&E, and the book value declines. Debits match credits, and book value does a good enough job of reflecting the reality of valuation. This approach worked to some degree when Graham was seeking value. Industrial, capital-intensive companies ruled the market. Over time, intangibles have become increasingly prominent, and valuable franchises have strengthened their moats and pushed up return on equities and fair-value P/B ratios. Then quants entered the field, arbitraging away what remained in the way of excess returns from buying low P/B stocks. The use of P/B as a secondary valuation tool for certain companies may still work, but caution is warranted.

Some Valuation Advice

> We look for mispriced stock opportunities with less capital. I can't give you a formulaic approach to intrinsic value and don't use one. I mix all the factors, and if the gap between value and price isn't attractive, I go onto something else. Costco at 13x earnings was a ridiculously low value because of the brand. I liked the cheap real estate and the good competitive position, and even though

it traded at 3 times book, it was worth more. There was not a formula. If you want one, go back to graduate school, as formulas don't work.

—CHARLIE MUNGER, BERKSHIRE HATHAWAY
ANNUAL MEETING, 2018

Most businesses cannot be valued with a high degree of confidence. The future may be too murky, management action may be unpredictable, competitive uncertainty may be too great, and an industry's staying power may be unclear. The foundation of valuation, however, is crystal clear. Use the principles espoused in part 1. Think of any investment as if you were an owner of the underlying business. Value that business conservatively by remaining humble as to future successes. Use a range of outcomes in your estimates. Investments requiring less capital reinvestment are better businesses, as FCF will be greater and earnings are most likely to be inflation protected. Mental flexibility is a must. Some names will screen attractively on P/E, P/B, or P/cash flow, and some not. None is more correct. They are just markers providing pieces of evidence. Any investment must be scrutinized in its entirety.

Evaluating Multiple Factors Relevant to Valuation

If you're going to learn to drive a car, it doesn't do any good just to know how to use the accelerator. There are four or five things you have to know before you understand the system correctly. I do think some things are way more important than others, and in the game we're in, understanding the advantages of scale, scale of experience, efficiency in the plant, scale of experience in leasing, other advantages of scale. (Take) Adam Smith's pin factory, I think that' a very important basic concept, but it's just one.

—CHARLIE MUNGER, QUOTED IN DAMN RIGHT,
BEHIND THE SCENES WITH BERKSHIRE
HATHAWAY BILLIONAIRE, 2000

Munger claims that he retains one hundred different mental models that he pulls out as needed when evaluating a company. No list of his various models exists to my knowledge, but he pulls liberally from biology, physics, psychology, and other fields. Interlace the principles of psychology and economics to understand that stock prices are a combination of fundamental variables and behavioral biases. Incorporate multiple models to better understand any subject.

The same holds true for valuation, which, at its core, is the in-depth study of business fundamentals. How did it get here? Why has its performance been X? What are its competitive advantages and disadvantages? What has happened, and might happen, to its moat? Why don't earnings reflect economic reality? Or cash flows or book value? How might management behavior injure or benefit the earnings power? Ask yourself what mental models are relevant?

Keep It Simple

We don't do a lot of involved math with schedules of investments. Certainly we expect a decent return or we don't do it. We use a lot of experience and do it in our heads. We distrust others' systems and think it leads to false confidence. The harder you work, the more confidence you get. But you may be working hard on something you're no good at. We're so afraid of that process that we don't do it.
—CHARLIE MUNGER, WESCO ANNUAL MEETING, 2006

Many years ago, I was the analyst on Pechiney, a French aluminum company. My financial model had less than one hundred lines of assumptions, with no future projections, just an added column on the right for my estimate of "normal." Meeting the CFO for dinner, we walked through my model. He chuckled at its simplicity. Less than three months later, a takeout materialized, coincidentally, at my precise estimate of intrinsic value per share.

Complicated valuations cause trouble. Simple models allow the analyst to focus on the primary drivers that determine intrinsic value. Move one estimate and you can immediately see the consequences. Every layer of complexity moves the analyst one step away from the intrinsic value per share. Make changes and eventually lose track of the drivers. Errors become buried, making mental arithmetic to confirm assumptions impossible.

Behaviorally, greater complexity built into financial models raises the level of presumed precision. Remember that most any model results in an answer down to several decimal points unless intentionally suppressed to a round number. A calculated intrinsic of $100 does not feel as satisfying as one arriving at $97.96 per share. Peers and clients can't help but be impressed when presented with a complex model, raising confidence in your investment process. It is easy to forget that most individual future inputs are assumptions subject to a wide variance. Overlay assumption upon assumption and conclusions can quickly border on nonsensical. Keeping it simple brings investing back to the basics, where it belongs.

The Foundation of Valuation

But nowadays I would describe the graph as U-shaped. At the left, where the company itself is speculative and its credit low, the common stock is of course highly speculative, just as it has always been in the past. At the right extremity, however, where the company has the highest credit rating because both its past record and future prospects are most impressive, we find that the stock market tends more or less continuously to introduce a highly speculative element into the common share through the simple means of a price so high as to carry a fair degree of risk. . . . Returning to my imaginary graph, it would be the center area where the speculative element in common-stock purchases would tend to reach its minimum.

—BENJAMIN GRAHAM, "THE NEW SPECULATION
IN COMMON STOCKS," FINANCIAL ANALYSTS
SOCIETY SPEECH, 1958

This is not intended to be a book specifically on valuation. Plentiful other resources exist. Rather, consider this a warning to be skeptical of all valuations. None is gospel!

Valuation is a game of give and take. Franchise quality and structural growth go up, and so does the price. Amazon at one hundred fifty times earnings in 2010 was a fantastic buy price given its incredible growth and ever-improving moat. Foot Locker, a weakened retailer well before the advent of COVID, traded below ten times earnings but was likely worth even less: no barrier to entry, no pricing power, and no premium valuation. When a company has a capital-efficient dominant competitor gaining market share, apply a heavily discounted valuation.

There is no one best-in-class valuation methodology. One excellent hedge fund shuns all current run-rate metrics, focusing on buying a portfolio of growing companies at low-price-to-earnings estimates five years out. Price to normal earnings is a staple with some investors, dampening out cyclical movement and attempting to build a portfolio of low-price-to-normalized-earnings companies. Conservative DCFs can work as well as price to free cash flow, or combinations of various methodologies. Be flexible.

Quality Adjustments to Valuation

Time is the friend of the wonderful business, the enemy of the mediocre.
—WARREN BUFFETT, BERKSHIRE HATHAWAY ANNUAL LETTER, 1989

Investments of various quality can become viable investment candidates at the right price. High-quality concerns offer more room for error as they are more likely than average to (1) offer protection in a downturn, (2) retain access to capital at reasonable prices, (3) be periodically expensive allowing for good exit opportunities, and (4) grow above the market over time. Overpaying for high-quality concerns will affect your IRR, but extended holding periods are unlikely to result in material impairments of capital.

Lower-quality companies can be good investments at selected prices. Price discipline is paramount: be stingy and patient. Wait for large margins of safety without regret if price never enters your buy zone. There is no shame in passing on marginal companies regardless of their future returns. *The intrinsic value range will often be wider, quite possibly very wide. If it is too wide, just pass. It's not worth the risk of speculating on a name for which you may or may not have an edge.*

Cyclical Adjustments to Valuation

As we've long said, we prefer a lumpy 15 percent return to a smooth 12 percent.
—WARREN BUFFETT, BERKSHIRE HATHAWAY ANNUAL LETTER, 1998

Cyclicals can be great investments, the caveat being that economic cycles, which drive the volatility of earnings, are hard to predict. Cyclicals may earn high returns on capital, although results are unlikely to be a smooth ride. Investors are too often tempted to avoid cyclical names because of fear that an impending downturn will take their names lower. There are three ways to approach cyclical concerns. First, ignore them completely because of uncertainty around cyclical projections. Second, only buy cyclical companies after downturns materialize to protect against unfavorable entry prices. Third, attempt to discriminate in various parts of the market cycle. See part 2, chapter 12, "Deep Cyclical Companies Near Cycle Peak," for an in-depth discussion. More moderately exposed cyclicals possibly can be investment candidates at any point in the economic cycle, whereas deep cyclicals should be targeted when not near an economic peak.

Growth Adjustments to Valuation

In fact, according to the arithmetic, if a company could be assumed to grow at a rate of 8 percent or more indefinitely in the future its value would be infinite, and no price would be too high to pay for the shares.

—BENJAMIN GRAHAM, *THE INTELLIGENT INVESTOR*, 1973, CHAP. 11

High long-term growth rates obviously overwhelm any valuation formulas, driving the denominator of a dividend discount model toward zero. Realistically, above-market growth rates always prove temporary, and a growth factor provides both upside and downside risk. Looking forward, several years of above-market growth (1) acts as a margin of safety as intrinsic value growth compounds, (2) allows the benefit of scale to aid margin improvement, and (3) keeps the stock price high, which increases the value of its currency should it be needed. Downside risks include (1) the market tendency to overprice growth stocks making for a disadvantageous entry price, (2) a heightened competitive response as new entrants clamber for market share, and (3) the tendency for growth companies to consume rather than distribute capital.

Growth investments can be excellent long-term holdings as long as the company is in the process of building a moat that will allow it to monetize its fair share of any industry growth. Paying too much for a high-quality growth company may impair returns, but it is unlikely to result in material permanent capital impairments given a long enough holding period. To protect capital, gravitate to market leaders, first movers, and better franchises and only to those not dependent on the capital market for funding in the short run. Nothing hits stock prices of growth companies more than a continued need for new capital to fund operating losses right after disappointing the market with its latest subpar growth projections.

Is a Fundamentally Based Valuation Reliable?

Over the long term, it's hard for a stock to earn a much better return than the business which underlies it earns. If the business earns 6 percent on capital over 40 years and you hold it for that 40 years, you're not going to make much different than a 6 percent return—even if you originally buy it at a huge discount. Conversely, if a business earns 18 percent on capital over 20 or 30 years, even if you pay an expensive looking price, you'll end up with a fine result.

—CHARLIE MUNGER, "A LESSON ON WORLDLY, ELEMENTARY
WISDOM AS IT RELATES TO INVESTMENT MANAGEMENT,"
UNIVERSITY OF SOUTHERN CALIFORNIA SPEECH, 1994

Stocks can deviate from intrinsic value for extended periods of time—months and even years. Investors worry endlessly about timing entry prices of their investments and then are disappointed if prices decline shortly after purchase. This makes sense for shorter-term-oriented investors looking to turn portfolios regularly, but truly long-term-oriented shareholders will be well heeded to focus more on sustainable long-term business returns than on pricing. Do not completely disregard pricing because there is an opportunity cost of paying too much, but over the very long run, returns will converge toward results seen by the underlying business.

Reasons to Pass

Excessively high valuation is a clear risk factor. Unfortunately, no magic formulas guarantee that you will be able to ascertain the price at which investments should be passed over. In some ways, you know it when you see it. If in doubt, just pass. Never forget that you need only twenty to forty names to populate a fully invested portfolio. Learn the basics from a valuation book and keep these caveats in mind. Price discipline provides a margin of safety, as does a high-quality franchise. Consider high barriers to entry and other competitive advantages to be intangible forms of a margin of safety that are suitable for consideration with any long-term-oriented investments.

18

Lollapalooza Effect

The most important thing to keep in mind is the idea that especially big forces often come out of these one hundred models. When several models combine, you get Lollapalooza effects; this is when two, three or four forces are all operating in the same direction. And, frequently, you don't get simple addition. It's often like a critical mass in physics where you get a nuclear explosion if you get to a certain point of mass—and you don't get anything much worth seeing if you don't reach the mass.

—CHARLIE MUNGER, *POOR CHARLIE'S ALMANACK*, 2005

Nassim Taleb, author of *The Black Swan: The Impact of the Highly Improbable* (2017), has since built a successful hedge fund that attempts to protect against adverse events at the tail of the distribution. Charlie Munger has captured something similarly imaginative with his Lollapalooza effect—that is, the combination of multiple adverse events working together to wreak havoc on investments' prospects. This effect is so obvious yet so overlooked. Munger speaks to nonlinear systems that emerge periodically that catch most everyone by surprise. The COVID outbreak in early 2020 might have become one of these systems in which a confluence of events caused great despair, mostly unforeseen by the investing public. Factors at play in the COVID outbreak included the following:

1. Lean inventory management across companies to reduce capital tied up in mundane items.

2. Reduced governmental stockpiles of personal protective equipment, ventilators, and testing kit materials as budget pressures pushed short-term thinking into government decisions.

3. Supply chains that leaned heavily on China during a period of heightened trade tensions.

4. The trend of globalization, centuries in the making, had reached a peak relative to history.

5. High corporate debt relative to history gave companies less operating flexibility when faced with an external shock.

6. High government debt relative to history, with debt to gross domestic product (GDP) reaching near record levels in many countries, provided less leeway for stimulus to cushion the blow of a GDP collapse.

7. A high cost and relatively inefficient U.S. healthcare system faced two primary pressures. First, investment in hospital bed capacity per capita lagged relative to some countries outside the United States. Second, the multitude of uninsured and underinsured in the United States placed limits on the system's abilities to adequately service the sick. Many other countries, particularly emerging markets, faced even more dire constraints.

8. Equity valuations at already stretched levels at year-end 2019 embedded assumptions of benign credit losses and strong future growth prospects. Negative sentiment shifts led to much larger movements of equity prices.

Unfortunately, the COVID disaster turned into a $5 trillion cost in the United States alone, with much broader economic damage worldwide, coupled with excess mortality and pain and suffering. Governments and some corporate balance sheets are now deeper in debt, leaving less available firepower for the next crisis and a smaller portion of the economics for shareholders. Lollapalooza systems are dangerous, and investors ignore risks that combine individually manageable concerns into unquantifiable combinations at their peril.

As Munger said: "A confluence of factors in the same direction caused Warren's success. It's very unlikely that a Lollapalooza effect can come from anything else" (Wesco Annual Meeting, 2007).

Enough said. Lollapalooza systems can materialize anywhere, including in Omaha, Nebraska, the childhood homes of both Buffett and Munger. Even if such systems can be beneficial, they're far too unpredictable.

In a 2011 conversation at the Pasadena Convention Center, Munger noted: "Of course Keynesian and monetary tricks do not work as well when everyone knows you are playing them. For example, things that worked in the 1930s might not work now. Back then the US had better credit and people did not use the polls to make themselves rich. Meaning, people did not get voted into power and then use their power just to become rich. This is a Lollapalooza system."

Political systems lend themselves equally well to Lollapalooza effects. Witness the mayhem that ensued at the U.S. Capitol in Washington, D.C., in January 2021. Most complex systems interconnected to other systems can experience an unexpected result.

The Lollapalooza Screen

Each chapter in part 2 has targeted specific types of names worth excluding in investment portfolios. The majority of the uninvestable names will be evident quickly and fall into the pass pile. Some names will slip through these filters because the particle sizes are toxic yet too small to be adequately trapped. In other words, the nature of their offenses are not egregious enough to justify immediate elimination. The toxin alone won't kill you. Now imagine that some of these names possess multiple toxins that in combination prove lethal. Pharmacists study drug interactions diligently. Investors, by comparison, should study Lollapalooza effects. Upon review, many potential investments possess multiple trappings identified in our *Reasons to Pass* that in combination create substantial and unpredictable risks to your capital. It is in this case that the Lollapalooza screen adds tremendous value, by identifying investment candidates that suffer from multiple transgressions. The combination of two or more less extreme transgressions may result in "unexpected" downside shocks. The Lollapalooza system identifies and removes these potential investments.

Which company appears to offer more appealing investment prospects? U.S. Steel is a high-cost commodity producer operating in a deeply cyclical industry with material yet manageable leverage. It has strong corporate governance and a compelling valuation. Hon Hai Precision Industries, an electronics assembler based in Taiwan, has an enormous net cash balance, is growing in excess of the market, has large customer concentration (Apple), faces potential geopolitical risk from its Taiwan domicile, and has questionable corporate governance yet an equally compelling valuation. Neither is perfect, and each possesses some combination of concerns that individually are not sufficient to completely derail an investment thesis.

No one bright line makes exclusion from a portfolio obvious when a Lollapalooza effect is concerned. Different investors will arrive at differing conclusions. My experience weighs the balance sheet more heavily, followed by the structural high-cost position and a company's cyclicality. Good corporate governance is not protection from a deficient competitive position, although bad corporate governance can destroy otherwise favorable economics. Growth can bail out investors of otherwise poor investment decisions, but strong growth on the back of one primary customer or a single technology presents substantial risks over the long run. My conclusion: an investment in Hon Hai is plausible at the right price, whereas an investment in U.S. Steel may be too hard to call.

The Virtuous Benefit of a Lollapalooza System

A truly great business must have an enduring "moat" that protects excellent returns on invested capital. The dynamics of capitalism guarantee that competitors will repeatedly assault any business "castle" that is earning high returns. Therefore a formidable barrier such as a company's being the low cost producer (GEICO, Costco) or possessing a powerful world-wide brand (Coca-Cola, Gillette, American Express) is essential for sustained success. Business history is filled with "Roman Candles," companies whose moats proved illusory and were soon crossed.

—WARREN BUFFETT, BERKSHIRE HATHAWAY
ANNUAL LETTER, 2007

Many investors speak, and this book is no exception, about high-quality or low-quality investments. While difficult to define, high-quality investment candidates offer protection from Lollapalooza systems that are similar to yet opposite of those forces that weigh heavily on low-quality investments. Investors often refer to "tailwinds" or "headwinds" experienced by specific names, labels that upon deeper examination reveal themselves to simply be multiple positive or negative factors working in combination. When Buffett speaks of his crown jewels, GEICO and Coca-Cola, or Munger speaks endearingly about Costco, it is because these names possess favorable Lollapalooza effects. Solid distribution, brand awareness, strong cash flow generation, high barriers to entry, low costs, excellent corporate governance and prudent, conservative managers work together to provide the moats so deeply cherished by investors.

Case Study: Norwegian Cruise Lines

Norwegian Cruise Lines is the third largest in a highly concentrated oligopoly. The industry is capital intensive, with new ships costing hundreds of millions of dollars. Cruise ship operations have high fixed costs, while the marginal cost of carrying one additional passenger is low. Ships need to be fully utilized to meet return objectives. The big three publicly traded cruise line operators, Carnival, Norwegian, and Royal Caribbean, are relatively interchangeable, leading to high rivalry.

Looking at results at year-end 2019, several areas of concern were evident. Financial leverage, at 3.5 times net debt to earnings before interest, taxes, depreciation, and amortization (EBITDA), was high. It was the most levered of the three dominant peers. Property, plant, and equipment (PP&E) had increased in the previous five years from $9 billion to $13 billion, and ongoing commitments to purchase more vessels would require additional debt capacity and capital consumption. The industry cycle was near its peak, with 2019 being the third year with greater than 15 percent return on equity, versus a long-term average of 10 percent. Margins were near peak levels as well, a function of revenues growing from $4.3 billion in 2015 to $6.5 billion in 2019. High fixed costs and growing revenue with high incremental margins equals rising profitability. The year-end 2019 stock price implied a 20 times price-earnings (PE) ratio, which is high for a cyclical name near peak conditions.

This was a "no-buy" stock at year-end 2019. The stock was priced for near perfection with an asymmetrical profile. A combination of high fixed costs, a near commodity offering, at a cyclical peak, with high valuation, high debt, and high capital commitments, should have made one ask what could go wrong. Limited upside with significant downside was inevitable if the cycle turned. Irrespective of the emergence of COVID, an eventual decline was likely given that the level of permanent impairment was uncertain but potentially material. This was a Lollapalooza pass.

Reasons to Pass

First, academic psychology, while it is admirable and useful as a list of ingenious and important experiments, lacks intradisciplinary synthesis. In particular, not enough attention is given to Lollapalooza effects coming from combinations of psychological tendencies.

—CHARLIE MUNGER, "PRACTICAL THOUGHT ABOUT PRACTICAL THOUGHT," 1996

Psychology experiments tend to focus on one isolated trait, such as loss aversion. These experiments are easy to construct and can be more successfully measured. The combination of multiple behavioral biases working together can create havoc for otherwise muted responses yet are ignored because they are difficult to simulate and measure. Loss aversion combined with overconfidence and recency bias lead to far poorer decision-making and more adverse outcomes for investors than any one of these three cognitive errors individually. One plus one plus one does not equal three. Cognitive errors can shift decision-making exponentially in the wrong direction.

Over time, experience will provide a guidepost for warning signs related to Lollapalooza effects. Simply being aware of the possibility that combinations of undesirable traits may amplify in a downside scenario will instill a necessary degree of caution. *When multiple borderline reasons to pass combine, and your compass is still uncertain, just pass.*

3

Reasons to Buy

Introduction

Passing on companies is liberating. The world is an overwhelming opportunity set, filled with many thousands of possible investments that may outperform the market at large. It is tempting to have an opinion on each investment because the fear of missing out outweighs the rational reality that analytical bandwidth is limited. No person, no team of analysts, and no quantitative processing power adequately covers the breadth of investment candidates available in the market. The intentional act of passing on a large swath of available investments provides three tangible benefits. First, it removes names from consideration for which the odds of success are low or cannot be quantified. Second, it frees up scarce bandwidth to focus on companies that are analyzable with odds that can be quantified. Build a manageable portfolio with odds tilted in your favor and the results are bound to please over the long run. The third benefit relates to portfolio construction. The key to managing an investment portfolio is to understand the portfolio. Portfolios with fewer moving parts are inherently easier to understand and therefore to analyze. We are simple beings with limited capacity for multivariate thinking. Risk management becomes a simpler and cleaner exercise when there are fewer names.

In a 2010 Berkshire Hathaway annual letter, Warren Buffett explained:

> It's easy to identify many investment managers with great recent
> records. But past results, though important, do not suffice when
> prospective performance is being judged. How the record has
> been achieved is crucial, as is the manager's understanding of—
> and sensitivity to—risk (which in no way should be measured by
> beta, the choice of too many academics). In respect to the risk cri-
> terion, we were looking for someone with a hard-to-evaluate skill:
> the ability to anticipate the effects of economic scenarios not pre-
> viously observed. Finally, we wanted someone who would regard
> working for Berkshire as far more than a job.

Risk Management

Catastrophe bonds became all the rage in the mid-2000s. These investments pay higher than market rates of interest, impairing capital only if
a predefined catastrophe hits a certain loss threshold. Hedge funds out to
make excess returns bought these instruments on two or three times leverage, borrowing short term to generate a massive spread that translated
to "uncorrelated" alpha. Clients praised these astute investors for their
stable and high returns, although the results were nothing more than a
calculated gamble that the weather would remain calm or that the ground
wouldn't shake.

Reasons to Pass is first and foremost a book about risk management.
Many investments turn out well, and historical returns signal praiseworthy
results, but past performance tells only part of the story. Certain investments and strategies perform well in bull markets, and some prove defensive
in downturns. An insurance company may experience solid underwriting
results for years before facing an "unexpected" loss that impairs value.

Risk management is a controversial topic, which is obvious in principle
but challenging in implementation. Many sophisticated investors use some
version of beta and cross-correlations of asset prices to measure portfolio
risk. The primary problems with this approach are threefold: (1) most of
these indicators are shorter term in nature and market environments can
change dramatically, (2) risks can emerge that are not well represented by
historical events, and (3) the implicit assumption is that asset prices are
tightly linked to underlying fundamentals.

Government leverage globally sits at unprecedented levels, as did corporate debt at the end of 2021. Negative interest rates had not been seen in material doses until Japan implemented 0 percent rates in 1999 and the market took its long-term debt yields negative in the early 2000s. COVID, emerging in 2020, was a threat not seen in a century. Cracks in the European Union are widening, while socialism is experiencing a rebirth not seen since the mid-1950s. Many risks are not well encapsulated in historical price movements and cross-correlations. Investors need to assess these prospectively. Price movements contrary to efficient markets offer ever-increasing evidence that the hard form of the efficient market theory (EMT) is nonsensical. Price movements as a component of risk management is ridiculous. The world is nonlinear, more Lollapalooza effect than Gaussian distribution. Tails are fatter, and distributions skew left, to the downside. Traditional risk management works well on a day-to-day basis until an "unexpected" event materializes, at which point those models break down. Liquidity, for example, is available until sentiment turns or large losses evaporate sources of capital. Historical price correlations do not offer much guidance, and the past may not be a prelude to the future.

In a *Wired* interview, Jeff Bezos, noted: "Our first shareholder letter, in 1997, was entitled, 'It's all about the long term.' If everything you do needs to work on a three-year time horizon, then you're competing against a lot of people. But if you're willing to invest on a seven-year time horizon, you're now competing against a fraction of those people, because very few companies are willing to do that. Just by lengthening the time horizon, you can engage in endeavors that you could never otherwise pursue" (November 13, 2011).

Long-term investors are the least likely to benefit from traditional risk management efforts. Long-term investors are well equipped to weather short-term price volatility. Very few points in history, whether it be in the United States or abroad, have provided below-inflation equity returns over a ten-year holding period. Most pension funds have a thirty-year-plus liability profile, whereas many large endowment funds are perpetual. Individual retirement portfolios build up and then run off over similar long-dated timeframes. These investors benefit most from a long-term time horizon and should focus on risk metrics that evaluate the underlying investment fundamentals. Short-term price movements are irrelevant, except when they provide occasional opportunities for enrichment.

Risk management needs for long-term investors revolve around three equally relevant factors: (1) sticking to your core principles, (2) structural risks surrounding individual positions, and (3) understanding structural cross-correlations to gauge permanent impairments from exogenous events.

Core principles protect investors from faulty decision-making. Pass on most names, require a margin of safety, and remain within your core competency. These guideposts keep investors laser focused on situations in which the odds of success remain forever in your favor.

Every investment faces greater than zero odds of some structural downside risk. This fact cannot be completely avoided. Legal frameworks can change, governments behave unpredictably, destructive acquisitions or divestments are made, and scientific advancement may disrupt seemingly wide moats. The goal of establishing a range of intrinsic values is to take into consideration the most likely disrupters of value to lower the odds of negative surprises. The application of a disciplined margin of safety concept protects against most possible adverse "surprises." The selection process filters out most of the names that are likely to experience adverse effects. The Lollapalooza effect is the final filter, removing names facing potentially nonlinear risks.

Benjamin Graham wrote: "Even with a margin in the investor's favor, an individual security may work out badly. For the margin guarantees only that he has a better chance for profit than for loss—not that loss is impossible. But as the number of such commitments is increased the more certain does it become that the aggregate of the profits will exceed the aggregate of the losses. That is the simple basis of the insurance-underwriting business" (*The Intelligent Investor*, 1973, chap. 20).

Portfolio construction is the final risk management overlay. An equally weighted portfolio of twenty widely diversified names should be adequate in most circumstances. Unexpected losses in one name should on average be more than offset by accretion in the remaining portfolio. Raising the number of names when conviction sits below maximum levels is reasonable, as the law of slightly larger numbers offers greater natural diversification. Portfolio concentration is still paramount—analyzing portfolio risk is purer and simpler with fewer names. Managers should have the ability to understand how their portfolios generally should behave in various states of economic disequilibrium. This expectation should be communicated to clients in advance, and managers should be held to account when results deviate from expectation.

Many portfolios at the end of 2020 were geared toward economic stabilization. Fundamental investors focus from the bottom up, finding attractive investments first and then assessing the high-level portfolio exposures. Stocks still well below midcycle at year-end 2020 include energy names and financials. These should be expected to recover once economic activity resumes at more normal levels. Investors see the margins of safety and construct portfolios. A prudent process incorporates some limits no matter how attractive the opportunity. Energy should not become 50 percent of any portfolio, the structural correlation within the group is too high. The same holds true for financials, which are beholden to interest rates, credit losses, and regulation. Managers prudently build portfolios that include attractive names in meaningful allocations. Like dessert, indulge in the sweets, but don't eat the whole cake. *Never set a portfolio up in which structural losses from cross-correlations or over allocations create a hole too deep from which to recover.*

Investors should have a decent idea how their portfolios will respond to a variety of higher-level risks. Consider, for example, how your portfolio is likely to react to the following:

1. Unexpected Inflation or Deflation—Equities typically do best in benign inflation scenarios. Markets prefer predictable and stable environments. Inflation above 3 percent and deflation below −2 percent per year creates fundamental challenges for certain businesses. Managers may reduce investment due to the greater uncertainty, and inventory challenges lead to unpredictable results. Most equities do poorly in these circumstances.

2. Terrorist Attacks or Other Major Events—These events are often temporary earnings shocks rather than permanent earnings impairments and thus are more likely to be buying opportunities as markets temporarily react to perceived increases in risk, although undue concentration can cause impairments. A major California earthquake might bring stress to insurers and locally focused businesses, while simultaneously presenting opportunities to infrastructure companies. The World Trade Center terrorist attack temporarily cratered all travel-exposed businesses.

3. A Financial Crisis in China or Another Major Market—An unexpected crisis will spill over to other markets. Australia, Brazil, and Canada all produce commodities that could trigger significant economic impacts if China enters a crisis and ceases to be the marginal purchaser. Chinese real estate investing reached 25 percent of GDP in 2021. High residential home prices could hinder its economy, or worse.

4. Political Crises—The height of Soviet influence in the 1950s and 1960s saw a surprisingly large part of the world experimenting with

socialism. The intensity of the debate in the United States is currently rising. Implications to investment portfolios are obvious as taxes and regulations become more burdensome and redistribution policies reduce returns to owners. The European Union faced jitters in 2012 because a Greek exit from the European Union was speculated as peripheral EU countries grappled with fiscal stresses. The Brexit vote in the UK in early 2020 brought with it the threat of geopolitical instability.

5. Wars—The consequence of political unrest, bad policies, bad actors, and blame. Equities did poorly entering World War II, bottoming in 1940 as France conceded defeat and became German occupied. Wars destroy capital investments, reduce productivity, increase sovereign debt, and take a tragic economic and social toll. The elimination of property rights, the foundation of capitalism, is jeopardized during wartime.

6. Majorly Disruptive New Technologies—Newspapers became obsolete distributors of information because of the internet, and cable companies' monopoly on content distribution similarly has come to an end. These can portend very large shifts in future earnings power.

7. Spikes in Commodity Prices or Other Supply Shocks—Semiconductor manufacturing came to a standstill because of unexpected flooding in Thailand. These events most often are temporary, but any company facing substantial supplier power may become vulnerable.

Generally, it is important to know whether your portfolio would react favorably or unfavorably to the following:

1. A large increase in the equity markets: Is the portfolio heavily geared to an upcycle?
2. A large decrease: How defensively postured is the portfolio?
3. A credit crisis: Will certain investments perform poorly when credit spreads gap out?

Ripple Effect Theory

Drop a stone in a pond and watch the ripples lap outward. A Greek exit from the Eurozone, for example, is the epicenter, rolling the most forcefully near the center. Other Southern European countries (e.g., Spain, Portugal, and Italy) are next in line, hit with large ripples as credit default swap prices spiked and capital withdrew. They are implicitly linked with Greece, creating stress almost as intense as that seen in Greece. Germany and France would see sizeable, slightly smaller ripples, forced to plug any capital holes to reinstate confidence. The U.S. government would provide liquidity to mitigate any fallout, and some U.S. companies would feel the consequences, although widespread economic damage would be smaller still. Pebbles of varying size drop regularly, most of which are too small to cause widespread harm. Risk management attempts to prepare portfolios for these unprecedented events.

Portfolio diversification can include any acceptable asset class. Investors specialized in real estate may diversify geographically or by asset type. Others build equity, debt, or private market portfolios, seeking lower fundamental correlations across a portfolio. The key is understanding the risks of structural impairments to avoid situations in which permanent losses cannot be adequately recouped by the remaining portfolio. A concentrated portfolio of twenty to forty names will include a mix of various assets and exposures, providing natural diversification across industries, countries, and asset classes. An opportunity set will vary over the years as some companies improve their positioning while others deteriorate. Have the mental flexibility and the ability to look at names with fresh eyes every few years, and more often during periods of large economic volatility. In 2008 and 2009, enormous shifts opened an investment window for assets previously uninvestable because valuations had been too rich. The Eurozone crisis of confidence in 2012 created many opportunities across Europe. Emerging markets are multiyear underperformers against global peers through 2021, making them possible areas of interest. The COVID cycle again shifted the laundry list of winners and losers. Each cycle will target a somewhat different set of assets, providing unexpected opportunities. The dynamic of the unpredictable creates some of the greatest joys of investing, uncovering opportunities to invest at discounts in names you never expected.

For those concerned about a dearth of available investment opportunities, I offer this thought: *You need only twenty to forty names out of many thousands.*

19

Screening

> But basically all investment is value investment in the sense that you're always trying to get better prospects than you're paying for. And so, but you can't look everywhere at once, just any more than you can run a marathon in 12 different states at once. And so you have to have some system of picking someplace to look, which is your hunting ground. But you're looking for value in every case.
>
> —CHARLIE MUNGER, DAILY JOURNAL
> ANNUAL MEETING, 2020

The process of whittling down the opportunity set will require, at some point, some form of screening. Determining how to screen for investment candidates should be predicated on your core competencies and your overall knowledge of global markets. Some investors target quantitative screens as a starting point, whereas others rely on more qualitative screens. Either one, or some combination, can work as long as you can meaningfully interpret results.

Quantitative Screening

As Warren Buffett wrote in a 1983 Berkshire Hathaway annual letter, "Book value is an accounting concept, recording the accumulated financial input from both contributed capital and retained earnings. Intrinsic business value is an economic concept, estimating future cash output discounted to present value."

Many databases are available in the marketplace to assist in your quantitative screening efforts. These databases provide financial information and price data on thousands of mostly equity securities. Equities lend themselves better to quant screening than to fixed income or real estate because somewhat standardized financial information must be provided for public companies. Book value is the classic example: it is easy to identify for any company back in time that has a long data series. As a result, book value has been used heavily in academic circles and by practitioners in their research. Book value is not a great measure of intrinsic value, however, particularly for names relying on intangibles to generate profits. An ideal screen targets equities trading at discounts to their intrinsic value.

Fixed income and real estate is more often bought and sold in the private markets without the involvement of exchanges. Pricing in this case is more opaque, and financial information does not have to be disclosed for most of these available investments. General reading of periodicals, searches on credit spreads, and conversations with brokers and real estate experts are great sources of information for these asset classes. Opportunistic investors should keep their eyes open. Identify countries or regions that are struggling, such as industries facing challenges or real estate downturns. Tight credit spreads in the United States and the historically low level of interest rates in 2021 should be enough to pass on all corporate debt with a greater than two-year duration. Record low cap rates in Seattle, seen at year-end 2021 , should be enough to justify passing on any local real estate investments—except perhaps one's primary residence meant for a multi-year holding period. Quant screens occasionally uncover nuggets not otherwise on the radar, such as high-quality mostly smaller names neglected by the news. Boring, low-tech, well-managed companies devoid of controversy, and low-growth companies in particular are ignored by the market and thus may be ideal candidates for quant screens. How else would you ever learn about them?

My recommendation is for any equity investor to attempt quantitative screens at least periodically. Results can be sorted individually to further reduce candidates to a manageable number of likely candidates, which then require more extensive work. All quant screening activities should encompass the following general principles:

1. Set appropriately constraining criteria: Many screens let through too many investment candidates—oftentimes one hundred or more. Investors' instincts are often to include all possible investment

candidates to ensure that the best possible investments are not overlooked. A list of a hundred names is overwhelming. Resist this urge.

2. Stick within your areas of competency: Including small-cap Chinese equities in your search may be futile for inexperienced investors. If you are ill equipped to deal with these nuances, simply exclude China in your quant screens. Quant screening for financial stocks is complicated by the obtuse disclosures and industry-specific terminology. Those who do not know how to analyze financials should study the industry first or just pass.

3. Include balance sheet metrics: Excessive leverage is often, though not always, identifiable through quant screens. Do your best by researching leverage metrics relevant to each industry. Some manual filtering will be required of any short list of results, but even a screen that is only 80 percent effective reduces the bandwidth necessary to filter out this important reason to pass.

4. Embed reasonable valuation metrics: No investment is a good investment at any price. The 1970s U.S. market eventually synthesized into the Nifty Fifty (i.e., fifty stocks that investors needed to have in their portfolios regardless of valuation). It is no surprise that these were among the worst performers in 1974, down over 50 percent on average. Pundits in the late 1990s urged investors to build a basket of any and all dot-com stocks, assuming that this basket would surely build wealth regardless of valuation levels. Benjamin Graham, Warren Buffett, Charlie Munger, and most all fundamentally oriented professional investors reinforce the discipline of price sensitivity. Paying too much will cost you money. Contrary to the teachings of famed investor Joel Greenblatt, quant screens do not have a magic valuation formula. Investors have found price to book, price to earnings, price to cash flow, price to free cash flow, quant-structured discounted cash flows, and other measures of replacement cost all may be effective in screening for names. Study your industries' and your countries' long-term financial history to get a sense of what normal is. The United States, for example, has traded at an average of sixteen times earnings over the past fifty years. High-growth companies justify higher multiples. Small caps have traded at similar price to earnings (PE) as large caps, as higher average earnings-per-share growth is offset by higher structural riskiness. Emerging market (EM) stocks have traded mostly

at discounts to developed stocks, with the occasional premium PE successfully signaling the need to dial back on EM exposure.

Qualitative Screening

At least a portion of your investment screen will be qualitative in nature, and for some professional investors, this is their primary screening lens. Buffett has been an astute observer of global capital markets for more than seventy years. He has read thousands of annual reports and reads at least two periodicals each day to further his areas of competency and find worthy investments. The image of Buffett incorporating a FactSet screen into his process is comical. The rest of us are not so privileged. A general rule is that the more experienced the investor is, the more likely he or she is to rely on qualitative screens. I come across names every day, sourced from articles, peer discussions, and even CNBC. Most are immediate discards, but a handful go into my "to review" pile for further study.

> How do you get worldly wisdom? What system do you use to rise into the tiny top percentage of the world in terms of having sort of an elementary practical wisdom? I've long believed that a certain system—which almost any intelligent person can learn—works way better than the systems that most people use. As I said at the USC Business School, what you need is a latticework of mental models in your head. And you hang your actual experience and your vicarious experience (that you get from reading and so forth) on this latticework of powerful models. And, with that system, things gradually get to fit together in a way that enhances cognition.
> —CHARLIE MUNGER, "A LESSON ON ELEMENTARY,
> WORLDLY WISDOM, REVISITED," STANFORD UNIVERSITY SPEECH, 1996

Done well, qualitative screening should include the following parameters. Note the emphasis on vicarious knowledge capture rather than simply relying on direct experience. Direct experience can be expensive. Potentially painful lessons are better learned vicariously, and time invested in historical analysis accelerates the learning curve.

1. Cyclical Observations—Direct cyclical experience is invaluable as it tempers enthusiasm during strong up markets while tempering

fear during down markets. Much historical information is available in books and periodicals. History is a powerful learning tool.
Study previous cycles. Learn from the past or be cursed to learn the
expensive way.

2. Market Analysis—Each cycle is different, and markets move in
unpredictable ways. Study the markets both holistically and from a
bottom-up basis to get a better sense of when long-term opportunities are likely to emerge.

3. Books—Books are vital sources of information, as Munger wisely
explained: "In my whole life, I have known no wise people (over
a broad subject matter area) who didn't read all the time—none,
zero. You'd be amazed how much Warren reads—and how much
I read. My children laugh at me. They think I'm a book with a
couple of legs sticking out" (Wesco annual meetings, 2003). Study
various business models, and read biographies, industry tomes,
history, and any other resource that helps you build a mental
model. Reading is worth the time invested. History, oft neglected
during our youth, provides many clues to our futures. The world
may evolve, but human nature remains consistent.

4. Periodicals—Periodicals, such as *Wall Street Journal*, *Financial
Times*, *Forbes*, *Fortune*, *The Economist*, *Scientific American*, and many
others provide knowledge and insights.

5. Public Company Disclosures—Annual reports, presentations,
earnings releases, conference call transcripts, and news reports all
help investors understand individual stocks and their long-term
prospects. Each year invested in such disclosures builds greater
qualitative acumen.

6. Personal Investment Performance—Track and collect data on your
own process. Keep a file of names reviewed, whether you invested,
when you bought and sold, and how each situation turned out over
the long run. Did your investments outpace those you chose not to
invest in? Did you perform better in up markets or down markets?
Did you sell too soon? One spreadsheet should do the trick. Learning lessons from mistakes is futile after one year because they are
statistically insignificant and do not encapsulate at least one full
market cycle. Cumulative knowledge gains over a lifetime will be
substantial and decision-making will improve cycle over cycle.

7. Lessons Learned—Be humble enough to acknowledge mistakes
and learn the right lessons. Simply boycotting airline stocks because

of poor internal rate of returns may be irrational as the industry performed poorly for forty years until the late 2000s, when consolidation and an economic boom led to an extended period of prosperity. Perhaps the right lesson was to acknowledge that low barriers to entry, a hallmark of the airline industry, was likely to lead to uninspiring returns on capital through the cycle. The solution then was to improve analytical success related to low-barrier-to-entry companies rather than studying one industry myopically.

Conclusion

However you screen the available universe, be disciplined and rational, force personalized deep learning into your process while keeping your ego in check. Done correctly, screening eliminates most all candidates from consideration. The remainder will fall out in your company-specific work as you push investments into the pass pile. Screening is not only an efficiency tool and a behavioral tool but also a learned behavior. Make screening efficient, targeted, and effective to free up precious analytical resources, which can be deployed optimally to finalize your list of investments.

20

Growth Stocks

The philosophy of investment in growth stocks parallels in part and in part contravenes the margin of safety principle. The growth-stock buyer relies on an expected earning power that is greater than the average shown in the past. Thus he may be said to substitute these expected earnings for the past record in calculating his margin of safety. In investment theory there is no reason why carefully estimated future earnings should be a less reliable guide than the bare record of the past; in fact, security analysis is coming more and more to prefer a competently executed evaluation of the future. Thus, the growth-stock approach may supply as dependable a margin of safety as is found in the ordinary investment—provided the calculation of the future is conservatively made, and provided it shows a satisfactory margin in relation to the price paid.

The danger in a growth-stock program lies precisely here. For such favored issues the market has a tendency to set prices that will not be adequately protected by a conservative projection of future earnings.

—BENJAMIN GRAHAM, *THE INTELLIGENT INVESTOR*,
1973, CHAP. 20

Long-term investors embrace growth. Revenues expand cycle over cycle, while margins remain steady or expand when more units are spread over fixed costs. Earnings per share (EPS) growth is capitalized at a high and steady multiple, which translates into continuous intrinsic value compounding. Companies whose earnings compound more quickly can be rewarded with multiple expansion and accelerating price appreciation. When you buy these assets below intrinsic value, favorable long-term compounding results. High-quality growth stocks lend themselves especially well to long holding periods. Buy a portfolio of growth stocks, and your job is done, possibly for many years.

Definitions for growth stocks vary. Price to book (P/B) was the original proxy, with low P/B stocks considered to be value investments and high P/B stocks growth investments. High P/B stocks reflected both higher return on equity (ROE) and higher growth. Value stocks quantitatively generated lower ROE—hence, the lower P/B ratio. Book value has become less relevant as global industries' earnings power has shifted toward intangibles and inflation has revalued historical assets. Traditional behemoths in the twentieth century built earnings power through large long-lasting investments in property, plant, and equipment—think steel or manufacturing—while twenty-first-century business models frequently rely on intangibles that are not capitalized on the balance sheet. Brands, research and development (R&D), information technology development, and advertising costs are expensed, which decreases book value while increasing ROE and return on invested capital. Sales growth should be in excess of market to be considered a growth stock, not just in spurts but over an entire economic cycle.

Fixed income investors sit higher in the capital stack and do not participate in growth directly, although credit risk declines when enterprises generate prudent growth. Growth companies are often mostly equity financed because they burn cash, and because credit markets are not well equipped to assess growth prospects. High-quality growth companies with clear paths to a steady state make better credit risks, as do those whose free cash flow conversion is higher. As growth translates to rising margins and free cash flow generation, creditworthiness improves further. Amazon was a poor credit risk in the early 2000s compared with its near AAA reputation today.

High-dividend-paying companies are mostly slower growth because high payout ratios indicate fewer reinvestment opportunities. Utilities, real estate, and many financials pay out greater than 50 percent of earnings, leading to above-market dividend yields but lower earnings growth. This is a reasonably predictive growth factor.

Well-chosen equities with high five- or ten-year growth trajectories make excellent investments at the right price. With any asset, price is key, and growth stocks face both a headwind and a tailwind in this regard. Better than market prospects are clearly visible with high-quality growth stocks. This drives up valuations. Although some growth-oriented investors focus deeply on underlying fundamentals and will resist the siren call of growth at any price, others are driven primarily by the story that remains equally compelling whether the stock trades at thirty, sixty, or one hundred and fifty times earnings. Human behavior is to gravitate to good stories. Good stories command high, sometimes irrationally high, valuations. Buyer beware. Alternatively, investors often do not appreciate the margin effects that culminate once scale benefits are achieved. This natural skepticism—a "show me before I believe you" mindset—can translate into underpriced opportunities.

The flip side of the valuation argument relates to future earnings power. Well-chosen growth stocks will experience structural earnings growth over many years, allowing high multiple investments to grow into reasonably valued investments. Pay forty times earnings when only thirty times is warranted, and the likely ten-year compounding will still be positive—just less positive than if the buyer had been more price disciplined.

Alternatively, consider deep value stocks facing earnings challenges that must be addressed by astute management intervention. Investors allocate capital in this case because of the expectation of earnings recovery. This adds an additional element of speculation because earnings recoveries do not always materialize. Five years later, the odds are that the earnings impairment may have proved structural rather than temporary, thus causing large intrinsic value impairment as well as likely permanent impairment of capital. Consider this the confession of a recovering deep value investor.

Jeff Bezos wrote in his 2001 Amazon annual letter, "Growth spreads fixed costs across more sales, reducing cost per unit, which makes possible more price reductions. Customers like this, and it's good for shareholders. Please expect us to repeat this loop."

Traditional investors targeting growth stocks often begin their search with industries that are expected to grow more quickly than the market over the next three to five years. The next step is to identify the winners. Some investors pay little regard to the price paid, preferring to overweight a theme, whereas others diligently model forward results into a discounted cash flow. Above-market industry revenue projections are overlaid with share gains seen by the winners, leading to large revenue increases, whereas scale spreads fixed costs over an increasing number of units and thus raises operating margins materially. The logic is irrefutable, although historical

cases, including the following, give pause to the likely success when targeting companies in high growth industries:

1. Railroad Companies—It was evident to most in 1850 that rail was
    going to capture market share against legacy transportation meth-
    ods. The competitive advantages were immense. Abundant capital
    flowed into the industry, and dozens of new competitors were born
    laying track across the United States. Track grew forty-fold between
    1850 and 1900, while half of all railroad companies went bankrupt
    by the end of the century. Miles of installed rail lines peaked in the
    United States in 1916 at two hundred and fifty thousand miles. The
    benefits from the country's interconnectivity cannot be overstated,
    but investors mostly struck out. Identifying winners in 1850 was
    challenging and returns on capital were low for the few surviving
    competitors.

2. Auto Companies—Mechanical buggies began to replace horse-
    drawn carriages in the early 1900s. Ford's Model T started produc-
    tion in 1908, selling fifteen million cars by 1927. Industry growth
    was massive, and at least two thousand car companies appeared in
    the United States, although only three survived in the long run. Two
    of those car companies went bankrupt in the 2008 Great Financial
    Crisis. Because some companies were acquired, investors turned
    out okay; however, long-run industry returns were lackluster and
    picking the winners was near impossible.

3. Airlines: Air travel became commercially available before World
    War II, but subsequent plane developments led to a sizeable drop
    in costs, which allowed for lower fares. Incumbent carriers were
    forced to upgrade their fleets to remain relevant. Travel in the 1950s
    was expensive and highly regulated, which led to the emergence of
    unregulated nonscheduled airlines operating low-cost flights. The
    government eventually closed these companies, which temporarily
    rebalanced the industry, but deregulation in the late 1970s created a
    wave of entrants and then bankruptcies as fares dropped dramati-
    cally thanks to the emergence of new and leaner competitors, most
    notably Southwest. Several of these companies went under in the
    early 1980s, while Pan Am, founded in 1927, struggled through the
    decade, surviving until its bankruptcy in 1991.

    In a 1992 Berkshire Hathaway annual letter, Warren Buffett
offered this: "Investors have regularly poured money into the

domestic airline business to finance profitless (or worse) growth. For these investors, it would have been far better if Orville had failed to get off the ground at Kitty Hawk: The more the industry has grown, the worse the disaster for owners."

4. Dot.Com Mania—Discussed at length in part 2, it became apparent in the mid-1990s that the internet was a disruptive force to be reckoned with. Selecting winners in the private or public markets would have proven to be hugely accretive over twenty years. Two problems emerged. First, valuations were rich for companies with little revenues (one hundred times revenues were common). Second, identifying the winners proved challenging, as few could have selected Amazon or Google as the eventual winners of the dot.com craze. Most of these companies went bankrupt by the early 2000s.

5. Fiber Optics Companies—Fiber optics became a replacement for coaxial cable in the 1990s, and companies came along to massively expand fiber capacity in preparation for the dot.com boom. More fiber was laid in 2000, the peak of the dot.com mania, than in any year through at least 2015. So much fiber was laid that in 2003 only 3 percent of fiber was lit. This low-capacity utilization led to a $2 trillion market cap reduction in telecom firms between 2000 and 2002, and much of the $1 trillion lent to the industry became uncollectable. Although fiber super-highways helped the proliferation of the internet and eventual survivors, including Netflix, three issues stifled the economics of fiber in the 1990s. First, evolving technological standards allowed greater bandwidth to be squeezed out of existing pipes leading to large, unexpected increases in capacity. Second, the last-mile issue had not been adequately solved. This slowed adoption of high-bandwidth services. Third, the mass of capital committed to fiber build-outs assumed high prices and utilization rates to justify investment with little regard to the competitive forces that drove down prices and overwhelmed returns.

6. Marijuana Companies—California became the first state to legalize marijuana for medicinal use in 1996. Colorado and Washington legalized recreational use in 2012, with a wave of activity leading to full legalization in eleven states and medicinal use in thirty-three states as of 2021. Canada became the first G–20 country to legalize marijuana in 2018, and more are likely to follow. This wave of legalization has created a wave of investment opportunities in both private and public markets. At least a dozen public companies have

emerged in the United States and Canada, with Canopy Growth being an early entrant and one of the largest. Its $10 billion market cap in 2021 suggested more than twenty times sales, and it is not forecast to generate positive earnings before interest, taxes, depreciation, and amortization until 2023. The current boom has been aided by intermittent COVID stay-at-home orders throughout 2020. The industry likely will face a day of reckoning as more capital floods into what is perceived as a historic opportunity.

7. Chinese Rental Bike Companies—Lyft and Bird created a massive inventory of scooters in public spaces during 2017 and 2018. In China, many entrants targeted the rental bike market that utilized manual pedal power. This trend linked the past traditions of pre-urbanized living to the growing awareness of environmental benefits. Adoption skyrocketed and many privately funded firms entered cities across China beginning around 2010. Available bikes overwhelmed natural demand in many cities, and some local governments deposited unused bikes into bike graveyards to clean out their streets' clutter. Capital destruction is ongoing but will culminate in billions of dollars of lost capital.

History rhymes. We could have listed dozens more cases, each with a fascinating anecdote of human judgment gone awry. Most readers will be familiar with Tulipomania, the South Seas bubble, the Japanese 1980s real estate market, the Roaring Twenties, the U.S. conglomerate craze in the 1960s, repeated booms and busts in Argentina, and the Asian crisis during which Hong Kong real estate prices fell 50 percent from 1997 to 2003 before beginning an epic boom that was only recently interrupted in 2021.

Each micro situation begins with a rational thought. Quite often, the thought revolves around a disruptive technology, or a market with competitive advantages gaining share, or industries poised to outperform over the medium run. Early investors reap spectacular returns, drawing in additional waves of investors. Price discipline fades as the allure of short-term gains outweighs rational thought, and a bubble begins to form. Growth investing is intertwined and expectations skyrocket. The key for investors is always to link fundamentals with price. Remain valuation sensitive to protect yourself from allocating capital near the late stages of a boom cycle.

Bruce Greenwald, the long-tenured, recently retired, head of the value investing program at Columbia Business School, once asserted: "Wrong.

It's barriers to entry!" Most of these booms and busts share one key characteristic, low barriers to entry. Growth is valuable only if a company so exposed is able to protect, or ideally expand, its market share while retaining its profitability. All too often, new entrants, flush with capital, drive down prices to irrational levels. Consumers are the beneficiaries; investors are the losers. Identify growth that offers some form of protection, a moat. Greenwald called this the only one of Michael Porter's Five Forces worth paying attention to. Each of the previous high-growth industry examples can be defined by low barriers to entry. Airlines had limitless expansion possibilities, as did railroads in the 1800s. High capital requirement does not provide protection because capital gravitates to perceived opportunity. R&D may or may not protect against entry, and the same is true of scale and other powerful economic forces.

High industry growth + low barriers to entry = impending disaster

The shape of any future bubble will vary. Timeframes from inception to peak differ, as do the magnitude of capital, which is eventually destroyed. Simplistically, three variables will determine the shape of any bubble:

1. Structural Growth Rates—High above-market growth rates are a necessary component of bubble formation. This is the link with growth investing, as bubbles will not form if the expected growth rates are low. Higher growth expectations lead to (1) a larger runway of rational investment opportunities, although that may be dwarfed by (2) a greater influx of investor capital.
2. Market Size Once Fully Saturated—The Japanese real estate boom began earnestly in the 1970s as Japan Inc. captured the market share globally with its lower costs and improved product quality. Increasingly, capital earned from successful businesses was reallocated into real estate both within and outside of Japan. The 1980s saw Japanese capital purchase prime assets in New York City, Hawaii, and Tokyo (of course). Even Pebble Beach Golf Resort in Carmel, California, became Japanese owned. Prices decoupled from fundamentals most extremely within Japan, where cap rates dropped nearly to zero. The impact abroad was limited, but property valuations in Japan became unhinged from fundamentals, leading to one of the world's greatest bubbles and subsequent collapses. The larger the market is, the more painful the bubble's pop.

3. Extent of Barriers to Entry—The dot-com bubble was perhaps the most extreme example of a zero barrier to entry market coupled with high growth expectations. Create a domain name, any online market, and a bit of favorable press. The result was a massive valuation. Cryptocurrencies possess similarly nonexistent barriers to entry. Many poorer cousins of Bitcoin sprung up after Bitcoin's success. Dogecoin, created as a joke currency in 2013 after the famous Doge meme, spiked temporarily to a $100 million valuation before crashing 80 percent in one day. Bitcoin's algorithm limits the number of future Bitcoins to be issued, but the industry barrier to adding new crypto currencies is zero. The lower the barrier to entry is, the more extreme any bubble peak and subsequent capital impairment likely will be.

According to Buffett, "Growth is always a component in the calculation of value. Growth hurts low return business requiring incremental funds. Value investing is redundant since investing should always seek value" (Berkshire Hathaway annual letter, 1992).

Conclusion

Investors often confuse high-revenue-growth companies with good growth investments. Growth is valuable to investors only if returns generated on that growth exceed a company's cost of capital. Another characteristic shared by the unsuccessful historical case studies is the reliance on low-return growth. Low barriers to entry inevitably lead to low returns. If incremental returns seem to be declining instead of improving, pass.

One favorable mental model to consider is the Amazon model. With high fixed costs, a market leader growing into its fixed cost will experience losses until those fixed costs are fully covered. Amazon's fixed costs grew slowly in the late 1990s and early 2000s, while revenues grew quickly, overtaking fixed costs in 2002. Free cash flow ballooned subsequently. It is plausible that Tesla reached that point in 2020 or 2021, at which time incremental investments and recurring fixed costs became more than fully funded by expanding revenues. These are powerful inflection points often propelling earnings and free cash flows well beyond expectations. Never short companies as they reach this inflection point. Quite often, these are excellent times to invest.

Growth is an investor's friend. Seek it out, appreciate its compounding attributes, and make it an integral part of a long-term investment strategy. The risks inherent in growth investing can be overcome with a prudent emphasis on valuation and underlying fundamentals. Finally, never forget to objectively evaluate industry- and company-specific barriers to entry. Find a company with high and improving barriers, even if at a premium price, and enjoy the benefit of long-term compounding of capital.

21

Core Characteristics of Successful Investors

A lot of people with high IQ's are terrible investors because they've got terrible temperaments. And that is why we say that having a certain kind of temperament is more important than brains. You need to keep raw irrational emotion under control. You need patience and discipline and an ability to take losses and adversity without going crazy.

—CHARLIE MUNGER, KIPLINGER INTERVIEW, 2005

Only nongeniuses claim that brain power above a certain threshold is wasted. This is a fair point. Mental horsepower always should lead to quicker, better outcomes, yet it does not work that way in real life. Our roadways limit the benefits of higher horsepower. Ferraris don't get to work faster. Traffic signals, other cars, speed limits, and turns impede progress. Although intellectual horsepower does not possess physical constraints, mental constraints abound. Barriers to full intellectual utilization are many, but some of the more prominent barriers are worth highlighting:

1. Decision Paralysis—High-horsepower investors question every-thing. They are curious and seek to optimize scenarios. Data defi-ciencies are pervasive in investing, and complete information does not exist. Judgments have to be made as to when enough data is sufficient for decision-making. It is not unusual for high achievers to freeze rather than act, as they seek additional layers of informa-tion to satisfy their need for optimization.

2. Effort-to-Outcome Ratio—High natural achievers succeed easily at earlier ages, creating a weaker linkage between effort and outcomes. Struggle, failure, and frustration are integral to development of internal optimizers. Even the best investors fail occasionally. Experiencing failure earlier in life prepares investors to better manage the aftermath and navigate through tough, unpredictable terrain with their emotions unaffected.

3. Overconfidence—The investments industry has drawn top talent for a generation because of intellectually stimulating work and high income potential. Top talent is used to arguing their way to success, and success breeds overconfidence. Overconfidence, in return, is a primary handicap to successful investors. They are more likely to ignore opposing data, listen less, speak more, act rashly, take bigger bets, and turn the portfolio more often.

Approaches to Successful Investing

It would be rather strange if—with all the brains at work professionally in the stock market—there could be approaches which are both sound and relatively unpopular. Yet our own career and reputation have been based on this unlikely fact.
—BENJAMIN GRAHAM, *THE INTELLIGENT INVESTOR*, 1973, CHAP. 15

Successful investing requires basic math skills, an understanding of probabilities, and an elementary understanding of accounting and finance. A core understanding of leadership and business strategy is necessary, maybe even a fascination with case studies and history. Anyone can learn these skills, and an MBA or a finance degree makes little difference to long-term performance. Although technical skills are unlikely to be differentiators, a handful of characteristics stand out. These skills may be innate but can be intentionally refined over time. Anyone can learn these skills, or at the least develop internal processes to ensure their utilization.

1. Be contrarian—Be willing to look at areas overlooked by the rest of the market. Being contrarian is not enough on its own. Quite often, investment selections appear that are accompanied by accolades and not antagonism. Google is a classic example. It was universally seen as a share gainer with its edge in search—yet its prospects remained underappreciated by the market for many years,

and possibly even still today. Being contrarian will uncover many excellent investment opportunities, but this is a little bit like being a rebel. A rebel with a cause is a visionary, but a rebel without a cause is merely destructive.

2. Exhibit curiosity—Why have Coke and Pepsi been such a successful duopoly for a century? How does that duopoly differ from Boeing versus Airbus? Why do national champion airlines routinely go bankrupt? Did labor unions contribute to the U.S. auto industry struggles? Relevant questions abound for any investment candidate, and successful investors will learn what questions to ask and where to find data that may help.

3. Study history—The history of Calvinism is interesting but not precisely relevant. Be a student of the past. It will broaden your range of expectations and accelerate your learning curve. Study various aspects of the past to complement knowledge that you acquire directly.

- Macro history—An in-depth read about the Great Depression, German hyperinflation in the 1920s, or Greece's repeated insolvencies over the past two hundred years and perusal of more recent cyclical forecasts gone awry will make you appreciate the frailty of a seemingly stable economic environment. How unique are negative interest rates? Only those conversant with financial history will fully appreciate this extreme, and they will be more readily equipped to activate their system 2 analytical efforts to better understand its consequences.

- Company history—Most investors believe the history of Coca-Cola is irrelevant to today's investment decisions. Nothing could be further from the truth because the seeds of their competitive advantage were sown in the distant past. Management decision-making varies widely, and assessing management competence is easier when well versed with historical examples.

- Latticeworks—Consider Munger's famous perspective that masses of seemingly disconnected information come together in a lattice. Rungs of wisdom apply broadly in unexpected cross-sections. Study fundamental science to learn about clean tech, and the link is logical. Study oceanography, and you just might find a link to investments in chemical concerns or hospitality companies. The future is deeply interconnected and influenced by many systems. Study the primary points of major systems to better understand interconnections.

260 REASONS TO BUY

4. Focus on broad versus deep—This is the perennial debate of institutional investors. Broad-based generalists believe in the 80/20 rule, uncover 80 percent of necessary information that is material to an investment decision and move on. Conversely, industry analysts believe that the 20 percent uncovered by specialists is where true alpha resides. Baidu, China's search engine, and the 80 percenters focus incessantly here, whereas the 20 percenters target Baidu's call options—their investments in autonomous technology, for example. Remain flexible, as either approach may be needed at times.

5. Have patience—Investment opportunities rarely appear overnight and disappear six months later. Many opportunities can take years to materialize and then can take years to converge to intrinsic value. Imagine the challenges faced by the new CEO of Wells Fargo as he attempted to right a culture in which poor sales incentives drove bad behavior. Incentives always have secondary impacts. Hiring practices drew in people who gravitated to those sales practices. Systems were set up to optimize incentives. Managers trained to make ethical concessions were promoted. A new CEO's first job is to correct sales practices, but secondary effects will linger for years until cultures are retooled from the ground up. Current investors in Wells Fargo require patience to see these changes through.

6. Be disciplined—Many people have attempted to translate success in their area of competence into investment success elsewhere: doctors trading options, lawyers in venture capital, equity investors in real estate, professional athletes starting restaurants. Confidence runs high with overachievers, which easily translates into an "I can do anything" attitude. Don't be afraid to expand your circle of competence, but have the discipline to know when to say no.

7. Embrace well-timed greed—Herding produces a powerful temptation to back off when others are fearful. Sentiment is contagious for us social beings. It is an obvious truth that prices decline when capital withdraws. Fear induces capital flight, triggering fewer bids and more asks with less price sensitivity. Find assets whose earnings power you can have confidence in five and ten years out and begin to provide bids at advantageous prices. Lower price provides an improved margin of safety, while also increasing your future upside. Fighting the temptation to herd produces better investment results with less risk.

Warren Buffett explained: "Imagine the cost to us, then, if we had let a fear of unknowns cause us to defer or alter the deployment of capital. Indeed, we have usually made our best purchases when apprehensions about some macro event were at a peak. Fear is the foe of the faddist, but the friend of the fundamentalist" (Berkshire Hathaway annual letter, 1994).

8. Have humility—Humility provides the inspiration behind *Reasons to Pass*. Some of us are born humble. We said, "I don't know" liberally in class and lost debates when acknowledging that the other side made excellent points. Professionally, we were seen as less persuasive or less passionate, even less confident in our judgments, demonstrating less conviction. Humility is not a trait rewarded in U.S. society and yet it is perhaps the most highly valuable trait an investor can possess.

The world is an incredibly complex system, and the data required to gain a full understanding is nonexistent. Much of investing is little more than guesswork. Predicting the future with all of its moving parts is nearly impossible for even the brightest and most studied. Encourage your children to acknowledge their ignorance. If possible, lead by example. They will grow up to astutely acknowledge complex systems incapable of analysis.

Once you embrace humility, investing becomes easier. A full day's work may include twenty "I don't know" answers. Saying "I don't know" is easy. It's stress free and really enjoyable. Try this exercise for one day: Read the *Wall Street Journal, Financial Times,* and *Barron's,* and sift through *Seeking Alpha.* Dozens of opinions will emerge—about countries, industries, companies, a political issue, whatever. How many times can you say, "I don't know" after reading the article and incorporating everything you know into the analysis? This likely will be your answer most often because a high-conviction answer eludes you. It's less likely an article will prompt inquiry. The answer may be unknown but can be sought out through a manageable effort. Finally, identify the one or two articles that sit solidly within your area of competence where you feel confident of having an edge in the debate. Put these articles in another pile. This is investing, day after day. It is that simple.

Behavioral Conclusions

We shall say quite a bit about the psychology of investors. For indeed, the investor's chief problem—and even his worst enemy—is likely to be himself.

—BENJAMIN GRAHAM, *THE INTELLIGENT INVESTOR*, 1973, PREFACE

Behavior drives decision-making, which collectively guides the investment markets. Market inefficiencies exist only because behavioral biases distort our investment decision-making process. Strive to understand your behavioral limitations as a partial inoculation against irrationality. Even small improvements over your status quo will favorably alter your investment returns. Graham wrote about behavioral pitfalls well before academics entered the fray and decades before the Nobel committee began to recognize behavioral economists as prize worthy.

Munger gave a speech at Harvard University in 1995 titled "The Psychology of Human Misjudgment." Behavioral errors are universal across time, rooted in evolutionary logic but outmoded in modern-day society. It seems only fitting to end this chapter with highlights from that speech. Keep these traits in mind when investing, and more broadly, in all your professional dealings. They will serve you well.

"The Psychology of Human Misjudgment"

The following excerpts are from Charlie Munger's 1995 speech at Harvard University.

Herding

"Now this is a lollapalooza, and Henry Kaufman wisely talked about this, bias from over-influence by social proof, that is, the conclusions of others, particularly under conditions of natural uncertainty and stress. And here, one of the cases the psychologists use is Kitty Genovese, where all these people, I don't know, 50, 60, 70 of them just sort of sat and did nothing while she was slowly murdered. Now one of the explanations is that everybody looked at everybody else and nobody else was doing anything, and so there's automatic social proof that the right thing to do is nothing."

Baby Steps to Bad Decisions

"I have this worthless friend I like to Bridge with, and he's a total intellectual amateur that lives on inherited money. But he told me once something I really enjoyed hearing. He said, 'Charlie,' he says, 'If you throw a frog into very hot water, the frog will jump out. But if you put the frog in room temperature water and just slowly heat the water up, the frog will die there.' Now I don't know whether that's true about a frog, but it's sure as hell true about many of the businessmen I know."

Envy

"I've heard Warren say a half a dozen times, 'It's not greed that drives the world but envy.' Here again, you go through the psychology survey courses. You go to the index: envy, jealousy. Thousand page book, it's blank! There's some blind spots in academia. But it's an enormously powerful thing, and it operates to a considerable extent at a subconscious level, and anybody who doesn't understand it is taking on defects he shouldn't have."

Probability Assessment

"Bias from the non-mathematical nature of the human brain in its natural state as it deals with probabilities employing crude heuristics and is often mislead by mere contrast. The tendency to overweigh conveniently available information and other psychological rooted mis-thinking tendencies on this list when the brain should be using the simple probability mathematics of Fermat and Pascal, applied to all reasonably attainable and correctly weighted items of information that are of value in predicting outcomes."

Stress-Induced Decision-Making

"Stress-induced mental changes. Here, my favorite example is the great Pavlov. He had all these dogs in cages, which had all been conditioned into changed behaviors, and the great Leningrad flood came, and it just went right up. The dog's in a cage, and the dog had as much stress as you can imagine a dog ever having. The water receded in time to save some of the dogs, and Pavlov noted that they'd had a total reversal of their conditioned personality."

Humility

"The use of post-mortems at Johnson & Johnson. At most corporations, if you make an acquisition and it works out to be a disaster, all the paperwork and presentations that caused the dumb acquisition to be made are quickly forgotten. You've got denial, you've got everything in the world. You've got Pavlovian association tendency. Nobody even wants to even be associated with the damned thing, or even mention it. At Johnson & Johnson, they make everybody revisit their old acquisitions and wade through the presentations. That is a very smart thing to do. By the way, I do the same thing routinely."

22

Viable, and Buyable, Investment Opportunities

Part of our secret is that we don't attempt to know a lot of things. We have a pile at my desk that solves most of my problems. It's called the too hard pile and I just keep shifting things to the too hard pile. Every once in a while an easy decision comes along and I make it. That's my system. Everything is in the too hard pile except for a few easy decisions which I make promptly.

—CHARLIE MUNGER, DAILY JOURNAL
ANNUAL MEETING, 2019

Reasons to Pass focuses heavily on areas of investments to avoid. If you protect capital, you will live to invest another day. Passing on most investment candidates is critical. Only a small number of ideas should pass your screens and analysis, and only these will warrant serious consideration. The good news is that some investment candidates will exist in any market environment, and investors should be open-minded to these opportunities. Following are some possible hunting grounds to explore as you search for accretive opportunities:

1. Chapter 14 Companies—One of the most influential chapters of Benjamin Graham's *The Intelligent Investor*, chapter 14 recommends the purchase of high-quality companies at a reasonable price. This text is an absolute gem; it is simple and easy to understand, with an overriding message: Buy shares in good companies whose results have remained relatively steady, whose balance sheets are defensive,

and whose results have grown cycle over cycle, at reasonable valu-ations. These companies are likely to possess moats around their businesses and have the necessary scale to compete. Bargain-basement prices are unlikely, but intrinsic value should compound over time. This allows for long, tax-efficient holding periods and intrinsic compounding with less than market risk. Read, or reread, chapter 14. Focus on the principles rather than on the formulas. As in most things timeless, the principles endure.

2. Deep Cyclicals Away from Peak—Look to buy deep cyclicals when not near peak macroeconomic conditions, and ideally, near the trough of the cycle. The majority of industries globally are linked to the economic cycle and correlation varies. Even utilities, the ultimate safe haven, see muted revenue growth during downturns as electricity, water, and gas usage slows. Cyclicals can make great long-term investments as their earnings power compounds cycle over cycle. Some cyclicals have strong moats around their busi-nesses. Siemens, for example, has a long history of earnings growth with its research and development (R&D) portfolio and brand and distribution advantages that continue to provide it with competi-tive advantages. Its earnings may decline during cycle troughs, at which point the stock price declines as investors flee the uncer-tainty of shorter-term earnings results. This is often an excellent buying opportunity.

Siemens is in the cyclical camp, but it is not a deep cyclical. Deep cyclicals are near the tail end of an earnings linkage with the eco-nomic cycle. Few people buy houses or cars during periods of eco-nomic uncertainty, whereas purchases are heavily concentrated in stronger economic times. U.S. auto sales declined during the 2008 Great Financial Crisis (GFC) by almost 50 percent from a peak of 17 million units per year in the United States to less than 10 mil-lion two years later. Some industries work in similar cycles, invest-ing heavily in capex when perceived economic visibility is high. Partly linked to confidence, partly to current cash flow, and partly to recency bias, both units and pricing power expand during peak environments. Capacity utilization is above average. Auto compa-nies, for example, will run their plants two or even three shifts per day to keep up with high demand. Margins expand while revenues grow above trend, producing peak earnings. These are dangerous times for investors who are considering deep cyclicals. It is difficult to pinpoint the shape of the cycle, although peak conditions are more readily evident. Avoid peaks and seek out troughs. Even economic environments between the peaks and troughs are likely to provide some opportunities. In the neighborhood of midcycle, some high-quality names will generate good returns and cash flows and strengthen balance sheets, with rising dividend payouts, all at reasonable valuations.

Credit investors focused on corporate bonds can target similar opportunities. Corporate bonds can be excellent investments as a component of portfolios. Yields normally will exceed government available yields with varying durations up to five years or more. Credit spreads over government yields will prove interesting when market spreads are around long-term average levels or higher. Credit quality for deep cyclicals can turn overnight as the cycle turns down, leaving what appeared to be prudent investments trading at par into deeply discounted credits. Junk bond spreads were incredibly tight heading into 2007, widening to 20 percent over treasuries by the end of 2008, creating huge losses for investors and enormous opportunities for astute investors. Spreads at year-end 2021 are incredibly tight, making corporate bond investments less attractive. Identifying the precise shape of the cycle is challenging, but identifying peaks is much easier and will help protect the portfolio from permanent impairment of capital.

Selecting survivors in the cyclical or deep cyclical camp around troughs is particularly important. The shape of a market cycle is uncertain, and troughs can last longer than you might expect. Balance sheet strength is important to successfully navigate through an extended cycle, as is overall business quality. Stick with high-quality cyclicals. The upside will still be significant, and the structural downside will be limited.

To this point, the emphasis has been on buying deep cyclical stocks away from the peak, either around midcycle or ideally in a trough. One other protection available to patient investors is to sit on the sidelines while a trough materializes. Deep cyclical stock prices will be down substantially, and low prices will prove tempting. Resist the urge to invest as the cycle declines. Eventually, the green shoots of a nascent recovery will take hold. Stock prices will react favorably, but most investors still anchoring off the stock price lows will resist the urge to invest unless stocks fall again toward their absolute lows. This point in the cycle may provide most of the upside with less downside risk. Catching a falling knife can feel rewarding, but no one can know how far it will fall.

3. Longer-Term Underperformers—Quite a bit of work has been done on whether stock price movements are indicative of future performance. Stock price data are easy to gather, and it is no surprise that academics and practitioners are drawn to analyzing trends. Shockingly, some Wall Street firms continue to employ technicians and chartists, whose job it is to predict entry and exit of stocks. A true fundamentalist should be agnostic to historical price movements, judging investment merits based on underlying fundamentals. Perhaps these investors believe in the weak form of the efficient market hypothesis?

Interestingly, solid research indicates that long-term underperformers, those whose stock prices have underperformed the market or their industries over the previous three to five years, are statistically likely to outperform over the following three to five years. Stock prices decline because of disappointing results. This chases away a broad swath of investors who focus specifically on growth or on higher-quality businesses. Management begins to restructure the business, only to be thwarted by the complexity of large-scale structural transitions. Legacy culture remains engrained longer than expected, and employee reconfiguration proves challenging. It is hard to lay off excess capacity, and even harder to fire employees who pollute a culture. Tenured employees often prove reluctant to structurally change their workflow or responsibilities, and they resist the adoption of new performance metrics or other measurements intended to make better decisions. Systemic resistance to change requires years to overcome, and the more complex an enterprise is, the greater the effort and time required for change. Labor unions may contribute to restructuring paralysis by inhibiting broad-based change.

No matter who's responsible, changing course is a key but difficult undertaking, as Munger explains: "How much can be achieved if the culture is right. In bigger and more complicated places like GM or AT&T it's difficult. One norm in culture is big businesses get very bureaucratic, and you see this in government too. I don't like bureaucracy. It creates a lot of error. I don't know how to fix bureaucracy in a big place. . . . There is no solution for corporate culture at monstrous places" (Daily Journal annual meeting, 2018).

Why undertake these painful restructurings in the first place? Management incentives and owner dissatisfaction are powerful forces, guideposts directing struggling institutions toward recovery. True restructuring efforts often begin in years two or three after disappointing results signal a warning, and management efforts take one to three years to begin to bear fruit. In the interim, many investors will have lost interest, making company valuations unusually attractive.

Warren Buffett cautioned: "We react with great caution to suggestions that our poor businesses can be restored to satisfactory profitability by major capital expenditures. (The projections will be dazzling—the advocates will be sincere—but, in the end, major additional investment in a terrible industry usually is about as rewarding as struggling in quicksand)" (Berkshire Hathaway annual letter, 1983).

Not every struggling enterprise makes an attractive investment, and statistically the majority do not. Companies with weak franchise quality are most likely to become engulfed in extended weakness, and some never recover their former glory because competitive forces left them behind. The challenge for investors is to differentiate weak franchises permanently impaired from those that possess excellent odds of recovery, with the necessary financial resources available to get there. Fundamentally oriented investors relish this challenge, and although many variables will influence your conclusion, certain questions can shed light on a company's turnaround prospects. Answer no to the following questions and quickly pass:

- Would the economic landscape miss this company if it disappeared tomorrow?
- Does the company have intellectual property that possesses value?
- Does the company have distribution advantages that possess value?
- Are there other barriers to entry that protect new entrants from easily displacing the underlying business?
- Are there switching costs that protect revenue streams over the medium run?
- Is the industry a likely survivor over the next twenty years?
- Can a high cost structure be turned around to become industry competitive?

4. Blood in the Streets—Baron Rothchild said, "the time to buy is when there is blood in the streets." The Rothschilds were enormously successful capital allocators, beginning in eighteenth-century Frankfurt, before the sons branched out to found profitable beachheads in London, Paris, Vienna, and Milan. The most successful investors instinctively gravitate to situations where asset prices disconnect materially from fundamentals. Situations in which short-term prospects are the most uncertain lend themselves best to such dislocations.

Any newsworthy event involving strife, conflict, protests, disruption, and armed clashes could fall within the category of blood on the streets. Government defaults or massive economic dislocation qualify. The COVID crisis qualifies, as did the housing debacle seen in the United States, United Kingdom, Ireland, Greece, and many other countries during the 2008 GFC. These situations, too many to list and ever increasing, lead to highly depressed asset prices. Buying high-quality issues so exposed, with the patience to see them through to normalization, can prove fruitful. Consider the following historical examples:

- The Asian Crisis—The 1997 Asian crisis saw precipitous falls in major indices, including Thailand, Korea, Hong Kong SAR, and Indonesia. Currencies plummeted against the dollar. Leverage was high and mostly in U.S. dollars, and the mismatch caused further struggles.
- Sovereign Defaults—Russia unexpectedly defaulted on its sovereign debt in 1998, causing ripple effects across various asset classes. Movements in spreads even caused Long-Term Credit Management (LTCM), a major hedge fund run by several Nobel Laureates with nearly $1 trillion in notional exposures, to fail. The U.S. Federal Reserve had to provide liquidity to keep the global system stable.
- World War II—Investing in assets during this era worked because the Allied Forces prevailed. Asset selection would have proved critical to protecting downside losses, as victory was not the obvious conclusion until the war's later stages. French industrial assets might have proved worthless to equity investors. Screening on domicile, geographic sales and asset mix, management flexibility, operating flexibility, capital mobility, and franchise quality all would have influenced risk-adjusted returns.

- U.S. inflation in late 1970s—Consensus investments were commodities, with gold hitting a high of $1,500 not seen again until the 2000s. Stocks retreated substantially as the specter of inflation surged, bringing many names, including solid franchises, to five times earnings. Equities turned out to be decent at passing through inflation to customers, making good franchises with pricing power an effective place to protect against the pain of inflation. Ideally, let inflation take a firm hold on an economy before allocating capital, ensuring the added margin of safety better preserves capital. Alternatively, wait for inflation to stabilize and start its reversal. As with many things, patience is a virtue.

Allocating to gold, other commodities, real estate, and other hard assets seemed obvious going into the early 1980s, but investors had no practical idea how high inflation was likely to get before stabilizing. Inflation eventually peaked at 15 percent in 1981, a moment in time from which long-term government bonds and most equities began enormous price recoveries. These situations are tricky. Be contrarian enough to slowly build exposure when uncovering quality assets at large margins of safety, deliberate and patient enough to average in over time, and patient enough to see the cycle through to extreme valuations before selling. The shape of any cycle is uncertain, and the more volatile the situation is, the less predictable the path will be. Buying inflation-proof assets in 1980 at inflated levels offered no actual inflation protection because the cost of the premium was too high, and normalization proved incredibly painful as exposed asset prices collapsed 80 percent or more as inflation declined.

5. Industry Overcapacity—Industry cycles ebb and flow based on capacity utilization. High utilization + high growth expectation = new supply. Beware of the point in the cycle at which large new capacity is emerging as downturns can unexpectedly materialize, leaving new capacity without customers. Leverage is often involved, and nothing drives prices down more quickly than financially leveraged companies that are desperate for any revenues to cover the fixed costs of debt financing.

   Seeking out survivors in the fallout, when capacity utilization is low, is quite often a successful investing strategy. Patience is required. Excess capacity can sit for years before absorption begins.

Fiber optics in 2000 and new home construction in 2003–2007 both saw enormous new supply additions that subsequently disrupted markets, taking years to rebalance. Steel production in 2001 saw the end of an extended deep downturn that culminated with 40 percent of U.S. capacity entering bankruptcy. The auto cycle and loan growth in banking have industry-specific supply-and-demand curves that can provide investment opportunities for those patient enough to wait for below-average utilization levels. One benefit of patience is that it takes time to determine how bad the cycle will get and which companies will remain relatively unscathed. Asset prices often collapse, creating distress for forced sellers and opportunities for astute investors. This process takes time. Do not be in a hurry to allocate capital here. Instead, let things unfold first.

6. Out-of-Index Names—The shift into index funds, exchange-traded funds (ETF), and other passive vehicles is in the process of creating a widening chasm as stocks included in an index find natural support from inflows that have zero price sensitivity. This widens the valuation divide with stocks excluded from indices, creating opportunities for long-term investors who are confident in the fundamentals of those out-of-index names. If or when passive investing falls out of favor, an opposing opportunity may emerge in in-index names.

7. Small-Cap Stocks—The equity business of Wall Street has changed. Fees are lower, regulations are higher, and management access is less exclusive, with limited support from the core investment banking business. The Markets in Financial Instruments Directive (MiFID II) in Europe has forced most asset managers to pay for Wall Street research in house through their own income statements rather than through commissions. This has further reduced fees to investment banks. Given the decline in fees, fewer small-cap names are covered by the sell side, and when they are, the quality of research is generally poor. Analysts just don't get paid to cover names that are thinly traded. This has created new inefficiencies in small-cap markets for opportunistic investors seeking greater return potential.

8. International Stocks—Valuations historically have been lower outside the United States. The U.S. capital markets are the most mature and well-covered globally, and home-country bias has led to enormous sums of capital overallocated to U.S. equity markets. The growth

trajectory historically has been a bit better in the United States as the more flexible economy and business-friendly culture has led to better revenue, profit, and job growth. This may be changing as political winds shift, creating headwinds in the form of higher corporate taxation and tightening regulations that stifle U.S. growth prospects. Growth prospects in the United States likely will decline relative to foreign stocks in upcoming years. The United States has done particularly well by global standards over the past five years, including its recovery post-COVID, and valuation premiums sit near record levels. This likely will balance out over the long run, leading to a convergence in valuations and substantial opportunities for long-term-oriented investors looking outside the United States. Investors always should focus on business quality and valuation, and the next three to five years may see more opportunities outside the United States.

9. Underappreciated Growth Stocks—Consultants and investors irrationally box investment styles into either value or growth. As discussed previously, growth is a component of value and is a core part of a fundamentally oriented investment process. Growth companies come in four distinct flavors, and investors ignore these differences at their peril:

- Inception to early adaptation—Investors in this phase must identify new innovation that will lead to long-lasting changes in consumer behavior and industry growth. Identifying the early participants is paramount, and valuation is purely guesswork as no numbers exist to reasonably bracket long-run earnings power. Questions include what is (a) the adoption rate, (b) pricing power, (c) the cost structure at various points of scale, and (d) the competitive environment? This phase is in the too-hard camp for all but the most specialized investors. Pass.
- Broad-based adaptation—Microeconomics and management acumen will dictate winners and losers. Fundamentally oriented investors with some expertise in the space may well find successful long-term investments, likely at high but well-justified valuation multiples.
- Mass euphoria—This is the most speculative phase growth stocks experience, reaching a crescendo as new capacity and second-tier competitors flood the market seeking to capitalize on what is now

a well-identified industry. Speculation runs rampant, reminiscent
more of a Ponzi scheme than an investment, as returns depend on
higher bidders entering the market. Pass on new investments and
divest existing investments as valuations drift beyond rational levels.

- Rotation away from growth investment—Growth forges its own
  anchor. Growth rates slow, disenchanted growth investors real-
  locate capital to higher growth prospects, leaving some durable
  franchises temporarily neglected. This is equivalent to forced selling, often with little price sensitivity or regard to valuation. This
  rotational process takes time—possibly several years, so patience
  is required. The difference between temporarily stalled growth
  and structurally declining growth rates is difficult to ascertain.
  Thorough analysis is required to understand the difference and
  to understand the company's true franchise value, including its
  moat, competitive advantages, and areas of differentiation. Microeconomics is once again heavily at play, and fundamentally oriented investors will find excellent investment candidates among
  those that are the prematurely discarded. Many situations will
  prove too tough to call. Should analysis not yield clear results,
  then pass. When an occasional unfairly discarded equity is uncovered, then buy.

Warren Buffett cautioned: "In a finite world, high growth rates
must self-destruct. . . . A high growth rate eventually forges its own
anchor. . . . Carl Sagan quote: 'bacteria reproduces by dividing into
two every 15 minutes. That means four doublings an hour, and
96 doublings a day. Although bacterium weighs only about a tril-
lionth of a gram, its descendants, after a day of wild asexual aban-
don, will collectively weigh as much as a mountain . . . in two days,
more than the sun—and before very long, everything in the universe
will be made of bacteria'" (Berkshire Hathaway annual letter, 1989).

10. Baskets of Similarly Exposed Names—Individually speculative
    names have no place in a concentrated portfolio. The risk of per-
    manent impairment is too high. Occasionally, one can find an
    opportunity in an industry or possibly a country where unique
    characteristics tingle the senses of fundamental investors, setting
    the stage for a viable investment through the construction of a bas-
    ket of similarly exposed names in smaller individual allocations to
    diversify the risks.

- Large price declines—Declines of 50 percent or more at a minimum for the basket, so-called falling knives, can make excellent investments if bought judiciously in a diversified fashion.
- In a critical subsector—An area of interest should be durable, that is, it cannot disappear because of its essential nature.
- That is highly correlated—Industry peers face similar threats and are exposed to the same negative factors. Stock prices move similarly because of these similar exposures, although company-specific nuances exist.
- Where selecting the winners is difficult—Losers and winners are identified by level of financial leverage, continued access to capital, cost position, management deft, customer loyalty, technology, and, to some degree, luck.
- And estimating the amount of economic carnage is futile—The shape of the cycle will be too tough to call. How long is Korea or Indonesia distressed following its 1997 collapse? When will oil prices recover from the spring of 2020? Nobody knew the answer to these questions, and a viable basket situation will leave you similarly perplexed with a large range of upside and downside scenarios. Many competitors may face financial distress or enter insolvency. The duration of the trough could span years.
- But to the winner go the next cycle's spoils—The deeper the trough is, the greater the next cycle's uplift will be. Ten-times-type returns are reasonable for the most successful names in a recovery scenario. An 80 percent decline amounts to a five times return just to break even, and an additional upside comes from successful names regaining credibility, expanding their market share and stabilization and eventual expansion of the overall market.
- Most important, patience is required—There is no need to pounce on a group of names immediately after they have collapsed in price. The washout takes time and will eliminate the first group of competitors, the weakest whose businesses were unlikely to survive in the long run. Sit patiently and watch the crisis unfold. As a downturn evolves, companies will begin to differentiate, with some accessing capital at reasonable prices and some more distressed. Customers may begin to flee perceived weaker competitors, and restructurings lower both the cost structures and industry capacity. Stronger competitors may begin engaging in mergers and acquisitions, taking out weaker competitors at low prices. The process could take months or

years depending on the industry and state of distress. Establishing a basket at a certain point of stabilization can accrue a massive upside. Patience is required from entry to exit. Expect to wait three to ten years for a full-fledged recovery.

Many examples illustrate what would have been successful baskets. Internet names at the end of 2002 were down 80 percent, but these names mostly dominated the list of technology outperformers over the next five and ten years. Auto parts companies, most of which were highly levered, declined similarly in the 2008 GFC. Japanese regional banks suffered greatly as Japanese interest rates went negative, trading as low as 20 percent of book value for some dominant local franchises. Greek equities in 2012, UK residential builder–exposed names in 2008, Hong Kong conglomerates in 1997 and again in 2004, junk bonds at year-end 2008, COVID-exposed travel names in the spring of 2020, and Brazilian companies after the currency devalued in 1997 are all examples of target areas that were completely blown out with massive upside potential once the cycle reverted.

The basket should be selective but inclusive. Stick with the better capitalized names and stronger competitors, although it may make sense to give small weights to weaker competitors with the greatest upside. Select names with plenty of liquidity, including those whose debt is well termed out and that have access to additional sources of liquidity and limited covenants. This creates a multiyear call option at a highly reduced price. Valuation must be highly compelling— the riskier the basket is, the higher the required return. Generally, return potential of five to ten times should be required to justify the hassle and risks. The hassle factor should not be ignored. These names will generate above-average material news flow, requiring a substantial commitment of time.

Build a basket of these names, more or less equally weighted, capped at 5 percent or a bit more when highly compelling opportunities abound. Individual position size will vary, but selecting five names at 1 percent, some stronger, some weaker, will spread risk while offering a substantial portfolio upside.

11. Gold as a Basket—Gold is a highly controversial asset class. It mostly is uncorrelated to equities but is not obviously anchored to underlying fundamentals. Gold is only marginally an industrial

276 REASONS TO BUY

metal. It is bought for speculation. The link with historical monetary systems is obvious, and the limited and predictable volume growth per year makes supply additions more stable than central bank monetary expansion over time since currencies decoupled from gold reserves.

Regardless of recent historical precedence, monetary expansion inevitably leads to devaluation. Currencies weaken in isolation when supply discipline is introduced. Foreign exchange (FX) is relative, so any country that manages its currency better than another currency should see strengthening over time. Because no country in recent history desires to be the world's strongest currency, relative devaluations lead to a slippery slope of new FX supply to keep their currency weak or at least "in line" with other currencies. Central bank asset purchases and monetary easing equal currency debasement. Given increasing pressures on central banks to conform to "modern monetary theory," continued currency debasement is more likely than in past cycles.

The strong macroeconomic environment in 2017–2019 was an ideal time for central banks to enact discipline with both higher interest rates and shrinking balance sheets. Neither appeared in substance. The Great Depression in the 1930s taught economists the lesson that Keynesian stimulus drove an eventual recovery. This lesson was reinforced in the 2008 GFC. Reticence to withdraw stimulus is natural, but the unintended consequences of low rates grow over time. Witness the record global leverage through 2019 even before COVID took hold. Trillions of dollars of new sovereign debt appeared shortly thereafter as rates again plummeted to zero, while asset purchases by central banks skyrocketed. Many central bankers and economists point squarely to 2008 as proof that not enough stimulus was done then with fiscal and monetary policy. Politicians now gleefully adopt this message. The formula of spend = votes has been solidified.

The system has become levered to the point at which only slightly higher interest rates may catalyze distress among companies and governments, triggering higher defaults, forced cutbacks, monetary suppression, and job losses. Central banks are already doing their part to suppress rates—rates were near or below zero in large parts of the world at year-end 2021. Rate suppression keeps the real rate negative, hurting savers and "hopefully" slowly bailing the world out from its debt burden. Inflation above suppressed interest rates raises nominal gross domestic product (GDP), while devaluing sovereign debt and slowly reducing sovereign debt to GDP. This worked in Germany in the 1920s, but with painful consequences for the population at large. Bankers today believe they can effectively navigate this path. It would be a first in financial history, and time will tell.

Increasing risk aversion is tied to the strengthening of gold and gold stocks. It is one of the world's best fear indicators. Macro uncertainty and economic downturns drive interest rates lower, which lowers real interest rates often to negative levels. *Aside from the fear factor, negative real interest rates are perhaps most correlated to a rising gold price. This fear indicator makes gold a unique and desirable asset class to protect against downturns.*

Gold exposure can be obtained through ETFs exposed to physical gold. The upside potential is limited to the underlying rise in gold prices, though so is the downside. Leveraged ETFs do not adequately track metal prices over the long run. One small tip: Never buy leveraged ETFs. Some hedge fund managers continuously short leveraged ETFs because of their directional downward tendency. Gold stocks have been severely punished since gold peaked in 2011, and many were down 80 percent or more through the beginning of 2020 trading near their net asset values (NAVs) using a gold price of $1,200. NAVs are sensitive to movements in the gold price, with many firms' estimated NAVs up 20 percent or more with a $100 move in the metal. This implies an upward move of roughly 100 percent as the gold price moved to $1,700, highlighting the leveraged nature of investing in gold stocks relative to the underlying metal.

The rise in the gold price through the COVID crisis was not unexpected, and gold equities responded mostly as predicted but with a lag as early innings of the crisis led to highly correlated, broad-based selling. Many gold mining companies, large and small, roughly doubled over the course of 2020. Equally predictably, news of a COVID vaccine began a partial unwind of the gold trade as fear dissipated. Only a partial unwind is likely because long-term damage has been done through added governmental leverage around the globe, and central bank interest rate suppression likely will last years. The extended zero-rate environment and continued massive fiscal stimulus further ensure a bid for gold at some level above its historical level.

Gold is one of a handful of insurance policies accessible to retail investors. A 1 percent to 5 percent allocation is a reasonable range for a basket of gold stocks depending on the current state of valuation, sentiment, and governmental policy. The cheaper the cost of insurance, as indicated by the price of gold, the greater the warranted allocation to a gold basket. Cheap options are ideal. Gold companies can become impaired, particularly those with high cost structures and levered balance sheets, so investors should avoid high-cost producers and those with too much leverage. Plenty of investible names should be available under most conditions that combine decent cost positions, moderate leverage, good production, and reserve profiles, without taking undue political or corporate governance risk.

Low gold prices eventually reduce exploration and development budgets and lead to mine curtailments. This supply decline, a microeconomic impact, propagates increasing stability of the forward-looking gold price, making it an even better hedge against monetary expansion. Some investors buy only the metal itself, likely because gold-mining stock volatility is so high and gold producers are subject to risks, including punitive taxation, labor strikes, mine impairments, and other governmental interference. This is a perfectly reasonable approach, although gold equities offer a leveraged upside, and price increases of gold stocks should readily precede government interference by some margin. Bear in mind that this basket will be highly volatile and unpredictable.

Writing in a 2011 Berkshire Hathaway annual letter, Buffett said:

> Today the world's gold stock is about 170,000 metric tons. If all of this gold were melded together, it would form a cube of about 68 feet per side. (Picture it fitting comfortably within a baseball infield.) At $1,750 per ounce—gold's price as I write this— its value would be $9.6 trillion. Call this cube pile A. Let's now create a pile B costing an equal amount. For that, we could buy all U.S. cropland (400 million acres with output of about $200 billion annually), plus 16 Exxon Mobils (the world's most profitable company, one earning more than $40 billion annually).

After these purchases, we would have about $1 trillion left over for walking-around money (no sense feeling strapped after this buying binge). Can you imagine an investor with $9.6 trillion selecting pile A over pile B?

Cryptocurrencies

I hate the Bitcoin success. And I don't welcome a currency that is so useful to kidnappers and extortionists and so forth. Nor do I like shuffling out a few extra billions and billions and billions of dollars to someone who just invented a new financial product out of thin air.
—CHARLIE MUNGER, ANNUAL MEETING, 2021

Another point that bears watching is that Bitcoin and other cryptocurrencies have again taken center stage because of large price increases through year-end 2021. The market cap of Bitcoin sat at $1 trillion at year-end 2020, up substantially from the year before. The volatility is shocking, with Bitcoin down 25 percent in one day recently. Larger institutions are beginning to embrace crypto as an alternative to cash, and the early movers have profited handsomely from their investments. Envy has taken hold, and greed has materialized as we exit 2021. This trend may well continue, and crypto may stabilize as a viable asset class. Conversely, thin liquidity coupled with several large orders and a retail investor craze may leave the space vulnerable to another major collapse.

New cryptos continue to emerge, as barriers to entry into the creation of new cryptos is zero. It is an irony of the asset class, that the appeal of the limited growth of Bitcoins outstanding seems maybe entirely offset by the ease of creating new cryptos. As of 2021, roughly four thousand cryptocurrencies exist, although 99 percent of the total $2 trillion market cap is represented by the top 10. Bitcoin is the presumed winner, and if successful, this market seems likely to be a winner-take-all market. The problem with Bitcoin is that its architecture is clunky, and slow, versus Ethereum, for example. It is quite possible that the eventual winner has not yet been determined.

Leverage is used extensively to purchase cryptocurrencies. Most borrowings are asset backed, secured by the cryptocurrencies themselves. AI startups claim to use machine learning to better predict who makes better credits, and what percent of the asset value to extend as margin. One possible weakness of the crypto market given its extreme volatility is the risk of a large margin call, leading to an unexpected circular price collapse. Crypto leverage going into 2022 sits at record levels, heightening the risks of an abrupt downward price adjustment.

Toughening regulatory standards present another potential risk to cryptos. The appeal of the asset class is its unregulated framework independent of central bank control. Any actions by larger governments around the world to regulate crypto, its use, or requirements that crypto transactions be registered, or possibly outright prohibitions against its use are among the barriers to its adoption.

This may be a well-deserved asset class, and future books may recommend crypto as an alternative to gold. The problem, predicting its odds of success, at this point is too hard. If successful, predicting which crypto will become the de facto standard is too hard. Determining whether governments will allow the evolution of third-party cryptos is too hard, and ideally the leverage issues would flush out of the system with one final, large-scale price decline. For now, this asset class is too hard to justify an allocation. Pass.

Buying the Micro Versus the Macro: Conclusion

More conviction to buy can be obtained from microeconomic analysis. Study businesses, strategies, winners, and losers, and microeconomic clarity occasionally can be identified. The vast majority of *Reasons to Pass* has focused on microeconomic analysis.

Macroeconomic forces are much more complex and, in many cases, are incapable of being analyzed with high conviction calls. *Reasons to Pass* places these decisions squarely in the too-hard camp. A gold allocation, and high-level thoughts on the crypto market, may seem contradictory because of the macro justifications. These assets are unique. They are insurance policies against reckless behavior, and they are not intended to be portfolio compounders. If they do compound favorably, it will be to the detriment of the remaining portfolio, which is a wish best left unanswered.

23
Selling Discipline

After we buy a stock, consequently, we would not be disturbed if markets closed for a year or two. We don't need a daily quote on our 100 percent position in See's or H. H. Brown to validate our well-being. Why, then, should we need a quote on our 7 percent interest in Coke?

—WARREN BUFFETT, BERKSHIRE HATHAWAY
ANNUAL LETTER, 1993

The sell decision should be simple, as simple as the buy decision. Except that it's not. We should buy when a large margin of safety exists between price and value and sell when the price has converged to intrinsic value. Behavioral impediments exist on both sides of the investment (avoid the phrase "both sides of the trade," as this implies speculation). The sales process, however, is polluted by a host of behavioral pitfalls that distort the simplicity of the sales decision.

1. Anchoring—Investors often anchor on their purchase price. Stocks drop, anxiety builds, which leads to quick sales when the price again approaches the cost basis. Or investors, demanding a decent return on their investment, refuse to sell unless return thresholds are met.
2. Let Losers Run—Investors will use their cost as an indicator of whether to buy or sell. Stocks trading below purchase price are more likely to be held irrationally. In actuality, the cost is sunk and irrelevant to decision-making.
3. Prune the Winners—Stocks trading above cost are more likely to be sold. "Lock in the gain" is a common heuristic. This approach is

as irrational as letting losers run. You should make decisions based on fundamentals rather than on the price relative to average cost.

4. Falling in Love with Stocks—Stocks that have done really well most likely demonstrate improving fundamentals. Many investors tend to aggressively increase the intrinsic value of these names to justify continued holding. Even investors who disregard fundamentals tend to fall in love with names that have done well. News flow often confirms a bullish thesis, reinforcing the decision to hold.

5. The Opportunity Cost Argument—"Where will I put this capital if I sell my position? Cash is earning zero!" The implication is that continued holding of an equity will exceed the return earned on cash. This opportunity cost argument runs hollow. Ignore it. The more an investment trades above its fundamental value, the riskier it becomes. Your goal is to achieve good risk-adjusted returns. The investment may continue to appreciate, but the increased downside risk does not justify continued holding.

6. Overconfidence—Most professional investors, and even many casual investors, are overconfident in their ability to select prudent investments for their portfolios. One negative consequence of overconfidence is high turnover, because these investors believe strongly enough in their intrinsic value to immediately consider a sale once breached. Rational investors accept the imprecision of their intrinsic value, as it is merely an estimate within a wide range. Be patient and let prices vary within your band of intrinsic value to avoid unnecessary turnover.

7. Margin of Safety—Buy decisions are made at positive margins of safety, which is a cushion to counter adverse surprises. This cushion disappears as stock prices approach intrinsic value, thus offering no more protection. Baidu's sum of its parts may indicate a fair value of between $150 and $350 per share, making an investment compelling at $100, which is where it traded at the depths of the 2020 COVID crisis. Complicating the analysis, however, the allocation doubles once shares hit $200, leading to a large allocation at a possibly low margin of safety. No wonder that conviction to hold is low. Conversely, Kimberly Clark, a consumer staples company with highly predictable earnings, may have an intrinsic value range of $120 to $150. A buy at $80 offers strong protection, while the downside risks at $130 are relatively limited.

Tax Considerations

There are huge advantages for an individual to get into a position where you make a few great investments and just sit back
and wait: You're paying less to brokers. You're listening to less
nonsense. And if it works, the governmental tax system gives you
an extra 1, 2 or 3 percentage points per annum compounded. And
you think that most of you are going to get that much advantage
by hiring investment counselors and paying them 1 percent to run
around, incurring a lot of taxes on your behalf? Lots of luck.
—CHARLIE MUNGER, "A LESSON ON ELEMENTARY,
WORLDLY WISDOM AS IT RELATES TO INVESTMENT
MANAGEMENT AND BUSINESS," UNIVERSITY OF
SOUTHERN CALIFORNIA SPEECH, 1994

Tax considerations matter to the sales process. Purists may argue that the
sales decision relates entirely to intrinsic value and that tax consequences
are irrelevant. Taxes are paid today, or in a future year, so why attempt to
delay the inevitable if an asset is no longer inexpensive? It is a reasonable
theory that does not hold up in practice.

1. Most successful long-term investors construct low-turnover, tax-
   efficient portfolios. Tax efficiency is a key component of building
   long-term wealth. Imagine the incremental wealth effect that Warren Buffett gains from his perpetual holding of Berkshire Hathaway.
2. The difference in short-term versus long-term capital gains taxes
   are almost always sizeable. Delaying monetization of appreciated
   investments to a one-year holding period almost always makes
   sense. Some price risk exists when holding names well above
   intrinsic value, but momentum is a powerful thing in the short
   run, defined as one year or less, that can stretch valuations far
   above intrinsic value. Meanwhile, paying short-term capital gains
   tax is a guaranteed penalty.
3. Selecting investments that compound through the cycle allows for
   pretax compounding for long-term investors. Purchasing those
   investments below intrinsic value offers two advantages. First, the
   convergence of price to value leads to excess returns. Second, the
   continuous compounding once the name hits intrinsic value allows
   for pretax capital to continue to compound, adding wealth down

the road. The longer this pretax compounding continues, the more accretive it becomes to wealth: liquidate, pay taxes, and reinvest. This process interrupts the compounding machine.

4. Much institutional money managed by professionals is tax exempt. In this case, compounding with a higher and lower turnover can lead to the same after-tax result. Transaction costs still exist, but these have been driven down substantially over the past twenty years as changes swept over Wall Street's equities' businesses. Turnover can be substantially higher in pretax portfolios to overcome the bogey of transaction costs. Stewards of capital should reward money managers who properly distinguish between managing pretax and after-tax portfolios.

Appropriate turnover varies depending on your investment strategy. A portfolio of high-quality names whose intrinsic value grows cycle over cycle requires a little pruning each year but low overall portfolio turnover. Dodge & Cox has successfully managed its portfolios with about 10 percent annual turnover, implying a ten-year holding period. Ruane Cuniff, the manager of The Longleaf Funds, manages its portfolios with similar turnover. Some fundamentally oriented growth investors strive to achieve similar holding periods by targeting high-growth names with barriers to entry and franchise protections. After-tax capital lends itself particularly well to this type of investment strategy as taxes are minimized over time.

Now consider more traditional value portfolios that invest in deep cyclicals and restructuring situations at large margins of safety. Quality of invested names may be lower and thus assurance of cycle-over-cycle compounding is low. These names are not forever names but rather are names that are more prudently sold as price converges with intrinsic. Empirical observation and academic studies indicate that these names converge toward intrinsic value within three to five years. Tax efficiency is lower with these reversion-to-the-mean portfolios, requiring higher hurdle rates to offset the tax inefficiencies when placed within a taxable portfolio.

Berkshire Hathaway virtually never parts with his holdings. Buffett explained: "A parent company that owns a subsidiary with superb long-term economics is not likely to sell that entity regardless of price. 'Why,' the CEO would ask, 'should I part with my crown jewel?'" Yet that same CEO, when it comes to running his personal investment portfolio, will offhandedly—and even impetuously—move from business to business when presented with no more than superficial arguments by his broker for doing so" (Berkshire Hathaway annual letter, 1993).

Although Buffett prefers purchasing whole companies, he will purchase high-quality equities at reasonable prices and hold on through most any valuation environment. His portfolio is incredibly tax efficient, more than the average index fund that actively rebalances its portfolio based on market weights. He likens an ownership position in a common stock to owning a subsidiary in say Coca-Cola or another of his holdings. He anchors on fundamentals, and high-performing companies' fundamentals will continue to improve. Most investors, by contrast, anchor on price. From a fundamental perspective, why would an equity investor seek to continuously turn over its best performing businesses?

Thoughts About Cash

Although it may appear to be contradictory advice, never be concerned about rotating "risky" exposures into cash. Cash is to be celebrated, not detested. The money management industry is fixated on relative performance, which is a function of high rivalry and intense pressures exerted by the institutional consultant gatekeepers. The financial system presses hard for investors to be fully invested because fees earned are higher for equity portfolios than for cash equivalents. Consistent pressure leads to irrational behavior, namely, forcing fully invested portfolios regardless of market conditions.

Reasons to Pass thinks holistically about portfolio construction. Consider that your financial net worth is one large consolidated savings account managed for a lifetime, which is no different than how a large plan sponsor thinks about a pie chart of its entire asset base. This account is unbound by any artificial constraints and is looking to gain an economically superior risk-adjusted return over many cycles. Cash is a critical component of the investment process. It is a safety valve when price ceases to accord any protection against large structural impairments. Cash is also an opportunity magnet and can be deployed without regard for the overall economic or investing environment when compelling new opportunities are identified. This access purifies the investment process by isolating an investment decision to one decision node—is a specific use of capital justified? If it is not compelling, sit in cash. If it is compelling, invest. Fully invested portfolios do not have this luxury. A buy decision becomes multivariate and is interlinked with other names in the portfolio. A harsh market decline may make a new name compelling, but much less so when considering the potential sale candidates who also now trade at a wide discount. This opportunity cost deliberation can freeze decision-making, limiting warranted portfolio rotation particularly at the peaks and troughs, when investment activity is most warranted.

Cash allocations as a percent of an investor's portfolio should vary widely over time, perhaps between 20 percent and 50 percent on average, and between 10 percent and 60 percent at extremes. Both extremes present risks and both can be costly—a 10 percent cash allocation faces the risk of unrecoverable impairments during material downturns, and a 60 percent cash allocation faces the risk of permanently reduced purchasing power in an unexpected long-lasting up-market or if inflation rates increase. A lower bound of 20 percent cash, in most instances, offers some cash cushion for unexpected financial needs. It is also opportunistic because at an extreme level, an unusually deep once-a-generation downturn should be expected that makes portfolio impairments likely. World War I, World War II and the Great Depression, the 1974 downturn, and the 2008 financial crisis are all examples of once-a-generation catastrophes. An additional 10 percent of cash rotated into productive investments at these deeply distressed levels will present enormous future gains that should mostly offset even large unrecoverable losses seen in these downturns.

Conclusion

Turn investment portfolios slowly and deliberately. Be patient with most names, especially high-quality names—even when they appear to be expensive. High-quality investments will continue to compound over time and often are bid up irrationally by the market, providing plenty of exit opportunities. Patient investors can hold high-quality securities under all but the most overvalued scenarios, with potential exits emerging when Mr. Market bids these names extremely high. Low-quality names can be pared sooner when allocations grow above maximum tolerance as well as when a limited upside appears to exist.

CONCLUSION

Capital allocation is a life skill. Children choose to buy candy or save up for a video game. Students determine whether a sizeable student loan is appropriate to complete their education. Families buy cars and houses, which is capital that has explicit opportunity costs. Professionals at P&G allocate scarce capital toward advertising and product development, while CEOs determine whether potential acquisitions meet their financial objectives. Capital allocation may be the primary responsibility of institutional investors, but it is an essential skill set in our modern world.

Individual, Family, and Investor Capital Allocation

Capital allocation is both tangible and intangible. Tangible capital consists of savings and debt deployed into assets. Savings is equity capital, while mortgages, credit cards, margin accounts, derivative purchases, and other borrowings are debt capital. Individuals allocate their tangible capital to primary residences and investment properties, to equities, fixed income, and other investments, targeting a return on their tangible assets. Families think hard about how to optimize tangible capital allocation. Money spent on consumption is just another tangible capital allocation decision—save it or spend it.

Intangible capital is an equally critical contributor to wealth. Teenagers weigh hours spent studying against hours worked, whereas adults balance hours invested in their jobs against time spent improving their skill set. Starting a company is no easy feat, and most entrepreneurs begin their original concepts in "off hours" because day jobs pay the bills. Recreational hours are a vital component of intangible capital, balanced against "working" hours, which is the equivalent of consumption versus investment.

Optimize lifetime tangible and intangible capital and you will maximize lifetime satisfaction. Hours allocated to the task of securing emotional wealth take away from hours invested increasing financial wealth. Should I go to the gym or work on my book? Should my teenager watch the Super Bowl with friends or attend her coding class? Is church attendance a cause worthier than catching up on much needed rest? Play with the kids or stay late at work? What percent of income should I save? Finally, how should I invest that savings?

Charlie Munger explained: Everything is based on opportunity costs. Academia has done a terrible disservice, they teach in one sentence in first-year economics about opportunity costs, but that's it. In life, if opportunity A is better than B, and you have only one opportunity, you do A. . . . All of you are in the game of taking the lot you have right now and improving it based on your opportunity cost. Think of how life is simplified if you approach it this way" (Wesco annual meeting, 2007).

The challenges of life are endless and seemingly dispersed and unconnected. In actuality, every financial and emotional decision is a combination of scarcity of capital and opportunity cost. Both tangible and intangible capital are finite. Allocation decisions are everywhere, but most go unnoticed because "it's just life." Opportunity cost is a framework for triaging your capital—directing it to the point of highest value. Your next hour has several options: eat, read, talk to someone, work, or sleep. Your next day has slightly broader options available, and your next year and beyond are even more widely bracketed. The next hour's investment is important, but the next ten years' allocations are critical.

Define goals, especially long-term targets, as guideposts for better financial and emotional outcomes. Financial targets can be quantitative, aiming for some arbitrary round number in the far-distant future. Far-distant numbers are tough to lock in because of the uncertainty surrounding income trajectory, future returns, and inflation. What does $1 million in twenty years really mean in purchasing power? A financial alternative more within your control is (1) setting a qualitative goal—perhaps to be financially free in thirty years, or (2) dedicating *x* percent of my income each year and accept my life's standing in thirty years. The power of compounding is well understood, and this is the reason deferred gratification works. Sacrifice a bit of lifestyle today and live better tomorrow.

Investment returns are just as critical as the dollars saved. Warren Buffett wrote: "Though investors were slow to wise up, the math of retaining and reinvesting earnings is now well understood. Today, school children learn what Keynes termed 'novel': combining savings with compound interest works wonders" (Berkshire Hathaway annual letter, 2019).

Enhancing investment returns by just 2 percent per year can double your future standard of living or dramatically accelerate the time to reaching financial freedom. Design a base-case investment scenario in the form of dollar cost averaging. Plan to put away *x* percent of your income each year no matter what the economic environment. Structure your life to allow for this annual investment on a sustainable basis from the earliest age possible. Invest in equities now and invest later in real estate and other asset classes.

Some years will see recessions, or worse. These are the particularly important years to continue with your annual investment contributions. Increase contributions during downturns, if possible. Prices will be lower, so your money buys more shares, more houses, more commodities, all leading to more future wealth. Some years will see enormous booms. Less wealth is created in these years, although you will feel wealthier because your investment accounts have grown. Two instincts naturally take hold during boom times. First, the wealth effect leads to greater confidence. Spending more money in this period feels natural. Many large purchases, such as larger homes, more expensive cars, and finer vacations, are made during the boom. Second, confidence in your investment prowess expands, leading to riskier investments being made at the peak. As expected, forward returns on risky investments made at the peak do poorly, leading to lower compounding or worse, wealth destruction. Third, high confidence leads to higher leverage. The peak is the time to reduce leverage. Pay down debt, and if possible, never expand leverage when times are good.

Investment contributions still matter at the top of the cycle because timing the tops is filled with missed opportunity. The risk of sitting out on sizeable gains is high. Witness, as one example, the 32 percent return in 2019 for the S&P 500 after many pundits called this market expensive at the beginning of the year. The stomach-churning 2020, with its ups and downs, ended 15 percent higher than where it began, and 2021 saw another scorching 26 percent. Live with your baseline contributions each year until asset prices drop materially, at which point you ideally increase contributions and overall portfolio risk. Increased investment contributions in the middle of 2020, when the market was filled with COVID concerns, were most likely going to generate higher returns. The goal when investing is simple. Get more for your money. Downturns are an excellent time to get more assets per dollar invested.

Buffett offered this: "In our opinion, the real risk that an investor must assess is whether his aggregate after-tax receipts from an investment (including those he receives on sale) will, over his prospective holding period, give him at least as much purchasing power as he had to begin with, plus a modest rate of interest on that initial stake" (Berkshire Hathaway annual letter, 1993). This may be the single most insightful quote highlighted in *Reasons to Pass*.

In the end, the goal of investing is not just to get your account value up but also to increase your real purchasing power. You have increased your purchasing power if your account value remains flat while home prices have declined, food prices are lower, and Hawaiian airfare and hotel prices drop. It won't feel like it, but you have become wealthier. Make increasing your purchasing power your constant and wealth creation will come.

Corporate Capital Allocation

I should emphasize that we do not measure the progress of our investments by what their market prices do during any given year. Rather, we evaluate their performance by the two methods we apply to the businesses we own. The first test is improvement in earnings, with our making due allowance for industry conditions. The second test, more subjective, is whether their "moats"—a metaphor for the superiorities they possess that make life difficult for their competitors—have widened during the year.

—WARREN BUFFETT, BERKSHIRE HATHAWAY
ANNUAL LETTER, 2007

Even the wealthiest corporations face scarcity of capital—opportunity costs that affect decision-making. Alphabet and Microsoft have to justify their capital allocations internally and to investors in spite of their net cash balance sheets. Large corporate cash balances often lead to declining hurdle rates, expected of any entity with an abundance of capital. Microsoft's purchase of Nokia's cell phone business in 2013 may be one such example. Would this $7 billion acquisition, fully written off just two years later, have occurred in a world in which Microsoft was net debt instead of net cash?

Although mistakes happen, attractive projects will prove almost universally compelling. Moat-widening investments increase future pricing power and expand franchise longevity because they keep competitors at bay. It is difficult to quantify in year one, but Amazon's investment in state-of-the-art distribution facilities enabling one-day delivery was such an investment, providing a point of differentiation solidifying its moat over retail. In his 1997 Amazon annual letter, Jeff Bezos wrote:

> We have a window of opportunity as larger players marshal the resources to pursue the online opportunity and as customers, new to purchasing online, are receptive to forming new relationships. The competitive landscape has continued to evolve at a fast pace. Many large players have moved online with credible offerings and have devoted substantial energy and resources to building awareness, traffic, and sales. Our goal is to move quickly to solidify and extend our current position while we begin to pursue the online commerce opportunities in other areas. We see substantial opportunity in the large markets we are targeting. This strategy is not without risk: it requires serious investment and crisp execution against established franchise leaders.

Return matters, as does risk taken to achieve a return. *Reasons to Pass* offers guideposts to raising risk-adjusted returns, most importantly emphasizing the value of humility in rational decision-making. Risk is everywhere because the future is cloudy. Genuine fortune tellers would rank high in the Forbes 400. Allocating capital prudently when odds are in your favor builds wealth without the need for a crystal ball. Prudent risks taken by companies to increase their moats, and future earnings power, should be celebrated by investors, even if the eventual outcome is disappointing.

Mistakes will be made and can be tolerated without materially affecting long-term returns. Identical to individual goals, expanding a corporation's real earnings power over time builds wealth for managers and its investors. Compound earnings over many years, expand the moat, increase the intrinsic value, and loyal long-term investors will onboard. Incentivize management fairly and effectively, practice good corporate governance, manage risks prudently (including the balance sheet), maintain a contrarian bent for large investments (both capex and acquisitions), and long-term investor loyalty will increase further. Communicate fairly to all stakeholders, and Mr. Market will be less likely to sway your stock price far afield from its intrinsic value. This further strengthens the connection between shareholder partners and the corporation.

Buffett shared this insight: "In a partnership, fairness requires that partnership interests be valued equitably when partners enter or exit; in a public company, fairness prevails when market price and intrinsic value are in sync" (Berkshire annual letter, 1996).

Having spoken to hundreds of CEOs, most evaluate the success of their investment communications efforts by upticks in the stock price and investor enthusiasm. Stock promotion rather than investor education is the norm. Management incentives encourage stock promotion because bonuses are linked to rising share prices. CEOs consider investor outreach a sales job. Fairness and trust, however, come from honest, candid communications. Eventually CEOs receive the shareholder roster they deserve.

Investment Portfolio Construction

The world is too nuanced for absolutes, and the future is too unpredictable, but the following generalities may help in the construction of a durable portfolio:

1. The status quo is to pass on investment candidates. Seek out only obvious additions.
2. Target names whose intrinsic value per share is likely to increase over the next ten years.
3. Be price sensitive—less so for high-quality investments and more so for lower-quality investments.
4. A minimum and maximum allocation should be between a low-single-digit and a high-single-digit percent, except for baskets. Anything lower than this minimum indicates a lack of conviction, while the maximum allocation should be reserved for absolute no-brainers with limited structural risk of loss.

5. A fully invested portfolio consists of twenty to forty names that are widely diversified by sector, country, and other exposures. The top ten will account for a significant portion of the portfolio (50 percent is reasonable). The portfolio may include any combination of equities, real estate, and fixed income instruments. The higher quality the portfolio, and the more diversified their operations, the fewer names will be required to protect from permanent capital impairment.

6. Cash is a welcome relief valve when market conditions do not present obvious opportunities. A cash weighting of 20 percent to 50 percent is to be expected on average; more extreme allocations, 10 percent to 60 percent, are possible in unusual circumstances and near deep economic troughs and peaks.

7. The typical holding period will be ten years for high-quality names and will be shorter for cyclical reversion-to-the-mean investments.

Summary

Anyone with an appropriate temperament, basic knowledge of accounting and finance, and genuine motivation can become a worthy capital allocator. Establishing a high-level strategy, the foundation to success, requires investment principles that endure over time and that provide the basis for navigating through the seemingly complex investment landscape. Your principles will become the lens through which investment opportunities are evaluated.

Cocktail party investment pitches always sound enticing. "A friend of mine at Qualcomm says that AMD is working on something big, so I bought some AMD." Often these pitches practice hindsight bias. "As soon as COVID hit I knew gold was going to be huge." These stories trigger envy, and its cousin greed. No one wants to be left behind. Irrational actions are not far behind once envy is invited to the party.

The objective of this book is to reinforce humility into your investment process. Humility anchors an intellectual framework that begins with "I don't know." Let that drive your investment process and conversations at cocktail parties. Behaviors drive decisions, and behavioral biases distort decision-making, so build a process that minimizes irrational behavior. The proof of the process will be in the portfolio construction, and eventually in its long-term results.

There is no shame in indexing your assets. It is easy, stress free, and can be done without the aid of an adviser and thus is a particularly low-cost option. Many investors feel more comfortable paying a professional adviser to oversee their investment accounts. Adviser's incentives are clear: to collect fees for service. Their intentions may be genuine, and many are honest and hardworking and keep a watchful eye over your long-term best interest. Unfortunately, many advisers resort to complexity to differentiate themselves in a crowded marketplace. When you hear complex, think expensive. Having said that, some investors can benefit from professional advice, even if more for the psychological peace of mind than the financial enrichment.

As final advice from an investor still seeking absolute humility, don't succumb to the siren call of market noise. Think independently and begin every decision with a framework of simplicity. We have outlined so many reasons to pass. Use them all. Liberally. "I don't know" is the password, freeing you from forced decision-making in an uncertain and complex world. Rare should be a reason to buy, a decision so obvious that any risk reward framework skews heavily in your favor. Relish these opportunities and pass on the rest.

INDEX

Page numbers in *italics* indicate figures or tables.

prudence, 37
psychology, 5, 7, 63, 73, 262–63
"Psychology of Human Misjudgment,
    The" (Munger), 63

qualitative criteria, 72
qualitative screening, 245–47
quality, of data, 53
quality adjustments, to valuation, 222
quantitative criteria, 72
quantitative screening, 242–45
quants, 53–62

railroad industry, 101, 251
Rand, Ayn, 9–10
rational thinking, 33
R&D. See research and development
real estate: Buffett on, 154; cyclical
    elements in, 149–50; in global
    valuation, 20–21; housing crisis, 31;
    in Japan, 76–77, 254; NAV in, 109; in
    U.K., 159
real estate investment trusts (REITs), 20,
    91–92, 109, 154, 210
reclassifications, 114–15
regulation: of banking, 118–19, 123;
    bankruptcy and, 127–28; ethics and,
    148; by FDA, 206; of health care, 123–
    25; of technology, 117, 122, 126–28; of
    telecoms, 126; uncertainties in, 117–22;
    of utilities, 119–20, 122–23
REITS. See real estate investment trusts
research and development (R&D):
    for biotech, 206; brands and, 249;
    by companies, 88, 192; costs, 213;
    diversification and, 83; expenses,
    102, 104; information from, 84–85;
    investing in, 154; PP&E and, 153; ROE
    and, 134; success, 25
retail industry, 120–21, 178–79, 206, 221
return on equity (ROE), 78, 118, 125, 134,
    167, 199, 249
return on invested capital (ROIC), 72, 94,
    191–92

revenue. See earnings
revenue declines, 172, 197–204
ripple effect theory, 240–41
risk management: Buffett on, 35, 95, 236,
    290; in COVID crisis, 156; with debt,
    171; in digital age, 51–52; in equity
    investing, 35–38; with investment
    opportunities, 273–75; for investors,
    170, 235–41, 291–92; Munger on,
    24; obsolescence risk, 35, 205–13;
    with quants, 61; with rollovers, 155;
    structural elements of, 238; with
    valuation, 224–25; VaR, 115
Robertson, Julian, 35
ROE. See return on equity
Rohr, James, 137
ROIC. See return on invested capital
rollovers, 155
Rothchild, Baron, 269
Russell 1000 Growth Index, 11
Russell 1000 Value Index, 11
Russell 2000, 88
Russia, 165, 269
Ryan Air, 181

sales, 102–3
sales, general, and administrative
    (SG&A) expenses, 102
sample size bias, 46–47
Samsung Electronics, 15
SAP, 72
scandals, 111–13
SCCO. See Southern Copper Corporation
screening, 242–47
Sears, 86
SEC. See Securities and Exchange
    Commission
securities, 11, 16–18, 23–25, 162
Securities and Exchange Commission
    (SEC), 48
Security Analysis (Graham), 11
segmental data, 53
segment disclosures, 111–12, 114–15
segment information, 146

Lightning Source UK Ltd.
Milton Keynes UK
UKHW012137210223
417408UK00005B/101/J